THE LAST VIKING

BOOKS BY STEPHEN BOWN

*Scurvy: How a Surgeon, a Mariner and a Gentleman Solved
the Greatest Medical Mystery of the Age of Sail*

*Forgotten Highways: Wilderness Journeys Down the Historic
Trails of the Canadian Rockies*

Merchant Kings: When Companies Ruled the World, 1600–1900

*1494: How a Family Feud in Medieval Spain
Divided the World in Half*

THE
LAST
VIKING

The Life of
Roald Amundsen

STEPHEN R. BOWN

Douglas & McIntyre

Copyright © 2012 by Stephen R. Bown
First paperback edition, 2013
Published in the United States as a
Merloyd Lawrence Book by Da Capo Press,
a Member of the Perseus Books Group

13 14 15 16 17   5 4 3 2 1

Douglas and McIntyre (2013) Ltd.
P.O. Box 219 Madeira Park BC Canada V0N 2H0
www.douglas-mcintyre.com

Cataloguing data available from Library and Archives Canada
ISBN 978-1-77162-000-0 (paper)
ISBN 978-1-55365-937-2 (cloth)
ISBN 978-1-55365-938-9 (ebook)

Editing by John Eerkes-Medrano
Front jacket design by Jonathan Sainsbury
Text design by Brent Wilcox
Front jacket photograph © Bettmann/CORBIS
Back jacket photograph courtesy National Library of Norway
Printed and bound in Canada

We gratefully acknowledge the financial support of the
Canada Council for the Arts, the British Columbia Arts Council,
the Province of British Columbia through the Book Publishing
Tax Credit and the Government of Canada through the
Canada Book Fund for our publishing activities.

PRAISE FOR *The Last Viking*

And yet even today we hear people ask in surprise: What is the use of these voyages of exploration? What good do they do us? Little brains, I always answer to myself, have only room for thoughts of bread and butter.

—Roald Amundsen, *The South Pole*

In spite of the long time I had spent in the Arctic I was always longing to go back again. Kipling says that the man who hears the East a-calling never hears anything else, but the Arctic and the ice call just as strongly to some people.

—Helmer Hanssen, *Voyages of a Modern Viking*

No man more than the explorer is tempted to adopt the doctrine of ends justifying the means. An explorer soon discovers that the world is full of busybodies righteously ready to save him, as they probably think, from himself. The only way to deal with such people is to agree to their terms and then go ahead as one pleases. There are enough legitimate discouragements in the world without submitting to artificial ones.

—Lincoln Ellsworth, *Beyond Horizons*

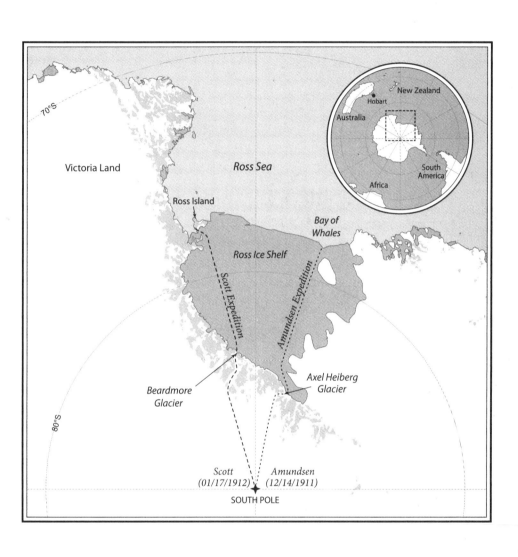

Contents

PART FOUR
NORTH

PART FIVE
LOST

The Last of the Vikings

I tried to work up a little poetry—the ever-restless spirit of man, the mysterious, awe-inspiring wilderness of ice—but it was no good; I suppose it was too early in the morning.

"THE STANDARD OF Fascist Italy is floating in the breeze over the ice of the Pole," radioed General Umberto Nobile, commander of the dirigible *Italia*, on May 24, 1928. The enormous airship and its crew of sixteen had flown from their base on Spitsbergen the day before and were now leisurely circling the frozen expanse at the top of the world. In the tiny main cabin strapped underneath the monstrous gas chamber, a gramophone scratched out the Italian folk song "The Bells of San Giusto," and the men celebrated with a homemade liqueur.

A month earlier, Pope Pius XI had publicly blessed the crew and commander in Italy, urging them to "consecrate the summit of the world," and had presented them with an enormous ceremonial oak cross for that purpose. It was impossible for the crew to disembark from the cabin onto the ice due to winds that kept the airship 150 metres in the air, and the men struggled to manoeuvre the great cross out the cabin door. They solemnly watched it plummet to the

ice with the flag of Italy's National Fascist Party attached to it, fluttering in the polar wind. Then, in a "religious silence," they tossed out
a Milanese coat of arms and a little medal of the Virgin of the Fire.

After the brief ceremony, which also included playing the Fascist
battle hymn "Giovinezza" followed by a flourish of salutes, the airship
slowly turned around and began to struggle against headwinds and
fog on its way back south to Spitsbergen. The visibility being poor,
Nobile couldn't determine the *Italia*'s location. The crew became disoriented, and Nobile ordered the airship to descend closer to the pack
ice for a better view. They were still almost three hundred kilometres
northeast of Spitsbergen when the rear of the airship became "heavy"
and lurched toward the ice. Alarmed, Nobile and his officers tried to
regain control over the *Italia* by increasing the speed of the propellers.
But it was too late. The rear end of the dirigible hit and scraped along
the jagged surface of the ice. "There was a fearful impact," Nobile
wrote later. "Something hit me on the head, then I was caught and
crushed. Clearly, without any pain, I felt some of my limbs snap.
Some object falling from a height knocked me down head foremost.
Instinctively I shut my eyes, and with perfect lucidity and coolness
formulated the thought: 'It's all over!'"

During the impact one man plunged from the cabin onto the ice
and died instantly. Nine men scrambled from the wreckage and
leaped or were thrown to the ice. As flames erupted from the crip-
pled airship, it spun away in a trail of smoke. Six men were trapped
in the cabin, never to be seen again. The nine survivors, several of
them severely injured, huddled on the ice amid the detritus of boxes
and equipment that had been thrown from the airship while Nobile's little dog Titina, uninjured in the collision, explored the bleak
surroundings. After several days without radio contact, Nobile finally accepted that the expedition was indeed in trouble and in need
of rescue; only a month of provisions had survived the crash.

Roald Amundsen was attending a public luncheon when news
of the disaster reached Oslo. Upon hearing the news he stood up

and announced, "I'm ready to leave at once to do anything I can to help." But as the Norwegian government began planning a rescue expedition, astonishing word came from Italy. Benito Mussolini had refused all assistance from Norway (despite the fact that the airship had probably gone down off Norway's northern border), particularly if the rescue were to be led by Amundsen. Nobile and Amundsen had been caught up in a nasty public feud for the past eighteen months—the fallout from a previous joint dirigible expedition to the North Pole—and Mussolini did not want the honour of Italy besmirched by Nobile's being rescued by his enemy. It would be an affront to Italian dignity. To the budding strongman, then beginning his scheme to reinvigorate Italy's image in the eyes of the world and to reposition his country as a powerful player on the international stage, the prospect of the nations of the world coming to Italy's rescue was humiliating. Captain Hjalmar Riiser-Larsen, an organizer of the Norwegian rescue operation and a past colleague of Amundsen's, wrote in astonishment: "I could not rid myself of the idea that it was preferable for the expedition to suffer a glorious *death*, [rather] than a miserable homecoming."

To avoid offending Mussolini, the organizers of the Norwegian expedition quietly dropped Amundsen from the rescue operation. It was a slight the aging but proud adventurer, officially retired for over a year, would not easily accept. Over six feet tall, weatherbeaten and still powerfully built at fifty-six years of age, he could not resist the urge to step into the spotlight one more time, perhaps to find closure for his quarrel with Nobile and redemption from the sordid publicity of the past two years.

In the 1920s, dirigibles were considered the future of air transport. A spectacular airship crash in the howling wastes of the polar sea commanded public interest; both nations and publicity-seeking individuals were eager to be seen as part of the thrilling escapade. So Amundsen began to arrange a private rescue plan. Money, as it had been throughout his tumultuous career, was Amundsen's chief concern. He had only recently cleared most of his debts, so his friends and family were not enthusiastic about financing his participation in what had become an international game played for national prestige.

There was strong sentiment in Norway that passing over Amundsen to please Mussolini was not only foolish but also a national embarrassment. Through the intercession of Fredrik Petersen, a Norwegian businessman in Paris, the French government quickly approved the use of a Latham twin-engine biplane equipped with pontoons, and a crew, to be put under Amundsen's command. The aircraft would help scour the ice for the stranded survivors of the *Italia* and ensure that France was a player in the great game of rescue, a drama that was generating voluminous columns of print in newspapers and magazines throughout Europe and North America. Although his fiancée was travelling from America to meet him, the Norwegian adventurer readied himself for the dangerous dash to Spitsbergen.

There was a reason Amundsen was able to command such international attention on short notice: he was the most famous of Norwegian explorers, and probably the most famous living explorer in the world. For nearly two and a half decades, his many thrilling exploits had pushed the frontiers of geographical knowledge and entertained millions. There was no one alive more deserving than Amundsen of the honour of a commanding role in the international extravaganza that would eventually include eight nations, dozens of ships and planes, and over 1,500 men.

In the early twentieth century, many of the great geographical mysteries that had intrigued adventurers for centuries remained unsolved, leaving unexplored blank spots on otherwise increasingly detailed global maps. Whereas Tibet, Africa and the Amazon had been repeatedly visited, every ocean navigated and every desert traversed, the Northwest Passage, the South Pole and the North Pole, sirens to generations of seekers, had not yet been conquered. Yet one man would undisputedly claim all these prizes within a twenty-year span.

Although he is known for being the first person to reach the South Pole—which, ironically, he didn't consider to be his greatest accomplishment—the Norwegian Roald Amundsen should also be remembered as one of the greatest explorers of all time. Like the accomplishments of the revered British mariner James Cook, Amundsen's feats are unrivalled. Unlike the expeditions of others—particularly British empire-against-the-world, our-way-as-the-civilized-way excursions—Amundsen approached his goals as physical and mental challenges. They were planned like military operations. The Norwegian explorer's style—a rational, as opposed to a romantic, approach to travel and exploration—proved successful where others had failed: in the harshest, most unforgiving places on the planet, where a single mistake could result in failure and perhaps death. His military-style execution of his objectives, carried out with gusto and flamboyant self-promotion, changed forever the way the geographical world would be perceived and future expeditions planned.

Amundsen was a skillful publicity seeker. To fund his exploits, he made the rounds of the lecture circuit telling hair-raising tales of his death-defying adventures and geographical conquests. In the press he was referred to as "the last of the Vikings," and he learned early never to do anything without securing advance publicity (and payment for exclusive rights to his story). Larger than life, arrogant and competitive, Amundsen was a meticulous organizer and avoided the extreme sufferings and early death so common among other adventurers. He could be taciturn and rude in public, and his accomplishments were tainted by the perceptions that he was devious and cold-hearted, that his quest for glory and public acclaim in the exploration game was somehow unseemly or ungentlemanly and that he had violated some unwritten code that dictated how respectable adventurers were to conduct themselves. In fact, while Amundsen viewed exploration as an exciting undertaking to settle his restless spirit, he somehow failed to appreciate, or ignored, the underlying political and nationalist motivations that inspired and financed others, making him the object of much vitriol, as occurred when Robert Falcon Scott of the British Antarctic Expedition perished while racing Amundsen to the South Pole.

Amundsen has been contrasted and compared with Scott by biographers and polar historians for the past century. His life and accomplishments have been condensed to this single episode, in which he is often portrayed as an uncouth bit player in the tragic drama of Scott's death. But Amundsen was not universally regarded as a cold and austere man. His American friend Lincoln Ellsworth claimed that "he was like a child whose confidence has been betrayed so often that it finally trusts nobody. So he encased himself in a shell of ice. . . . Nobody was warmer hearted, no boy could frolic more joyously than Amundsen in his fifties, as he was when I knew him." Amundsen also had an intuitive sense of other people's moods and thoughts. When he sensed that others found it uncomfortable to be constantly looking up at him, he would indicate that everyone should be seated.

Although he strove for respectability, cloaking his exploits in scientific accomplishment, Amundsen pursued his objectives as a series of conquests, as records to be broken and listed on his résumé, metaphorical trophies for his mantel, much like professional adventurers do today. He commented to a friend when he heard of the American Richard Evelyn Byrd's plan to fly to the South Pole: "Of course Byrd can fly to the South Pole, if he wants to, but what is the use? I don't understand such a thing. I was there, Scott was there—there is nothing more to find. Why should anybody want to go to a place where somebody else had already been? Or go there for the sake of doing it a different way?" On another occasion he wrote that he was glad he hadn't been born later, because then there would have been nothing left for him to do but go to the moon. He was the supreme man of action, an actor in a grand drama of his own devising. The only reason he didn't endorse equipment in order to fund his expeditions was that adventure tourism as a form of middle-class recreation did not yet exist and there was not much equipment to promote, although he did promote other products—shoes, toothpaste and tinned meat—whenever he could.

During the early twentieth century, Amundsen was a towering public figure. In an era before the Internet, television, radio and easy travel, he excelled at selling excitement and adventure to the public. A casual search of the *New York Times* archives between 1903 and 1928 reveals over four hundred articles about Amundsen. These articles include gushing tributes to his accomplishments, notifications of his honours, decorations and citations, notices of his upcoming lectures, news of his opinions on global events and details of his future plans. Some of the pieces read like the society pages, announcing which prestigious prize Amundsen would receive in Paris, what President Theodore Roosevelt had written in a public letter read aloud at a dinner in Amundsen's honour in New York, or which German scientific medal the Norwegian explorer had renounced during the war. Even the auctions of his manuscripts to publishers made the papers.

Amundsen wrote about his exploits with a wry, self-deprecating sense of humour free of the nationalist bombast and pedantic cereal-box philosophy, the fake moralizing and shallow introspection, that was so common in the pronouncements of many other explorers of the era. Much of his own writing is tongue-in-cheek and deliberately lurid; he was a natural story-teller chuckling at his own tales. "I tried to work up a little poetry," he wrote just before setting off on skis for the South Pole, "the ever-restless spirit of man, the mysterious, awe-inspiring wilderness of ice—but it was no good; I suppose it was too early in the morning." After surviving a dangerous situation in the Arctic, he observed that "my nerve-wracking strain of the last three weeks was over. And with its passing, my appetite returned. I was ravenous. Hanging from the shrouds were carcasses of caribou. I rushed up the rigging, knife in hand. Furiously I slashed off slice after slice of the raw meat, thrusting it down my throat in chunks and ribbons, like a famished animal, until I could contain no more." On another occasion, quoting the novelist Rex Beach, he mused that "'the deity of success is a woman, and she insists on being won, not courted. . . . [Y]ou've got to seize her and bear her off, instead of standing under her window with a mandolin.'"

Amundsen was an entertainer of the highest order, and his geographical conquests were his art, executed with simplicity and grace. People sought out his opinions, snapped up his books and lined up to attend his lectures. Yet for much of his professional career he teetered on the cusp of bankruptcy, pursued by debt collectors even at public venues and ceremonies. He was indifferent, if not incompetent, when it came to dealing with the business aspect of his adventures, pouring all his earnings and borrowings into his next great adventure. At one point he was even involved in a lawsuit over debts to his own brother. Ellsworth, his friend and adventuring partner, remembered that in the 1920s, "In his room at the Waldorf, I frequently heard a mysterious rustling of paper on the floor—another court summons for Amundsen being slid under the door." It speaks to his character, however, that he always paid off his creditors as soon as he was flush with cash from his latest book or tour.

Like all larger-than-life characters, Amundsen had several nicknames: "Last of the Vikings" invoked his national heritage for bold undertakings, "Napoleon of the Polar Regions" referenced his style of operation and the planning of his geographical conquests, and "White Eagle" was a concession to his striking appearance. Like his Viking ancestors, he was an imposing figure. His stride was confident and his stance defiant, his great beak of a nose a cartoonist's delight, his bald head dominated by the white tufts of his imperial mustache. His face was weathered and prematurely aged from ploughing his way through blizzards on skis and dog sleds and from endless fretting over the state of his foundering finances. The skin around his piercing blue-grey eyes was crinkled from a lifetime of squinting into the sparkling ice and vast, frozen seas. These eyes, one friend noted, bored "through one as their gaze passed on into infinite distances."

Amundsen lived with verve and enthusiasm. According to Ellsworth, who knew him for four years in the 1920s and joined him on two polar adventures, he inherited "from those half-wild ancestors who voyaged to America centuries before Columbus . . . a heroic physical appetite that matched the strength of his restless spirit." He could eat almost anything, from multiple hard-boiled eggs to a succession of greasy meatballs. He seemed to thrive on a monotonous diet of pemmican and oat biscuits, but was never averse to hunting and eating unfamiliar animals such as dolphins, seals and penguins, which he proclaimed made for excellent eating, "not unlike beef." He even ate his own sled dogs once. "His throat seemed to be lined with asbestos," Ellsworth recalled, "and his digestion was that of an ostrich." Amundsen was known to gulp burning hot chocolate, place his empty mug on the ground and proclaim "That is good" while others patiently waited for their drinks to cool. Never a routinely heavy drinker, Amundsen nevertheless poured himself a glass of aquavit or other liquor, eyeing his watch to await the precise moment of 5 p.m. each afternoon before drinking it.

The Last Viking was stubborn and intractable. He had many strong opinions, many friends and many enemies. It was nearly impossible to compel him to do anything he didn't want to do—even to deliver a speech if he wasn't in the mood—yet when he disappeared it was while dashing to the rescue of a man he hated. Ever restless and on the move, to the very end Amundsen was out to prove that he still had what it took to be a leader, that his glory days did not lie in the past. He shied away from the role of elder statesman, from

becoming an object of morbid curiosity while fading away on his remote property. Unlike his mentor and countryman Fridtjof Nansen,
the celebrated Norwegian patriot famous for the first recorded crossing of Greenland, Amundsen was not a scientist or an academic—
he did not crave comfortable respectability but, rather, sought
continued acclaim for daring exploits. He was a professional with a
lifelong dedication to his skills and craft, and he had no other career
to fall back on.

Amundsen was loved by his men, commanding a devotion of
which others could only dream. He repaid loyalty with loyalty, even
at considerable cost to his reputation, as was the case with the disgraced American explorer Dr. Frederick Cook. Revealing his own
leadership style, Amundsen once admitted in a rare critique that
"Nansen is too kingly. He will not hobnob with the common herd."
Some of Amundsen's men even claimed they would sacrifice themselves for him. "If we were in want of food," claimed Oscar Wisting, who was with Amundsen at the South Pole, in the Northeast
Passage and at the North Pole, "and he said one must sacrifice himself for the others, I would gladly go quietly out into the snowdrift
and die."

Amundsen himself had a few qualities he demanded of his men,
in addition to physical strength and quiet competence: "courage and
dauntlessness, without boasting or big words, and then, amid joking
and chaff—out into the blizzard." Ever the optimist, who often
counted on luck and always came out ahead, one of his favourite
maxims was "When it is darkest there is always light ahead." Yet he
could share the complaints of his men in a down-to-earth way even
while remaining the indomitable commander—he somehow was
both leader and comrade. "There are two times a man is happy up
here," he claimed about the North Pole. "When his belly is full of
hot liquid, and when he is in his sleeping bag." Once, on a small
ship that was bucking and corkscrewing in an ocean storm, a companion remarked that he didn't like the sea. Amundsen, pale from

seasickness himself, replied, "I don't either. It is something we have to put up with."

But as with any public figure, there was more to the explorer than the press revealed. An intensely private and secretive man, Amundsen rarely discussed things that were not part of his public persona— the elaborate façade of invincibility and determination that captivated the public for decades. He was as guarded and circumspect in his private life as he was flamboyant in his public exploits. Never, in any public documents or lectures, did he mention his three complicated affairs, all with married women, nor his quarrels with his family, until his strangely imprecise and erratic autobiography was published, barely a year and a half before his death.

Perhaps it was a chance to redeem his reputation, a gambit to claim the limelight, that propelled Amundsen on his final dangerous and hastily planned flight in a French biplane. Perhaps he feared the arrival of his American fiancée. Whatever his reasons, on June 18, 1928, the Last Viking set off on his last great polar adventure. The twin-propeller biplane, with a Norwegian co-pilot and four French crew, soared into the blue northern sky from Tromsø, in northern Norway, toward Spitsbergen.

Oddly, many observers had premonitions of Amundsen's fate in the days before takeoff. One even noted tears on Amundsen's cheek the day he belatedly boarded the train north to Bergen, twenty-five years to the day since he had set sail on his first great conquest, of the Northwest Passage. "Ah, if you only knew how splendid it is up there in the North," he said to an Italian reporter at his home in Uranienborg, on the coast outside Oslo. "That's where I want to die, and I wish only that death would come to me chivalrously, that it will find me during the execution of some great deed, quickly and without suffering." His last hours, spent with his friend Fritz Zapffe, were also notable for unusual musings. Amundsen handed his broken lighter to his friend, and when Zapffe said he would have it repaired, Amundsen replied that he shouldn't bother: "I'll have no more use for it."

It was almost as if there were warring factions within him: a nostalgic melancholy in his final days at home, pushed aside by a sense of duty that was propelling him to fulfill the expectations of his public. Even the sailing from New York of his bride-to-be did not deter him from his quest for yet more acclaim in the polar regions, which had for two and a half decades served as the set for his grandiose life. We will never know his thoughts about the imminent arrival of his Alaskan paramour who planned to marry him in Norway, because Amundsen was never seen again. A few weeks after the biplane lifted off from Tromsø, a seven-foot-long blue pontoon and other detritus were spied floating in the choppy waters of the Barents Sea. The pontoon had clearly been used as a life raft.

Amundsen's final bow on the international stage was an oddly fitting conclusion to the life and career of the most enigmatic and dynamic of the pioneers of the golden age of polar exploration. His disappearance was a neat conclusion to his adventure-novel life. Yet it was also somewhat anticlimactic. With Amundsen, the way he died is far less intriguing than the way he lived.

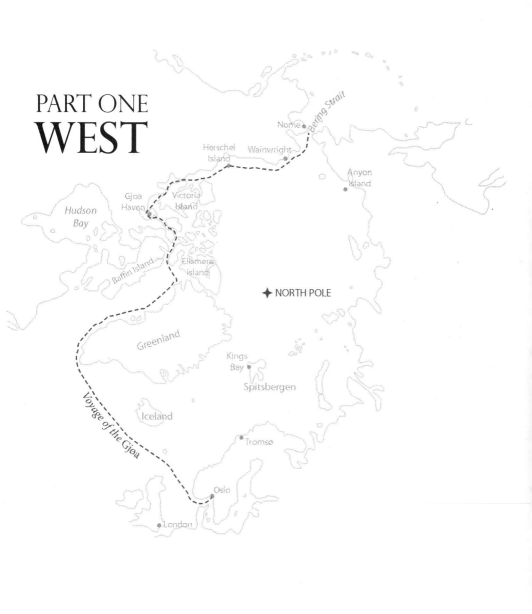

PART ONE
WEST

Nome

Bering Strait

Herschel
Island

Wainwright

Anyon
Island

Gjoa
Haven

Victoria
Island

Hudson
Bay

Baffin Island

Elismere
Island

✦ NORTH POLE

Greenland

Kings
Bay

Spitsbergen

Iceland

Tromsø

Voyage of the Gjoa

Oslo

London

1

The Boy from the Mountain Kingdom

This is the greatest factor: the way in which the expedition is equipped, the way in which every difficulty is foreseen, and precautions taken for meeting or avoiding it.

ON JUNE 16, 1903, the single-masted fishing smack *Gjøa* was moored to the pier in Christiania Fjord. The deck of the small ship was pounded by a "perfect deluge of rain" as a terrific storm whipped the waves into dangerous cross-currents. The captain of the ship was an exhausted, worry-worn thirty-one-year-old dreamer and schemer named Roald Amundsen. So far in his life he had dabbled in medicine at university, worked as a sailor and an officer on fishing and merchant ships, and overwintered in the Antarctic on a poorly organized Belgian expedition. Most importantly, he had come into a considerable inheritance, which he had spent on his ship and a crew of six experienced young mariners in preparation for his grand adventure, one that had animated his dreams since boyhood: the navigation of the unconquered Arctic waterway known as the Northwest Passage.

Unfortunately, his inheritance was insufficient to fund the ambitious voyage. He had begged for money from many "learned societies and private patrons of science," but to little avail. The remainder of the financing was to be credit. He had not yet paid for the years of supplies and equipment he had stowed aboard, and his creditors had been hounding him for months. The previous day, his principal creditor had demanded payment within twenty-four hours. He had threatened to seize the *Gjøa* and to have Amundsen arrested for fraud. In a desperate move, the explorer had called a meeting with his crew, laid bare the sorry state of his finances and urged his men to a bold scheme.

Just before midnight, while the storm heaved the *Gjøa* and the rains pelted down, the first mate leaped aboard, yelling the news: the creditor was on the wharf, along with the bailiff and officers, waiting for the storm to pass before impounding the ship. Amundsen "seized an ax, dashed out into the cloudburst and cut the mooring hawsers," and the ship plunged into the storm, steering south through the fjord into the Skagger Rack and North Sea—out of the jurisdiction of the bankruptcy courts and toward the deadly Northwest Passage. "When dawn arose on our truculent creditor," Amundsen gleefully recounted later in his life, "we were safely out on the open main, seven as light-hearted pirates as ever flew the black flag, disappearing upon a quest that should take us three years and on which we were destined to succeed in an enterprise that had baffled our predecessors for four centuries."

The young man who conquered the Northwest Passage could easily have been destined for a life of sailing and adventure. Born Roald Engelbregt Gravning Amundsen on July 16, 1872, he was the fourth and final son of Jens Engebreth Amundsen and Hanna Henrikke Gustava Sahlquist. His mother was the daughter of a middle-class government official, and his father was a successful business owner and sea captain sixteen years her senior. At the time of their marriage, Jens was prosperous and well travelled. In 1854 he and a partner had purchased an old hulk at a scrap auction, refurbished it in a small shipyard and rechristened it *Phoenix*, displaying a sense of the symbolic power of words and prophecy that would later be shared by Roald.

The *Phoenix* voyaged to the Black Sea the following year, when the Crimean War pitted Turkey, France and England against Russia. By good fortune the ship, moored near Sebastapol, was eagerly received by the British and converted into winter quarters for their officers. Afterward it serviced the British cavalry, hauling forage and straw throughout the war. Jens returned to Norway with the foundation of a fortune in 1856, the beginning of his commercial empire. His business enterprise flourished with freer maritime trade in the second half of the nineteenth century, when Britain repealed its Navigation Act, opening the world of commercial shipping to ambitious but poor maritime people from commercial backwaters like Norway. Jens was a shrewd and uncompromising captain, business minded if unscrupulous by modern standards: among other cargoes, he shipped Chinese indentured labourers around the world—a practice little better than the slave trade. When he met Gustava Sahlquist he was a respected member of the commercial elite, the owner or co-owner at one time of thirty ships that circled the world. In the Norwegian tradition, ship owners were usually the captains of their own vessels, so marriage didn't change his life much. Jens and Gustava's first child was born in China.

Gustava—after many years of living aboard world-girdling merchant ships; several more years of living at Hvidsten, their secluded home on the mainland coast near the shipping centre of Sarpsbord; and the births of three more boys—persuaded her husband to move the family to Christiania, as Oslo was then called. Although more urban than Sarpsbord, Christiania was still dominated by sprawling wooden structures built along a fjord surrounded by pine-clad mountains and snowy peaks. The Amundsens' new home was located near the city centre, had two stories and was staffed by several servants, yet it also backed onto forested backcountry. It was as urban as anything then in Norway yet still under the spell of the hinterland, a good place for children to experience the blending of urban and rural worlds. For the boys—Jens, Gustav, Leon and Roald—it was undoubtedly an idyllic place to grow up: They learned skiing and skating at an early age in the forest behind their home and had great latitude in outdoor play. They learned knot tying and wood carving, and forestry and boating skills, yet they also had the city to explore.

Jens Sr. was a good but stern father, respected by his family and larger community, and also well liked. He regaled his children with tales of his adventures at sea and in exotic foreign lands. When he was not on a voyage he was involved in the boys' lives, dispensing practical wisdom such as his comment on their fighting: "I don't want you to get into any fights. But if you must, get in the first blow—and see that it's enough." Roald seems later to have taken this to heart as a general philosophy: if you start something, go in strong and finish it. But although he inherited his father's sense of adventure, he certainly did not inherit his father's superior business sense, a lack that would haunt him for most of his life.

Gustava appears to have been unhappy. During school holidays and Christmas, she did not often travel with her sons to visit their cousins at Hvidsten. She either remained at home in Christiania or visited her own relatives. It is tempting to attribute Amundsen's later wanderlust and international ambitions to his father and the family's international shipping business, but it was Gustava who encouraged the boys' formal education, which gave them a different window into the world, one that was less pragmatic and more intellectual, than their father's outlook. It was she who urged the family to move to Christiania, where Amundsen was undoubtedly exposed to ideas and attitudes not commonly held in smaller, rural places. None of the Amundsen brothers was held back by the provincialism, feelings of inferiority or insularity that can come from growing up in remote places. Gustava saw to it that her sons were not disconnected from the larger intellectual and cultural currents of the wider world.

In the capital, the Amundsen brothers attended private school, but only Gustav, the second-oldest, had completed his studies before their father died in 1886 at the age of sixty-six. "It is hard to lose such a father," wrote the fourteen-year-old Roald, "but it was God's will, and the will of God must be fulfilled." Some have suggested that this and similar writings over the years are evidence of Amundsen's religious beliefs, but it seems just as likely that these platitudes skirt the desolation of a teenager's feelings upon losing his beloved father: they are the words of someone who knows he needs to say something but is unable to convey the enormity of it. Amundsen's three older brothers left home soon after their father's death. Amundsen himself, according to his cheeky retelling in his autobiography, "passed without incident through the usual educational routine of Norway."

With her three oldest sons gone to sea, Gustava pinned her desire for one of her children to pursue a career in medicine on Roald. "This ambition, however—which originated with her and for which I never shared her enthusiasm—was never to be realized." But his mother's respect for higher education was likely why Roald first came to read books in English about events outside Norway. And while he continued his education to please his mother, he developed an interest in British history, particularly in the tragic fate of John Franklin and his quest to locate the fabled Northwest Passage, but also Franklin's earlier expeditions in arctic North America. "I read them with a fervid fascination which has shaped the whole course of my life," Amundsen recalled.

His description of the return from one of his expeditions thrilled me as nothing I had ever read before. He told how for three weeks he and his little band had battled with the ice and storms, with no food to eat except a few bones found at a deserted Indian camp, and how before they finally returned to the outpost of civilization they were reduced to eating their own boot leather to keep themselves alive. Strangely enough the thing in Sir John's narrative that appealed to me most strongly was the sufferings he and his men endured. A strange ambition burned within me to endure those same sufferings. Secretly . . . I irretrievably decided to be an Arctic explorer.

"Roald" means "the glorious" in Norwegian. As a youth, Amundsen dreamt of a glorious future for himself, one in which he would live up to his name and perhaps his father's legacy. He had visions of vanquishing, against great odds, geographical chimeras, enduring incredible suffering in the process and emerging a hero.

Amundsen plodded on through his studies, passing each year with grades that reflected indifference and muted enthusiasm, barely good enough to keep his mother pleased. Meanwhile he continued to dream and to train in the outdoors during every possible break from school. "From November to April," he recalled, "I went out in the open, exploring the hills and mountains which rise in every direction around Oslo, increasing my skill in traversing ice and snow and hardening my muscles for the coming great adventure." He loved skiing but had little interest in football, the other sport then popular in Norway. He joined football teams anyway, just for the physical challenge. Amundsen slept with his window wide open at night even in the winter, claiming to his mother that he loved fresh air, but really "it was a part of my hardening process." He organized small expeditions for himself and a few friends, such as overnight treks on skis under a star-studded sky, enlivened by the otherworldly swirling of the aurora borealis, into the winter wilds to improve his toughness.

If one were looking for a challenge in late-nineteenth-century Norway, there were two ever-present opportunities: the sea and the mountain wilderness that constituted much of the country. Amundsen's dream of suffering and endurance was given a substantive boost in the summer of 1889. That summer, Fridtjof Nansen returned to Christiania to a hero's welcome after skiing across the frozen expanse of Greenland. Nansen sailed up the fjord toward Christiania surrounded by a mob of small boats proudly waving the national flag while bands played on the decks of larger ships, "his tall form," Amundsen remembered, "glowing with the admiration of a whole world for the deed he had accomplished." The whole city joined the celebration; on shore, the streets were lined with cheering crowds as Nansen and his hardy companions snaked their way through the city in a festive parade. Nansen and five other Norwegians had seized a geographic prize that had eluded many international teams before, including that of British mountaineer Edward Whimper, who had scaled the Matterhorn; American naval officer Robert Peary, who would later lead a dash to the North Pole; and Swedish explorer and aristocrat A. E. Nordenskiöld, who achieved fame for being the first to navigate the Northeast Passage.

Norway was not yet an independent nation, but was under the dominion of Sweden and eager for international recognition for its nascent independence movement. For succeeding where others had failed, and for giving Norway its first international recognition, Nansen was now a big man in a small country. Amundsen hoped to emulate this new national hero in terms of bold vision as well as technique; the seventeen year old remembered vividly that "with beating heart I walked that day among the banners and cheers and all the dreams of my boyhood woke to storming life. And for the first time I heard, in my secret thoughts, the whisper clear and insistent: If you could do the North-West Passage!" Amundsen was maturing at the dawn of the golden age of Norwegian exploration, when national pride spurred heroic exploits not seen for nearly a thousand years. Norwegians fondly recalled the time when Viking raiders plundered the coasts of Europe as far as the Mediterranean and pushed their dragon-headed knarrs west through the unexplored Atlantic as far as North America.

Modern Norway's coming of age was a period of optimism, of expanding horizons and ambitions for the tough, individualist people. A sparsely populated country on the fringes of Europe (it had fewer than two million inhabitants in the late nineteenth century, about one tenth the population of Britain and one thirtieth of the United States), Norway could be an insular society. It was a place where merchants looked elsewhere for profits and where dreamers could view the greater world as a legitimate theatre for their ambitions; to succeed at endeavours other than the traditional industries one would have to leave. A Norwegian could achieve recognition at home simply by being recognized elsewhere.

The teenaged Amundsen barely passed his school exams. But in those days a pass was sufficient, and in 1890 he dutifully enrolled in the Royal Norwegian Frederick University of Christiania. He planned to study medicine, according to his mother's wishes. "Like all fond mothers, mine believed that I was a paragon of industry," he reminisced, "but the truth was that I was a worse than indifferent student." Not recognizing her son's shortcomings, she paid for a private apartment in the city for him. But he continued to pursue his outdoors training and dreaming, all the while pretending to be making headway in his medical studies.

During these years Amundsen continued his extensive ski touring in the rugged hills around the city, growing in skill and stamina. He mastered touring while the sport and its equipment were rapidly evolving, from the use of a single stick to the development of more effective methods of waxing that involved pine sap, candle tallow or even soft, fatty cheese, depending on the conditions. The skis then in use were heavy wooden planks, and the bindings were a cumbersome system of straps.

In early February 1893, Amundsen attended a lecture given by the Norwegian explorer Eivind Astrup, who regaled his eager audience with tales of his adventures in the Arctic with the American explorer Peary. Astrup spoke about the superiority of skis over snowshoes in this environment, the benefits of using dogs to pull sleds (the standard method of travel in the Arctic) and the wealth of knowledge possessed by local peoples. It was a revelation to the young Amundsen that "civilization" did not always provide superior methods and technologies. That people who had for generations survived in the Arctic could be relied upon to have better knowledge regarding how to survive there, that native peoples were not in fact benighted savages but rather should be emulated, was an eye-opener to the young Norwegian.

Amundsen was a serious and principled young man who had a small group of friends and led a quiet social life. But he seldom attended classes and was on his way to expulsion from university. In fact, he had recently failed his exams, but he kept the secret from his mother—he must have been nervous about telling her. The only thing that saved him from embarrassment and family discord was that his mother died in the fall of 1893, when he was twenty-one. Her unexpected death "saved her from the sad discovery which she otherwise would have made, that my own ambitions lay in another direction and that I had made but poor progress in realizing hers." Later that year, Amundsen left the university with "enormous relief." Although he had stayed in school only to please his mother, during these years he had enjoyed a great deal of latitude in how he spent his time. His mother had provided him not only with an apartment but also a housekeeper, as well as a stipend that allowed him to live without worry. Despite his poor grades, university life provided him with access to the intellectual and cultural currents of Europe and a great deal of free time in which to pursue his true interests.

Freed from the responsibility of maintaining the charade of actively pursuing a medical degree, the young Amundsen now inherited a

substantial sum of money from his parents' estate. Counterbalanc-
ing his grief, throughout the spring of 1893 there was excited talk
in Christiania about the imminent departure of another expedition
led by the famous Nansen. This time, Nansen enjoyed considerable support for his plans from the Norwegian government and
had a doctorate to bolster his scientific claims. He had designed
and built a special ship with a tougher and rounder hull to better
resist the pressure of pack ice. He planned to sail his new ship into
the Arctic, deliberately wedge it into the ice, and observe where
the ship was taken, in an effort to follow and better understand
the polar currents. That was the scientific goal of the voyage; the
excitement in Christiania sprang from the fact that it was a daring
undertaking.

The expedition was launched to great fanfare in June, further gal-
vanizing the young Amundsen's plan of becoming an explorer. He
saw and felt the excitement of the crowds and wanted the thrill of
that attention for himself. Although he had no direct experience of
what life would be like for the men aboard the ship during the actual
voyage, he continued working toward this goal. Fortunately for him,
a large number of North and South polar expeditions were being
planned and undertaken, not just in Norway but in the United States
and Britain. The North and South Poles were the least explored and
least understood lands on the planet, and polar exploration was in
the air, so to speak.

A few months later, in October, Amundsen wrote a letter to
Martin Eckroll, the leader of a planned Norwegian expedition to
Spitsbergen, outlining his credentials and requesting a position on
the expedition, which was being planned for the following summer.
"I have long been possessed of a great desire to join one of these interesting Arctic adventures," he wrote, "but various circumstances
have prevented me. First and foremost, my parents wanted me to
study. . . ." The young man then outlined his family history, men-
tioning that he was now free from familial obligation because his

mother had recently died. He noted to Eckroll that he planned to spend the winter "in the study of Meteorology, mapmaking, surveying" and other practical vocations that he believed might be valuable on an expedition. The would-be explorer indicated that he wanted no pay and would be "willing to submit to anything whatsoever." He sent out similar applications to other expeditions being planned for various remote locations, but his lack of experience limited his prospects.

Without waiting for replies—which, in any event, were not favourable, owing to his lack of experience in wilderness exploration and not having spent any time at sea—Amundsen launched himself into further training in mountain wilderness skiing. He organized a ski trip across the vast, uninhabited plateau of Hardangervidda to the sparsely inhabited western mountain ranges. It was a dangerous and difficult trek over windswept terrain, and it had never been completed in winter. His two companions were Laurentius Urdahl, an experienced mountain skier and a brother-in-law of his brother Gustav, and his friend Villhelm Holst, a medical student. After long planning sessions in the fall of 1893, the eager trio departed on Christmas Day by train to the trailhead, commemorating what they evidently believed would be their assured success with a now-amusing studio portrait: three skiers in fake gear and large packs, looking jaunty and well groomed, skiing purposefully onwards against a painted background of snow and pine trees.

But with youth can come the underestimation of difficulties or the overestimation of one's abilities. After many months of having "smoked perfumed cigarettes," according to Urdahl in his reminiscences, the trio started out "sluggish and completely out of the habit of taking exercise." Amundsen's equipment proved inadequate, causing him to frequently slide and sink into deep snowdrifts, which exhausted him but provided some amusement to his companions. His bindings did not fit his boots, which resulted in his tumbling forward on downhill sections. An unseasonal thaw and a temperate blizzard made good skiing nearly impossible, and several days into the trip the thaw was followed by plummeting temperatures approaching −40°C, which nearly froze them at night in their specially constructed reindeer-fur sleeping bags. Then there was another blizzard. Despite a great deal of preparation, the three young men did not reach even the farm at the eastern edge of the plateau before they were forced to turn back. It was a humiliating defeat. They had skied barely fifty kilometres. Wilderness exploration was even harder than it had seemed.

Amundsen, however, was not deterred by one setback. A few months later, in the summer of 1894, he signed onto a commercial sealing ship bound for Norway's northern waters. He wanted to accustom himself to polar weather and gain some practical skills and experience as a sailor. This might also help cover his expenses, since his only income came from his inheritance. His plan was to work toward his master's certificate, a qualification required to become a ship's officer. This career path required years of sea time, performing many tasks as a ship's crew member and passing a series of written tests. This was a profession he could happily throw himself into, and he spent the next several years working on ships mostly in the waters around Iceland and Greenland, where he reported that, "concerning life in the Arctic Ocean, I like it a lot. Its bad reputation is as usual an exaggeration."

Next on the young explorer's agenda was fulfilling his military service. This was a duty of all young men in Norway, but also an experience that Amundsen thought would help develop some of his practical and wilderness skills. For several years he harboured the fear that he might be disqualified from military service due to a physical imperfection: his eyesight. Although he assured the readers of his autobiography that his eyesight was "especially powerful," he admitted that he never wore the glasses that had been prescribed for him, concealing his near-sightedness. Fortunately, according to his own later account, his physique distracted the military physician from examining his eyes and pronouncing the humiliating disqualification. "The old doctor looked me over and at once burst into loud exclamations over my physical development. Evidently my eight years of conscientious exercise had been not without their effect," Amundsen fondly reminisced. "He said to me 'Young man, how in the world did you ever develop such a splendid set of muscles?' . . . So delighted was the old gentleman at his discovery, which he appeared to regard as extraordinary, that he called to a group of officers in the adjoining room to come in and view the novelty. Needless to say, I was embarrassed almost to extinction by this exhibition of my person in the altogether." He was admitted to the army, which required only seven months of service and left him plenty of time to work on the skills he would need for his dream.

Despite his lack of interest in formal schooling, Amundsen began reading "all the books on the subject [of polar exploration] I could lay my hands on." The conclusion he reached after his study of several explorers' journals was that there was a "fatal weakness common to many of the preceding Arctic expeditions": the leaders of these expeditions were not ship's captains.

They had almost invariably relied for the navigation of their vessels upon the services of experienced skippers. The fatal defect of this practice had been in every case that, once embarked at sea, the expedition had not one leader but two. Invariably this resulted in a division of responsibility between the commander and the skipper, incessant friction, divided counsels, and a lowered morale for the subordinate members of the expedition. Always two factions developed—one comprising the commander and the scientific staff, the other comprising the captain and the crew. I was resolved, therefore, that I should never lead an expedition until I was prepared to remedy this defect. The only way to remedy it was to equip myself with experience as a skipper and actually qualify as a ship's captain.

Only then could he lead an expedition as both a navigator and an explorer and "avoid this division into two factions." This lesson served him well for many years and many expeditions. On the one occasion when he didn't follow this rule, he experienced problems exactly as he had imagined, dealing with two semi-hostile factions who did not work well together, causing years of frustration and quarrelling.

Though he was only in his early twenties and had no direct experience in leading expeditions, Amundsen was already imagining himself as the leader rather than just as a member of one. He wrote to an official in the Norwegian government about the national status of the island of Spitsbergen, inquiring whether an expedition there might be in the nation's interests. But then his attention turned to the Antarctic, and he wrote more letters to government officials inquiring about snow and ski conditions there, as well as the number of seals there that could be used as food for dogs.

In the end, however, he must have realized that he was still too inexperienced to be considering these ventures. He returned to putting in his hours working toward his captain's certification instead of pestering government officials. He sailed on merchant ships owned by members of his extended family to destinations as far south as the west coast of Africa, but mostly in the mid-Atlantic from Europe to the Americas. His interest in a voyage quickly waned when it had no northern destination. Nevertheless he held to his studies, and on May 1, 1895, he was awarded his mate's certificate, an important stepping-stone toward acquiring the leadership and practical skills needed to lead an expedition.

During the winter of 1896, Amundsen began planning another ski adventure across Hardangervidda, starting from "the mountain farm Mogen on the east to the farm called Garen on the west coast." It was similar to the trip that had defeated him years earlier, and still "there was no record of any person having ever crossed the plateau in winter. There were no tourists in those days in any season of the year." Years later, he recalled that the adventure "nearly wrote 'finis' to my life, and involved dangers and hardships fully as severe as any I was destined ever to encounter in the polar regions." Indeed, the plateau in winter is very like the polar regions in its wind-lashed barrenness, unpredictable storms and erratic temperatures.

Amundsen's companion this time was his brother Leon, then on holiday from his work as a wine merchant in Europe. But the weather again wreaked havoc on Amundsen's carefully laid plans. He and Leon had barely started before they were forced to spend a week holed up in a tiny farmhouse with six peasant farmers, waiting for a ferocious blizzard to peter out. Knowing the dangers of the plateau in winter, the farmers argued with Roald and Leon not to attempt the crossing before bidding the two young men a sad farewell. "Of course we were lighthearted about the enterprise," the younger Amundsen recalled. The plateau was only 115 kilometres across and, at their speed of skiing, should have taken only two days to traverse. Two days didn't seem like such a long time, so they packed only meagre supplies.

At the end of an exhausting day, the two brothers made it to the halfway hut to find that the door was nailed shut. Exhausted and chilled, they broke in and quickly kindled a fire, the hearth having been conveniently stacked with wood. After eating a warm meal, they fell quickly asleep. That night a storm rolled in, so severe that "it would be folly to venture out in it." For two days the brothers huddled in the hut with warmth but little food. Without food, remaining in the hut was not an option, so they set off in the semi-darkness of winter in the north, navigating by compass. Soon it was snowing again; they could not reach the western edge of the plateau before full darkness was upon them. They settled down to a cold, miserable night, sleeping in the open because they had not brought a tent in order to save weight.

Visibility remained poor due to fog and snow, and the trekkers became disoriented, wandering in circles without food for two more days. The skiing was exhausting them. On their fourth night out they again slept in the open, digging little pits to avoid the wind. They climbed into the pits as the snow piled up around them. Roald was covered completely. When he awoke in the morning, he was immobilized in ice. The warm snow around him had frozen when the temperature dropped. When he opened his mouth to yell for help, powdery snow filled his mouth, partially blocking his airway. He forced himself not to panic and breathed slowly around the snow. He could not move or yell, and felt like he was locked in an icy tomb. When Leon woke up, he was perplexed: he couldn't see his brother. After a while, searching where he remembered Roald lay down to sleep, Leon noticed a few hairs of a reindeer fur poking through the snow. It was the fringe of a sleeping bag. It took him an hour to chip his brother out of the icy pit.

After a few more hours of travel, they found themselves at the edge of the plateau. They descended to the farm hut where they had started out from a week earlier; the men were carving wood and the women were spinning yarn. When the residents looked up to greet the newcomers, they did not recognize the brothers as the same two who had stayed with them the week before. When the Amundsens said they had stayed in the cabin a week earlier, they were not believed. "Our scraggly beards had grown," Roald wrote, "our eyes were gaunt and hollow, our cheeks were sunken, and the ruddy glow of colour had changed to a ghastly greenish yellow. We were a truly awful spectacle." He later learned that a farmer on the far western side of the plateau had seen mysterious ski tracks one morning a few metres from his doorway, coming from the east. The Amundsens had no idea they'd been close to a dwelling. Roald recognized that the journey was a near disaster, but he did not try to place the adventure in any sort of heroic light. Nor did he shy away from taking the blame for many of the trek's problems, such as scant provisions. Despite the hunger and the frostbite that had nearly caused the amputation of fingers and toes, he shrugged off the dangers. It was, he claimed, "a part of my preliminary training for my polar career. The training proved severer than the experience for which it was a preparation." Certainly Amundsen learned to expect the unexpected and to plan for all eventualities, however unlikely they seemed. Many decades later, looking back on his career, he wrote, "I may say that this is the greatest factor: the way in which the expedition is equipped, the way in which every difficulty is foreseen, and precautions taken for meeting or avoiding it." No other expedition led by Amundsen could ever be said to be under-provisioned or unprepared.

He obviously learned a great deal from these amateur forays, undertaken with bravado and the light-hearted anticipation of easy success, but which turned almost deadly when he made the wrong decisions. It was not an accident that Amundsen became the leading explorer of his age. Late in life he claimed—and the claim has the feel of truth to it—that "my career has been a steady progress toward a definite goal since I was fifteen years of age. Whatever I have accomplished in exploration has been the result of lifelong planning, painstaking preparation, and the hardest kind of conscientious work." Certainly that is how he remembered it years afterward, and the meteoric trajectory of his life events seems to confirm it. Of course, a little good luck is always welcome in any story. For Amundsen, the luck came soon after this nearly fatal adventure.

2

Polar Apprentice

Snow and wind are forgotten, and one could not be happier in a royal palace. . . . These excursions are wonderful, and I hope to have frequent opportunities for more.

ON AUGUST 13, 1896, Fridtjof Nansen returned from his three-year expedition in search of the North Pole. He had, as planned, driven his ship *Fram* into the pack ice and drifted with the polar currents. In doing so, he had attracted condemnation and sneers from many within the scientific establishment. During the risky voyage he and a comrade, Hjalmar Johansen, left the *Fram* and with dog sleds skied across the windswept expanse of frozen ice and snow toward the North Pole. They reached 86 degrees, 14 minutes, before turning back—a new record that was 270 kilometres closer than any other recorded approach to the pole. Returning was a struggle, an 800-kilometre trek of endurance over shifting pack ice, futilely chasing their ship as it drifted away from them. The two men overwintered on an uninhabited island near Franz Josef Land before being rescued by a passing British ship. The *Fram* and the rest of its crew returned home to Norway a week after the duo arrived.

Nansen and Johansen were acclaimed as heroes. Tens of thousands thronged the Christiania Fjord to greet the victorious explorers and hear their patriotic speeches. This time, Nansen garnered even more international fame and recognition than when he had returned from Greenland, boosting enthusiasm for Norway's independence from Sweden and feeding a public demand for tales of adventure and danger in an era before the Internet, television or even radio. Tall, blond and muscular, Nansen fit the bill for an idealized Nordic hero figure, braving danger and hardship in a struggle to acquire valuable information for his people. Stereotypes generate easy stories for time-pressed or lazy journalists, and Nansen quickly became part of the endless parade of stock characters that formed the news. He essentially began what has become known as the heroic age of polar exploration, in which a pantheon of larger-than-life individuals competed for the glory of being the first to attain particular, although somewhat arbitrary, geographical milestones.

Around this time, in 1895, the Sixth International Geographical Congress passed a resolution at its meeting in London that "the exploration of the Antarctic regions is the greatest piece of geographical exploration still to be undertaken; it should be undertaken before the close of the century." The polar explorer was becoming a standard fanciful ideal, but one that nonetheless mirrored the young Amundsen's natural characteristics in both personality and appearance. A month before Nansen returned to Norway to international acclaim, Amundsen, now twenty-four years old, had just completed another commercial voyage, this time a sealing voyage in the polar seas off Norway's northern coast. Sealing was an undertaking that he had little liking for—he was never a sport hunter, and large-scale butchering of marine animals disgusted him. Nevertheless, the voyage gave him enough sea time to obtain his master's papers, which permitted him to command a ship in waters around Norway.

With his new certification in hand, he applied for a position with the latest exciting voyage of exploration: a Belgian expedition to

Antarctica, under the command of Adrien de Gerlache. Amundsen's application stood out from the hundreds of others that arrived from around the world. The expedition was grossly underfinanced, and Amundsen's offer to serve without pay undoubtedly was an advantage. But so too was the fact that Amundsen was countryman to the now-famous Nansen. He also had experience skiing and sailing. "The trip will last two years and will be most interesting as, of course, it is the first of its kind," he wrote his brother Leon.

The Belgian expedition was an international affair and stood out not only for being the first of its kind but also for being somewhat peculiar for a country without a significant maritime tradition. The crew included members from Norway, Belgium, Poland, Romania and the United States—among them the Brooklyn physician Frederick A. Cook, who had ventured to northern Greenland a few years earlier with Peary. While de Gerlache wintered in Norway to learn Norwegian and how to ski, Amundsen spent the winter in Antwerp learning French and taking a private course in navigation. In March he hastily returned to Norway, fleeing Antwerp after the suicide of his Flemish landlady. She had apparently died from carbon monoxide poisoning, and Amundsen had found her body when he came down for breakfast. His Norwegian biographer, Tor Bomann-Larsen, contends that she and Amundsen had become lovers and that her death had so shaken him that he could not continue with his studies: "The lady and I were good friends so I know the circumstances," he wrote to his brother. "If I were to start on this story I'm afraid I would never finish it."

The *Belgica* sailed for the Antarctic from Antwerp on August 16, 1897, for a two-and-a-half-year adventure with Amundsen aboard as second mate. The small ship, a converted Norwegian whaling ship, cruised south toward Cape Horn, reaching the Strait of Magellan in late December. Cook had joined the ship at Rio de Janeiro, and he and Amundsen soon became friends. The young Amundsen was eager to hear stories about Cook's trip to the north.

The crew of the *Belgica* spent several weeks exploring Tierra del Fuego. "In those days, little was known of this region scientifically, and our commander was so taken with the possibilities of discovery there that we lingered for several weeks, gathering specimens of its natural history, mapping its shores, and taking meteorological observations." They pushed south, past the South Shetland Islands and encountered icebergs. They were now in the uncharted waters north of the Antarctic Peninsula, and Amundsen noted that they "soon had an adventure that came near to ending the career of all of us." He came onto the bridge to take the afternoon watch and found the ship entering a terrific gale. In the driving sleet and snow, the ship was surrounded by deadly ice. The captain, who had been steering the ship in the lee of an enormous iceberg, instructed Amundsen to keep the course to shelter the ship from the worst of the storm. In doing so, one sailor was washed overboard, screaming as he plunged into the fog and ice. The men rushed to save him. One grabbed the sailor's arm and nearly pulled him back onto the ship, but his grip slipped and the sailor slid away and soon sank from view. Amundsen felt responsible because he was the officer on watch, although the mishap had little directly to do with him. He passed the remainder of his watch without incident and relayed the captain's instructions to the next officer on duty before turning in for the night. Then he "could feel the ship rolling in response to the swell," he recalled; the movement "was not the tremendous heave of the main Pacific, but was a modified rolling of the current which came around the iceberg to us," and Amundsen was gently lulled to sleep.

In the morning the water was calm, and Amundsen quickly dressed and rushed on deck with the others. They stared in awe, finding the ship in a small basin, "icelocked on every side by a complete circle of towering icebergs." The young man who had steered the ship into the enclosure had no idea how they came to be encircled. It had probably happened during the storm, when the ship might have been "lifted on one of the mighty Pacific swells through an opening between two icebergs and had landed us in the becalmed basin. . . . [N]othing short of a miracle of coincidence had saved us from being dashed to pieces by the bergs that formed the shallow entrance we had hurdled on the back of that swelling wave." The crew carefully eased the ship out again, with flags at half mast for the drowned mariner and with their fear growing stronger. It was around this time that Amundsen finally realized that this expedition was not a well-organized scientific foray into the unknown but an underfunded, poorly planned dash into danger. "I can only admire his audacity," Amundsen wrote of de Gerlache. "Onwards or bust. I will follow all the way, cheerful and smiling."

The *Belgica* wound its way along the coast of Graham Land, the northern portion of the Antarctic Peninsula, and slipped into an unknown channel between the mainland and a series of islands. De Gerlache named it after his ship, but now it is called De Gerlache Strait and is considered the great geographical discovery of the expedition. The ship toured the strait for several weeks, stopping often to collect rock samples, inspect glaciers and launch ski expeditions. Amundsen set off on several ski expeditions and joined the first Antarctic sledging expedition. De Gerlache, Cook, Amundsen and two others landed two great sledges and a week of supplies near Brabant Island and then slogged to the height of land for a better view of the strait to gain perspective when drawing up their map of the region. They man-hauled their sledges over the rough, frozen terrain, around "uncounted" crevasses and up slippery slopes. The South Pole expert Roland Huntford points out quite colourfully that to Amundsen this experience was game-changing in that it forever steered him away from man-hauling sledges on his own expeditions: "[M]an-hauling was vividly shown to be neither glorious nor heroic, but unpleasant, sweaty, toilsome and stupid."

It took a great and exhausting effort for the sledge party to reach the height of land on January 31, 1898. When the men stood on the promontory they beheld a desolate, wind-lashed plain of icy expanses broken by jutting black rock formations that were separated from the land by an ice-infested channel. Here they set up a historic Antarctic camp, the first ever. "The snow was very close," Amundsen wrote in his journal, "and we were compelled to dig out a place for the tent." The duties were split between setting up their camp and preparing the communal meal in the "lee of a sledge. . . . [I]t is not long before our little tent raises its ridge against the snow and wind. Our necessities for the night, sleeping bags and dry stockings, are put into the tent; the rest is left on the sledge, well protected by covers." The five companions settled in for a meal of pea soup and soon "snow and wind [were] forgotten, and one could not be happier in a royal palace. . . . These excursions are wonderful," Amundsen enthused, "and I hope to have frequent opportunities for more."

During the outing he took special care to observe and learn from "[t]he Doctor [Cook], the experienced Polar explorer," who was calm and competent, and a willing teacher. Amundsen observed that the doctor wore sealskin clothes rather than wool and praised "the practical and calm manner in which this man works." He went on, under Cook's tutelage, to evaluate the expedition's equipment, noting deficiencies such as the type of tent, which "presents too great a surface to the wind," and preparing a list of necessities for polar travel that included snow goggles, light wool clothing and a waterproof tin for matches. Amundsen devoted many pages to these seemingly mundane practical observations and assessments. As a result, his journal of the *Belgica* voyage is somewhat lacking in the lurid descriptions and semi-mocking musings of the entertaining accounts of his later expeditions, when he was the leader and his writing was both a marketing tool and a source of income. In 1898, however, Amundsen was a serious student of the practical aspects of organizing an expedition, and he knew he was not writing for an audience.

By late February, the *Belgica* had ploughed south into the pack ice in search of more geographical mysteries to solve, and de Gerlache was hoping to break through to the Weddell Sea (which proved to be impossible) and perhaps be the first to overwinter in Antarctica. He wanted to wedge the *Belgica* in the ice and float with the Antarctic currents, repeating at the bottom of the world what Nansen had so recently done at the top. The crew, even the scientific contingent, showed little interest in this speculative and highly dangerous plan. They were not equipped for an overwintering. The original plan was to proceed to the region of the magnetic South Pole on South Victoria Land and leave a four-person team for the winter while the rest of the crew sailed to Australia. Amundsen, who would gladly have supported de Gerlache's scheme if it had been made public, wrote that "unfortunately, the scientists are openly showing their fear. They are reluctant to go any further into the ice. Why, I ask, did we come here? Is it not to explore the unknown regions? That is impossible if you stay outside the ice."

On February 28, de Gerlache steered the *Belgica* into heaving ice as another "terrific gale" blew in. Instead of heading north into the open sea, he ordered the ship to ride before the storm through a tiny opening in the ice to the south. When the storm abated, the *Belgica* had been driven deep into an ice field. "Here we were, fast in the Antarctic ice drifting round in the uncharted southern seas at the beginning of the long Polar winter." Interestingly, later in life Amundsen blamed the manoeuvre on "a lack of experience in Polar navigation," when clearly de Gerlache's actions had been intentional. In his journal of the voyage, Amundsen recalls being "happy," writing that "nothing could be better" than this outcome. But these musings were penned before he realized that they had packed no winter outer clothes for most of the crew, had inadequate food for an overwintering and insufficient lamp oil. Writing thirty years later, he recalled the predicament as "a truly dreadful prospect." The ship lay 150 kilometres in the surging pack ice and was almost certainly locked in for the winter. De Gerlache made a half-hearted effort to extricate the *Belgica* from the ice swells, its engines roaring as the ship futilely surged against the congested ice. It was, however, an action intended to mollify the despondent crew rather than to escape. By this time de Gerlache had taken Amundsen into his confidence; the Norwegian knew of the deception and approved of it. "Here we were," he wrote in his memoirs, "drifting round in the uncharted southern seas at the beginning of the long Polar winter."

A polar winter can be a dreary, morale-sapping season even for those who are psychologically and physically prepared: living in cold and darkness for months on end, locked up together on a tiny ship, rehashing the same stories, brooding over the same resentments and reviving the same quarrels with the same people again and again. Add to this unwholesome isolation the constant fears that they might never again see the sun or return to their homes; that the ship might be frozen in the desolate wasteland until they perished from exposure and dwindling supplies; and that if the ice shifted the ship could be pinched in a vise and burst—it was hardly a wonder that morale plummeted on the *Belgica* as the months dragged on. Certainly there could be no rescue in this most forlorn reach of the planet. The crew's dissatisfaction increased when it became known that they had been tricked by de Gerlache. Two of the men were driven mad, and others teetered on the edge of sanity. Cook wrote of life on board the *Belgica* that "mentally, the outlook was that of a madhouse."

Amundsen seemed to thrive on the hardships and continued absence of the usual comforts of life: variable and fresh food, new conversation partners, even female company. He relished the absence of these comforts, the shrinking of his daily joys. His apparent pleasure in suffering may have been a coping mechanism that enabled him to endure the monotony and discomfort of extreme conditions, or perhaps an ascetic quest for deprivation fuelled his desire for harsh expeditions, so that he could suffer just like Franklin did. This relishing of hardship stayed with him his whole life, but it was limited to the times when he was on expedition. Between adventures, he wholeheartedly embraced the daily pleasures to be found in food, companionship, warmth, variations in scenery and intellectual stimulation. Even in the midst of perpetual darkness, he deliberately kept his spirits up: "Tomorrow the sun will reach the end of its northward journey and start to make its way back. Of course I am looking forward to seeing it again, but I haven't missed it."

Perhaps like many adventurers today, whether canoe-trippers, backpackers, sailors, mountain climbers or polar skiers, Amundsen had a great appreciation for the sense of accomplishment that the struggle against hostile elements provides, or the intense pleasure that comes from simple comforts like a cup of warm soup and a dry pair of socks after a day of hard labour in the freezing cold. There is a way in which a shared struggle in dangerous situations magically reduces the worries of a complicated life to an intense appreciation of even minor comforts, but even celebration in communal struggle eventually gives way to despair and hopelessness. The months of cold and darkness groaned on throughout 1898. Many of the *Belgica*'s crew were convinced of their imminent death. They became lethargic, depressed and anti-social, drifting away into near-catatonic isolation even while crammed together on the ship. Their hair and beards grew unkempt, their eyes became dim and bloodshot and their weary faces showed the strain of their predicament.

Amundsen and his friend Cook weathered the season better than most. Amundsen was eager to continue learning all he could of the techniques of polar travel and survival, and during the nine months they were locked in the ice he worked on testing new tent designs, perfecting new clothing and venturing on a sledging foray onto the pack ice, the first such trek in Antarctic history. He and Cook tested skis on the pack ice, comparing them with snowshoes and finding them faster, safer and better suited to distributing weight when crossing dangerous sections of ice. Cook, "of all the ships' company, was the one man of unfaltering courage, unfailing hope, endless cheerfulness, and unwearied kindness. When anyone was sick, he was there at his bedside to comfort him; when any was disheartened, he was there to encourage and inspire. And not only was his faith undaunted, but his ingenuity and enterprise were boundless."

It was the energetic Dr. Cook who spearheaded the solution to the greatest threat to the mens' survival during that gloomy winter: the insidious spread of scurvy. Many of the mental aberrations that beset the crew during those dark months—their depression, morose moping in their bunks, lethargy and lack of enthusiasm even to help themselves—are psychological symptoms of scurvy, whose physical symptoms include puffy, blackened and bleeding gums and loose teeth, foul breath, swollen joints, the opening of old wounds and the un-knitting of broken bones as the body's connective tissue disintegrates. All this is accompanied by a general inability to focus or to think clearly. Scurvy is one of the most ancient of diseases, although it is more properly considered a dietary deficiency. It is caused by a lack of ascorbic acid. Vitamin C is found primarily in fresh foods, and scurvy will show up anywhere that a diet is lacking in this essential ingredient, during famines or long winters and in impoverished populations.

During the Age of Sail scurvy was the bane of mariners, indirectly causing more deaths than storms, battles and shipwrecks combined. On long voyages it could claim the lives of entire crews, as they became too ill to pilot their vessel and it capsized or was driven against a rocky coast. The renowned British mariner Captain James Cook was able to keep scurvy mostly under control on his epic voyages in the late eighteenth century by imposing a strict diet. The problem was famously solved by the British Royal Navy during the Napoleonic Wars in 1795, when the physician Sir Gilbert Blane persuaded the admiralty to issue lemon or lime juice daily, mixed with sailors' rum ration, giving rise to the term "Limeys" to describe British sailors. In the early twentieth century, during Amundsen's time, scurvy's causes were still unknown and synthetic vitamin supplements did not exist. The methods for preserving food (drying, salting and primitive canning techniques) destroyed most, if not all, vitamin C. Thus it was on long expeditions in polar environments, or in armies subsisting on rations through long winters, that scurvy would show up to make history.

Nearly everyone on the *Belgica* was suffering from scurvy long before the winter was through. One man died of it on June 15, and many more would undoubtedly have followed, had not Cook recognized the seriousness of the problem from his experience in the Arctic and his observations of the diets of northern polar peoples. His solution was introduce fresh meat into the men's diet. He noted that the open channels near the ship were frequented by penguins and seals, which if cooked only lightly would provide the men with sufficient amounts of the essential nutrient. Amundsen recorded that "we had, therefore, spent many weary hours, after the day's work was done, travelling for miles over the ice in search of seals and penguins, and with great labour had killed and brought to the ship a great number of each. The commander, however, developed an aversion to the flesh of both that amounted to a mania." While Cook and Amundsen and several others frequently consumed the meat in a near-raw state and avoided the most severe symptoms of scurvy, de Gerlache opposed having the meat issued as a daily ration to the men, allowing the crew to eat it only occasionally and, even then, only if they wanted it.

The men hated the taste of the meat, and many ate it only as a medicine under the doctor's orders. Amundsen, in his typically contrarian and open-minded style, claimed that "the meat is excellent, not unlike beef." He preferred the daily ration of lime juice. As historians have noted, however, the production quality and consistency of bottled lime juice varied greatly, depending on how it was heated during the manufacturing process. The rapid development of scurvy in the crew of the *Belgica* was an indication that the lime juice supplied for the expedition was probably compromised and contained little or none of the vital vitamin.

Many of the crew became horribly ill before they saw the benefits of the semi-raw seal meat: those who ate it remained mostly free of the ravages of the deadly deficiency. The ship's cook then thawed the frozen seal steaks acquired through Amundsen and Cook's hunting forays and prepared the meat regularly for meals. As with all cases of scurvy, the men's improvement from their debilitated state was rapid and remarkable. Even de Gerlache, who was prostrate with the sickness, was soon going about his regular duties.

After pulling through the long winter, the men were faced with another serious problem: the pack ice that surrounded the ship remained thick and impenetrable, even as spring gave way to summer in the southern hemisphere. Yet more forced immobility was frustrating for everyone aboard, and it exposed another disagreement. Amundsen and Cook were annoyed at de Gerlache's intransigence in refusing to eat fresh seal meat, and, as captain, to order his crew to eat it even while the scurvy epidemic spread through the ship. His obstinacy had endangered the lives of all—indeed, the entire expedition.

Then, when November arrived, Amundsen discovered that a secret deal had been arranged whereby the *Belgica*'s normal chain of command was to be altered to give Belgian officers priority in commanding the expedition, regardless of their rank. De Gerlache informed Amundsen, who was second mate, that he was to be passed over in the succession of command by the third mate, a young Belgian officer. Amundsen, consumed with anger, viewed the decision as an attack on himself and on Norwegians in general. It was a seriously damaging lapse in the judgment of the expedition's organizers, founded in nationalism. He wrote to de Gerlache in frustration, "I followed you without pay. It was not a question of money, but honour. That honour you have insulted by denying me my right. As far as I am concerned, there is no longer a Belgian Antarctic expedition, and the *Belgica* is just an ordinary ship locked in the ice. It is my duty to help the men on board. For this reason, captain, I will continue my work as if nothing had happened."

The fact the ship was immobilized in ice, thousands of kilometres from any other ship or inhabited land, was certainly another consideration that kept the young Norwegian aboard and at his post. He felt that many of the crew and officers were incompetent—certainly an accurate observation if the word "inexperienced" is substituted—and that only through his efforts could he ensure that the ship would ever break free of the ice and return to civilization.

Several writers have seen his angry response to de Gerlache as evidence of Amundsen's "irrational" and "hysterical" reaction to any and all criticism, and that the slight was somehow insignificant or imagined. In fact, there is a reason de Gerlache kept this information secret for over a year and a half: it was not normal or accepted protocol in naval or maritime traditions. It was a serious violation of custom to have an erratic and random chain of command that was revealed by secret documents only when the need arose. The formalized succession of command exists for a good reason—law at sea—and is undermined by the issuance of secret papers partway through a voyage. Amundsen was right to be infuriated by the situation, not for personal reasons, but rather for institutional and structural reasons. Gaps in the hierarchy of leadership could lead to infighting and even mutiny, endangering both the crew and the expedition. De Gerlache later admitted that he was forced into the sly situation under duress—pressure from the Belgian Geographical Society.

Amundsen recognized an incompatible difference in style between himself and the Belgian crew when he wrote that "between us and the Belgian nation there exists in thought and deed such a vast difference, that we would never be able to work well together." This was the sort of insight that Amundsen became famous for, and this one led him later to consistently choose men who would work well together as a team. It is fair to note that much of the criticism Amundsen was frustrated with later in his life was levelled by people who had far less experience than he did. And, as was the case in the Belgian Antarctic Expedition, it was initiated for reasons that had little to do with Amundsen's actual competence as a leader.

Meanwhile, the *Belgica* was still stuck in the ice and showed no signs of breaking free after nine months and the return of Antarctic summer. If the crew couldn't get the ship free, the men would either have to stay a second winter or abandon the ship and march for land; neither option offered much hope of a happy ending. For the second time on the voyage it was Cook who roused the shipmates from their torpor. During his ramblings on the ice with Amundsen he had noticed, a kilometre or two from the ship, a large crack in the otherwise unbroken ice sheet. Cook's plan was to somehow cut a path through the ice to the crack and get the *Belgica* into it, so that as the thaw progressed the ship would have a chance of sailing out to open water. Indifferent at first to what Amundsen himself called a "mad enterprise," the men were soon enthusiastic; as Amundsen wrote, "at least it would give us something to do besides sitting and contemplating our probable fate."

The main problem was their equipment. The *Belgica*'s supplies contained only a small supply of dynamite and a few four-foot saws. The men were still weakened, despite the fresh meat in their diet. Nevertheless, by January 1899, Cook got them working together to cut lines in the ice and then place dynamite in them to blast a channel. After several weeks of hard labour the men had created a channel long enough to drag the ship to water, where they continued to wait. "Then," Amundsen related, "the miracle happened—exactly what Cook had predicted. The ice opened and the lane to the sea ran directly through our basin!"

The engineer fired up the boiler and the *Belgica* surged forward, struggling against two giant icebergs. "All day and all night we were subjected to a terrific grinding pressure, and the noise of the ice cakes battering against our sides and splintering off incessantly was at times so loud as to make conversation trying." To prevent damage to the hull, they lowered penguin skins over the side of the ship to serve as bumpers as the *Belgica* slowly ground against the pack ice. The struggle continued for another month before the crew even saw open water. By mid-March the ship was still grinding against the congestion of ice, making little headway, its engines roaring and belching smoke as it bucked ineffectually against a mighty frozen wall. But then, deliverance: "[T]he engineer comes on deck to say he cannot keep up steam any longer. He sees the gravity of the situation for himself. It is unnecessary to ask him to keep steam up. In the winking of an eye he is below again, and the engine is working as it has never worked before, and never will again. We fight our way ahead, inch by inch, foot by foot, meter by meter. We are saved. At the critical moment, the ice slackens." The battered ship surged ahead into open water, free.

Two weeks later, on March 27, 1899, the *Belgica* cruised into Punta Arenas, a Chilean port in the Strait of Magellan. Here Amundsen disembarked and sailed home to Norway on his own. He was disgusted with the incompetence, deceitfulness and nationalist prejudice of the expedition's Belgian officers. The *Belgica* had long been feared lost, so the public was surprised by its return; likewise, its crew members were surprised to learn of events that had transpired since they had entered the Antarctic ice at the end of 1897, such as the start of the Boer War in South Africa and the Spanish American War in the Caribbean and the Pacific. During the nearly two years of their voyage and imprisonment in the ice, the world had marched on. It was a phenomenon to which Amundsen would have to adjust. He returned home without fanfare, on a mail boat, escorting one of the Norwegian mariners who had gone mad during the terrifying Antarctic winter.

That the *Belgica* expedition was fraught with inefficiencies, inappropriate equipment, flaws in the chain of command and imprecise objectives is undoubted. Amundsen did, nevertheless, learn a great deal about how, and how not, to organize and lead an expedition in extreme polar conditions. The negatives came from observing the

innumerable deficiencies in leadership and crew that caused most of
the trouble and a near-fatal outcome for the *Belgica* expedition.
Most of the positives came from the many hours spent with Cook in
exploring and discussing various methods and types of equipment.

The German author Rainer K. Langer, writing in *Scott and
Amundsen: Duel in the Ice,* seems to accuse Amundsen of poor judgment for signing on to the expedition in the first place. "Amundsen
ought to have known better, but after the London congress he was
blinded by ambition to reach the place at de Gerlache's side that was
the center of world attention." An alternate view does not presup-
pose such responsibility on the young Norwegian: de Gerlache's was
the first exploring expedition that had accepted him as a member; he
had applied for many positions before and had been overlooked.
Amundsen was not about to turn down his first and perhaps only
chance to go on a voyage of exploration and gain polar experience,
and it's hard to imagine anyone in his place doing so. He was second
mate on the voyage, not the captain, and he was not responsible for
selecting the other members of the crew or for arranging the financing. Criticism of Amundsen as being blinded by ambition is
unwarranted, but it fits the stereotypical image of him that became
popular decades later.

Although Amundsen kept a journal of the voyage, he did not
publish his account of the expedition; that was the commander's
prerogative, and de Gerlache, as the official commander, published
a book in Europe. Cook, as an American physician, published his
book in the United States. When Amundsen wrote about the adventure in his memoirs three decades later, he omitted de Gerlache's
name—so great was his antipathy to his commander after the quarrel that occurred near the end of the expedition.

In his journal and memoirs, Amundsen generously gives Cook
credit for initiating the scurvy cure and for rousing the men into
sawing through the ice, creating a path to their freedom. Throughout his career, Amundsen freely gave credit where credit was due.

Conversely, when someone failed to live up to his expectations he could be ruthless and defiant. He would not accept criticism from individuals he did not respect, or from those whom he felt had no knowledge or experience upon which to base their critique. From now on, Amundsen hand-selected the members of each crew and, apart from a few notable exceptions, enjoyed remarkable harmony and cohesiveness among them in the astonishing feats of exploration that would define his life.

Amundsen took no pay for the *Belgica* voyage, but he had no expenses either, so he returned to Norway in the same financial state as when he departed. He did, however, earn one important thing on the two-and-a-half-year expedition: the first of his many nicknames. One of his shipmates, the Polish meteorologist Antoine Dobrowlski, after enumerating what he considered the main accomplishments of the *Belgica* voyage years later, wrote that "our voyage was the first school of that extraordinary explorer, the Napoleon of the Polar regions; Amundsen."

3

An Extraordinary Plan

*I have many bright and pleasant memories from those
days, of men who encouraged me and gave me all
the support they could. I have also other memories—
of those who thought they . . . had a right to criticise
and condemn whatever others undertook or proposed
to undertake.*

DESPITE ITS ACCOMPLISHMENT of overwintering
for the "first Antarctic night," the *Belgica* expedition attracted
little fame. Amundsen returned quietly to his home in Christiania,
moving on to the next phase of his career: planning his own expedition. He completed a final stint in the army and then sought an audience with Fridtjof Nansen, who was then, as Amundsen put it,
"the Grand Old man of Arctic exploration in Norway. I knew that
a word from him would be priceless to me in enlisting aid in my enterprise; on the other hand, a word of disparagement from him
would be fatal."

Nansen would go on to become one of the founders of the
League of Nations and also its high commissioner for refugees. In
the 1890s, he was entertaining the possibility of leading his own expedition to Antarctica, and he welcomed the young man's offer to

discuss his recent voyage to the southern continent. "I went, therefore, to see him and laid before him my plans and hopes and asked his benediction," Amundsen wrote. "This he graciously gave; and he even went further—he offered to commend me to the good offices of people who might help me."

What these people might help him with was still very much a private matter, but on the *Belgica* expedition one of the objectives highlighted by de Gerlache—an objective that proved impossible—was to locate the magnetic South Pole. Amundsen began to imagine combining his quest to sail the fabled Northwest Passage with the more prosaic and scientifically noteworthy objective of locating the magnetic North Pole. "My plans matured," he wrote after his first Antarctic voyage. "I wished to unite my childhood dreams about the North West Passage with the, in itself, far more important objective: to determine the magnetic North Pole's present position."

Encouraged by Nansen's support and encouragement, and inspired by his own developing plans, Amundsen continued wrestling with the less exciting technical hurdles that blocked his dream of sailing the Northwest Passage: completing the final hours of ship time to obtain his captain's licence, which would enable him to command a ship in international waters, and then passing an exam. He signed on to the *Oscar*, a small ship that was part of the family business, then stationed in Cartagena, Spain. Amundsen being who he was, rather than take some comfortable or practical method of reaching southern Spain, decided to cycle there with his brother Leon. Leon was in Norway, but he was planning to return to his wine-shipping business in southern France.

Cycling was not then a common activity in Europe, and the sight of two tall blond men pedalling south through the European countryside surely raised some eyebrows. It was an uneventful journey and Amundsen was soon at sea on a two-month voyage bound for Pensacola, Florida. He brought with him a large collection of books on polar travel and exploration—everything from Sir John Franklin's decades-old books to British naval officer James Clark Ross's account of reaching the magnetic North Pole in 1831 to the British explorer Frederick Jackson's more recent *A Thousand Days in the Arctic*, concerning his recent expedition to Franz Josef Land, northeast of Spitsbergen, in the late 1890s.

When he returned from this commercial voyage, well-read and finally with enough sea time to be a certified ship's captain anywhere in the world, Amundsen set out to burnish his scientific credentials. "My expedition must have a scientific purpose as well as the purpose of exploration," he noted. "Otherwise I should not be taken seriously and would not get backing." Amundsen was eager to accomplish heroic deeds, but who would pay for them? He went to visit Dr. Aksel Steen at the Meteorological Institute in Christiania and presented his case, emphasizing the magnetic North Pole and adding the navigation of the Northwest Passage as an interesting side project. The doctor was impressed and urged the young man to learn how to take the necessary measurements. He gave Amundsen a letter to take with him to Hamburg, introducing him to Professor Georg Neumayer, director of the German Marine Observatory.

In the seaport of Hamburg, Amundsen "hired a cheap room in the poor part of the city—my funds were low," he sheepishly related. Despite his letter of introduction, he was not overly optimistic about the reception he would receive from the distinguished professor, since he was "an undistinguished stranger." Nevertheless, "with beating heart, I presented myself at his outer office and handed in my card of introduction" to Neumeyer's assistant. Amundsen was then ushered into the presence of "a man of probably seventy years, whose white hair, benign, clean-shaven face, and gentle eyes presented a most striking resemblance to the famous musician, Franz Liszt." The young Norwegian introduced himself and stammered an erratic overview of his desire to go on a voyage and collect scientific data to justify the adventure. In his memoirs, Amundsen relates how he feared to aspire to something so prominent and prestigious.

"Young man, you have something more on your mind than this!" Neumayer exclaimed kindly. "Tell me what it is." Amundsen then admitted he wanted to conquer the Northwest Passage. "Ah," Neumayer responded, "there is still more." Neumayer waited while Amundsen overcame his reticence and blurted out that his scheme was indeed more grand, that he aspired to no less than the accurate measurement and observations of the magnetic North Pole to settle the longstanding controversy over whether it was mobile or static. The old man rose slowly to his feet, approached Amundsen and quietly embraced him. "Young man," Neumayer said, "if you do that, you will be the benefactor of mankind for ages to come. This is the great adventure."

For the next three months, Amundsen immersed himself in the study of magnetic science and the methods for taking magnetic observations at the institute. Neumayer gave him much personal instruction and attention, which Amundsen repaid by being the first student to arrive in the observatory in the morning and the last to leave at night. Amundsen was very serious in his studies, and the professor, impressed with his diligence, insisted on dining with him regularly at a luxurious hotel where the restaurant was "a fairyland of savoury delights, and its menu a Lucullian feast." The professor also introduced Amundsen to other visiting scientists and luminaries, "thereby providing me, not only with a much appreciated meal, but with the stimulation of contact with active minds and intellects of achievement. Never shall I cease to be grateful to this kindly old soul who so greatly encouraged and helped me." It is worth noting that Amundsen was turned down for similar training at the British Observatory at Kew and recalled this perceived slight when writing his memoirs nearly three decades later.

Back in Christiania in November 1900, Amundsen prepared for another meeting with Nansen, in which he would outline the details of his proposed expedition and the dual but linked objectives of navigating the Northwest Passage and locating the magnetic North

Pole. Nansen had given him encouragement the previous year, and now Amundsen was returning to get his mentor's solid support for a specific objective. "I think it is Mark Twain who tells of a man who was so small that he had to go twice through the door before he could be seen. But this man's insignificance was nothing compared to what I felt on the morning I stood in Nansen's villa at Lysaker and knocked at the door to his study." Amundsen soon stood before the man who had "for years loomed before me as something almost superhuman: the man who had achieved exploits which stirred every fibre of my being."

Nansen had a reputation for being stern and brusque, and was known for his attention to hierarchy and formality. As Amundsen wrote many years later, Nansen was perhaps "too kingly" toward his men, unchallenged as the world's foremost polar scientist. The older man was, however, an adventurer in addition to being a scientist, and he supported Amundsen enthusiastically right from the start, perhaps inspired by Amundsen's youthful enthusiasm and energy. "From that moment," Amundsen recalled, "I date the actual realization of the *Gjøa* expedition." The idea of relocating the position of the magnetic North Pole, and the adventure involved in doing it, was enough to secure the famous patriot's blessing. Without that support, Amundsen's life as a famous explorer might have ended before it even began.

Of the many lessons Amundsen had learned from the *Belgica* voyage and from his discussions and meetings with Cook and Nansen, a few were vital: (1) that a small, light-travelling group could be successful where a large, overly burdened one would fail; (2) that skiing was the best way to travel in polar environments and that a small, select band of tough, equally skilled skiers could prove successful where a large and varied group was more likely to disintegrate and fail (a group is only as fast as its slowest member, and therefore all its members need to be equally conditioned and skilled); (3) that the most effective means of travel in polar environments was not man-hauling large sledges but rather using dog teams to haul light sleds; and (4) that the best clothing would be based on designs used by the people native to those wind-lashed polar landscapes. So, when conceiving his expedition, Amundsen opted for simplicity—the absence of superfluous people, overly ambitious plans or complicated equipment. An expedition on a smaller scale also had the advantage of being more affordable, which was particularly important for an individual planning a privately financed adventure. He also came to a conclusion that was more common in the military: if an expedition leader provided no line of retreat, then the only way out was to follow the plan. Nansen, for example, when crossing Greenland, had his party dropped on the uninhabited east coast to work their way toward the settlement on the west—success and survival for him and his men lay in pushing forward, never to retreat.

Perhaps most importantly, on the *Belgica* Amundsen had learned a lot about poor management, poor organization and poor equipment. A hero, in his mind, was not someone who suffered disaster after disaster, heroically pulling through with great endurance, but rather one who focused his intelligence and skills to avoid disaster, thus succeeding by good planning and crafty decision making. Amundsen was not preparing for heroic disasters—he planned to succeed with as little potential for disaster as possible, even if this meant years of preparation. As he would demonstrate throughout most of his life, Amundsen had an innate sense of when he was ready for an undertaking; in 1900, he felt he wasn't prepared to tackle the Northwest Passage quite yet.

He also didn't have a ship, so he travelled north to one of the remotest places in Norway. The town of Tromsø is surrounded by deep fjords, and at the time, it was accessible only by sea. Tromsø was effectively the gateway to the Polar Sea and home to the Norwegian sealing industry. Here Amundsen wanted to seek out any additional information that might help him on a polar voyage, from people who routinely sailed in Arctic waters. He also wanted to purchase his ship here; a vessel that was seaworthy in these conditions. He settled in Tromsø for a few months and, in a classic example of his single-mindedness, interacted only with people whom he felt had knowledge that could help him. He had them over for coffee in his small room, listening intently and respectfully to the sometimes tall tales of the veteran sealers and ship captains. In January 1901, after learning from these practical northern mariners, Amundsen began negotiating for a ship. He asked his brother Gustav, who was then managing his finances, to send a large chunk of his inheritance to Tromsø.

The ship Amundsen had his eyes on was a forty-seven-tonne fishing smack, small but sturdy, designed for coastal and northern waters. Amundsen noted that the ship was twenty-nine years old, the same age as he was; it was named *Gjøa*, after the previous owner's wife. The little sail-powered vessel, he noted, "had ample opportunities of proving herself an uncommonly well-built boat." A small ship could sneak through the ice floes rather than crush against them. And he preferred a small ship because, as the north was harsh and unforgiving, it would be impossible to live off the land if there were too many people to feed.

Amundsen hired a small crew and set off on a summer voyage to test the *Gjøa* and to take some scientific measurements for Nansen. Cruising the waters between Norway and Greenland for six months, he tested the ship in all weather conditions. "The *Gjøa* performed splendidly under all conditions," he reported. He also commented that he was glad to see that northern Norwegians were not afraid of eating seal meat, which he knew was going to be a staple food on his voyage. He needed a cook who could make use of one of the most abundant northern food sources and a crew who would eat it, to stave off scurvy. On this first voyage, Amundsen broke even, barely covering his costs with the sale of seal pelts and a couple of walrus and polar bear skins.

During these first months at sea, he did note deficiencies in the *Gjøa*'s design, as far as his purposes were concerned. In Arctic waters, he knew the little ship would be working its way through pack ice and close to rocky, uncharted shores. It would require some modifications at the Tromsø shipyard, including iron reinforcements to the hull, supplementary petroleum tanks and a small engine, a thirteen-horsepower motor that could be "connected to everything that could possibly be driven with its aid." Years later, he commented that "our successful navigation of the North West Passage was very largely due to our excellent little engine."

In his memoirs, published two decades after the event, Amundsen wrote, "The winter and spring of 1902–1903 I spent in feverish preparation for my great adventure of the North West Passage. I besieged every possible source of funds—the learned societies and the private patrons of science. The rest of my time was spent in selecting and ordering supplies." The process was considerably more complicated and time-consuming than he admitted or remembered in his memoirs. It was from his base in Tromsø in 1900 that he began not only the search for a crew interested in a multi-year voyage of great uncertainty and danger but also the list of things necessary to outfit a ship for a voyage that might last three or more years. It was a daunting task for a single person, particularly since he was lacking the funds to provide even the most basic equipment and supplies.

As fortune would have it, in spite of Amundsen's habitual secretiveness during his months in Tromsø, there was a person who found his furtive planning and work on the *Gjøa* too unusual to ignore. Fritz Zapffe was an active skier, mountain scrambler and climber then working as a pharmacist in Tromsø. He was also a correspondent for a Christiania newspaper, *Morgenbladet*. Amundsen was initially reticent about answering any questions about his destination or the modifications to his ship. But Zapffe persevered, and finally Amundsen admitted that he was indeed planning something but didn't want anyone to know about it. He told Zapffe that he wanted people to know about his undertaking only when he had achieved something significant, something worthy of attention.

Amundsen was reluctant to toot his own horn, to publicly brag or strut; he believed that he deserved recognition only after he was successful. Zapffe tactfully pointed out that any success would depend on raising the funds to finance his expedition. For a private citizen, advance publicity might be the only way to get additional financial support. People or advertisers could donate or lend money only if they knew about this exciting new adventure and rallied around it—there could be no public support for a secret. Although Zapffe's point appears obvious, Amundsen had absolutely no exposure to or experience with publicity or fundraising. Fortunately, he took Zapffe's advice to heart and never made the same mistake.

Zapffe, who became one of Amundsen's life-long friends and supported many of his adventures with logistical assistance over the years, wrote a front-page story about the planned conquest of the Northwest Passage. Despite Amundsen's initial misgivings about getting publicity before he had done anything, the article led to a surge in financial support. Zapffe also helped Amundsen's endeavour in other ways: through his knowledge of outdoor equipment and his local contacts, he was able to help with the design and manufacture of key pieces of equipment and clothing. He advised Amundsen to consider Arctic clothes designed by the Sami, the indigenous reindeer-herding nomads of Norway's north, and arranged for him to acquire reindeer-hide boots, overcoats and sleeping bags. Amundsen was quick to recognize the superiority of the local clothing and gear. It made a strong impression on him, particularly when combined with what he had learned from Cook in Antarctica and his experience there with inferior clothing and equipment unsuited to the rigours of a polar environment. Through Zapffe, Amundsen was able to source equipment and clothing that were far superior to anything he could purchase in the outfitting shops of southern cities.

The next two years saw Amundsen travelling, fundraising, testing his equipment and continuing to study history and the science of magnetic observation. In the spring of 1902, he moved the *Gjøa* from Tromsø to Christiania for the final preparations, including making vast quantities of pemmican from dried meat and berry mixture. He knew that once he sailed for the Northwest Passage, anything he might need had to be aboard the ship in the right quantities—he couldn't count on being able to resupply or reprovision for several years, and the lack of something vital could easily result in death. He took a short voyage north with Aksel Steen to test the magnetic measurement instruments that were being supplied by the German Marine Observatory, and he also ventured abroad to London, where he met the president of the Royal Geographical Society, Sir Clements Markham, and several retired Royal Navy officers who were veterans of cold-climate voyages, in order to hear any suggestions they might have.

In the fall of 1902, Amundsen was back in Norway, where he officially passed his exams and received his master's certificate, enabling him to be both the expedition leader and the captain of the ship, avoiding the infighting between sailors, scientists and explorers that he saw had plagued innumerable previous expeditions. Qualifying for his master's certificate was one accomplishment Amundsen remained proud of throughout his life, always preferring the title "Captain" over any other. But his optimism and excitement about the expedition were tinged with disappointment and frustration. The modifications to the ship, the purchasing and stocking of supplies and the stockpiling of money to pay the salaries of his crew had burned through his funds and all the donations he had received.

Around this time, Nansen persuaded King Oscar II of Sweden to contribute to the venture. Although the Swedish king's gift was intended as a gesture of goodwill, Nansen had other hopes. He was a vocal and prominent advocate for Norwegian independence from Sweden, and his support of Amundsen was predicated not only on his interest in geographical exploration but also on increasing international recognition of and support for the Norwegian independence movement: if Amundsen was successful in claiming the geographical prize of the Northwest Passage, the reflected glory and international attention would go to Norway. Nansen believed that an increasing lexicon of great deeds done by native sons would go a long way toward boosting national pride and confidence in the country while elevating international awareness of Norway as a distinct culture with its own heroes and contributions to the world.

Nansen, who had dealt with the publicity from his own past adventures, helped Amundsen negotiate international newspaper rights to his story. It was again a steep learning curve for Amundsen, who had never considered these activities—putting a public face on the expedition, generating advance interest, securing financial support and publication rights and paying creditors afterwards—to be part of his job as expedition leader, but he quickly realized that for a privately funded individual they were just as important as succeeding at the expedition itself.

In the late fall of 1902 he travelled south to Christiania and gave his first public lecture, "My Journey," at a meeting of the Norwegian Geographical Society. Despite the increasing publicity and public awareness of his audacious voyage, Amundsen kept his cards close to his chest, revealing his full intentions to no one. Harald Sverdrup, the oceanographer and meteorologist who joined Amundsen on several later expeditions, recalled: "There is, however, no doubt that his reluctance to discuss plans, which was often considered a special form of conceit, had deep roots and that by nature he was a lonely man who preferred action to words." In this instance, Amundsen did not reveal that he was more interested in navigating the Northwest Passage than in locating the roving magnetic North Pole (which he suspected would turn out to be an unremarkable patch of snow surrounded by a vast wasteland of similar terrain). He understood that private investors would not support a sailing trip along a remote coastline, no matter how storied and famous; yet the general public would be interested in a tale of adventure and derring-do, not merely scientific discovery. By balancing these objectives—focusing on the magnetic North Pole to secure institutional support and on the Northwest Passage to entertain armchair adventurers—Amundsen sought to satisfy the establishment and to intrigue the public.

In the end, he chose the need to interest a general audience over the constraints imposed by a government's political and nationalist agenda. He came to realize that unless an explorer worked for the government, he was essentially an entertainer. Therefore, to become a successful explorer, he would have to become a successful entertainer. Still, he found fundraising to be the most tedious and disagreeable component of his preparation work, which never changed throughout his long career. Traipsing about the countryside with his cap out, begging for funds from well-connected and wealthy individuals, was something he always found undignified, even with Nansen's aid and blessing. "This was 'running the gauntlet' in a fashion I would not willingly repeat," he wrote in his book on the Northwest Passage. It was, however, entirely out of his control.

Many of his closest friends and family were a great encouragement to Amundsen during this time. Nansen had been "indefatigable in this matter as in all others," as were his three older brothers—once they overcame their initial reservations about him spending his entire inheritance to buy the *Gjøa*. "I have many bright and pleasant memories from those days," Amundsen recalled, "of men who encouraged me and gave me all the support they could. I have also other memories—of those who thought they were infinitely wiser than their fellow-creatures, and had a right to criticise and condemn whatever others undertook or proposed to undertake." Adding to his stress, his brother Gustav was at this time experiencing financial difficulties of his own, and Amundsen moved the power of attorney over his affairs to his brother Leon.

During this time, Amundsen had been interviewing and selecting his crew, the men who would spend years together with him under dangerous, isolated and monotonous conditions. He wanted only the best, and fortunately he was a natural judge of character with an innate sense of how to build a team that would work well to-gether. He searched widely and remained open to many possibilities before he settled on his team. He had the pick of the crop because he offered to pay well, more than a man could earn on other voyages. In the spirit of the best leaders, Amundsen went to great lengths to en-sure that his men were well taken care of, even if this meant finan-cial hardship and stress for himself. Harald Sverdrup recalled that Amundsen placed one characteristic in a potential crew member above all others: resourcefulness. "When preparations were still in progress, he might ask a question about a difficult task or give a man an impossible assignment. If he got the answer 'it can't be done' he was through with the man then and there."

A photo of Amundsen surrounded by his six polar pirates ap-pears in the first edition of his official book detailing their adventure, *The North West Passage: Being a Record of a Voyage of Exploration of the Ship Gjøa, 1903–1907*. All seven of the adventurers sport mous-taches and appear in starched collars. Their serious, formal expres-sions are partly the product of the primitive photography techniques of the early twentieth century and partly a device for portraying the respectability they wished to convey to the world as professional ex-plorers and as Norway's cultural ambassadors. Two of the men had come to Amundsen's attention through his friendship with Zapffe—first mate Anton Lund and second mate Helmer Hanssen, both northerners, both married and slightly older than Amundsen, and both with extensive experience on commercial whaling and sealing voyages in arctic waters. Lund, thirty-nine years old, first went to sea when he was twelve, and he was an experienced harpooner. Hanssen, who had briefly met Amundsen years earlier, before the *Belgica* sailed, would go on to become one of Amundsen's staunchest allies, joining him on many adventures.

As first lieutenant, Amundsen selected Godfred Hansen, a lieu-tenant in the Danish navy, whose sense of humour and thorough grounding in the theoretical aspects of sailing and command were skills that Amundsen valued to round out the practical experience of the other crew members. Hansen had made four voyages to Iceland and the Faeroes with the navy and had a keen interest in polar exploration. He also had many other skills; Amundsen described him as a "navigator, astronomer, geologist and photographer." His leave of absence from the navy was secured through the intercession and goodwill of Nansen. The expedition's engineer and meteorologist was Peter Ristvedt, a young and energetic mariner who had met Amundsen when they did their military service together and who had sailed with the captain on the trial voyage of the *Gjøa* in 1901. Gustav Juel Wiik, the second engineer, had been trained at the magnetic observatory in Potsdam and was to help with the measurements of the magnetic North Pole. He was also a gunner in the Norwegian navy, had a philosophical and scientific disposition, and at barely twenty-five years of age was the youngest member of the expedition. The final member of the expedition was the cook and general roustabout Adolf Henrik Lindstrøm, a jolly and practical man only recently returned from nearly four years sailing on the *Fram* with Otto Sverdrup in the islands of the Arctic Archipelago. A heavy drinker, fondly known as "the Polar Cook," he was perpetually cheerful, a trait that proved immeasurably valuable throughout the long polar winters.

Amundsen did not hire anyone with specific medical training. He didn't trust doctors aboard an expedition ship, feeling they might split his authority and endanger the expedition because of their priest-like role of administering to the sick. A doctor's opinions in favour of the perceived interest of the individual, Amundsen believed, could run counter to the best interests of the group. This was a response to his formative youthful experiences aboard the *Belgica*, and it's hard not to observe that in addressing the problems that surfaced on that poorly planned and badly led voyage, Amundsen went too far in the opposite direction. All was being planned to prevent problems arising with leadership and cohesion. But in eliminating one obvious problem, he perhaps laid open the possibility for others to arise—on the *Belgica* it was Cook, a doctor and the man who Amundsen respected the most, who was the greatest source of leadership and practical advice.

Amundsen also arranged a special meeting with Sverdrup to discuss the *Gjøa* expedition and to gain insights and advice from the older man about his recent experience in the Arctic. Amundsen was particularly interested in Sverdrup's thoughts on the use of dogs and sleds in Arctic travel. "Ah, the dogs," Sverdrup wrote. "[I]t is they who give a polar journey its character; without them travel would indeed be grim." Amundsen should use not just any dogs, he cautioned, but huskies, which were particularly bred for cold climates, harsh conditions and travel on snow and ice. Amundsen recalled hearing a similar opinion on Arctic dogs from Cook while on the *Belgica* expedition, and he no doubt remembered the unpleasant experience of man-hauling sledges across the icy Antarctic wastes. It would be preferable if dogs did the hauling. Arctic peoples had been using dogs for just this purpose for generations.

Even at this early stage in his career, Amundsen would learn from anyone if he thought it would benefit him or give him an edge toward success, and local and direct experience always held the greatest weight. He had never used dogs or sleds before, but he knew that his chance of locating the magnetic North Pole would be possible only if he harnessed the speed and extra hauling capacity of dogs and sleds to cover greater distances at a faster pace. Sverdrup not only passed along this most invaluable advice, he also offered to give Amundsen his dog team, which was not doing well in the warm climate of southern Norway. "Poor creatures!" Amundsen wrote. "It would have been better to let them remain in ice and snow than to drag them here, where they suffer sorely, especially this spring, which was unusually warm. They were now tied up along the rail and looked wretched in the rain—the greatest infliction to an Arctic dog. To get here they had made one voyage in the drenching rain, and now they had to endure another to get back. But, at any rate, back they were going, poor things—to their home."

A few months before the planned departure of the *Gjøa* on its historic voyage, Amundsen ran out of money to pay for the remaining supplies. He had long ago exhausted his access to additional credit. In fact, apart from the ship, its vast stores of supplies and provisions and the trust accounts holding the men's salaries, he was bankrupt. When creditors got wind of his predicament, several began agitating for the immediate repayment of the moneys they had advanced, in effect backing out of their agreement to support the expedition. Amundsen put them off as best as he could, but when the bailiffs were called he approached his men and explained his predicament—and then received their support to sail before they could be apprehended and their grand undertaking derailed. They cast off during a storm at midnight, just ahead of the creditors.

"The strain of the last days, getting everything in order, the anxiety lest something might yet prevent us getting away, and the desperate efforts to procure the money still wanting—all this had greatly affected me both in mind and body. But now it was all over, and no one can describe the untold relief we felt when the craft began to move." The Northwest Passage beckoned, and the thirty-one-year-old Amundsen looked like he had aged a decade: his hair had turned white, his face was lined and his scalp showed some new baldness. The Last Viking set off on his first great undertaking. "The great adventure for which my whole life had been a preparation was under way!" he wrote. "The Northwest Passage—that baffling mystery to all the navigators of the past—was at last to be ours!"

4

Where Franklin Died

*The voyage of the Gjøa was far more like a holiday
trip of comrades than the prelude to a serious struggle
lasting years.*

S IR JOHN FRANKLIN, Sir John Ross, William Parry, John
Rae, Robert McClure, Martin Frobisher, John Davis, Henry
Hudson, William Baffin, John Rae: their names are sprinkled over
the distinguishing features of maps of northern Canada, identify-
ing prominent bays, channels, inlets, islands and lakes. These famous heroes make up the pantheon of brave, or foolhardy,
explorers who tried to discover an ocean route around the top of
North America and into the Pacific Ocean to gain access to the
spices of Indonesia that for several centuries were worth nearly
their weight in gold. So valuable would this waterway be that maps
from past centuries depict the hopes and dreams of countless generations of merchants and monarchs rather than geographical reality. Lacking direct evidence, chart-makers embellished their maps,
depicting an enormous snake-like channel rounding the North
American continent, even a vast inland sea occupying the western
United States and Canada. If only this fantastic channel or this inland sea could be located, untold riches would be forthcoming. So,

< 55 >

obstinate mariners battered their ships against the barren shores of innumerable Arctic islands in a futile attempt to reach the Orient. Many died—stranded, starving and scurvy-ridden—in pursuit of this prize.

The Arctic Archipelago sprawls over a vast area occupying 1.4 million square kilometres and consists of more than 36,000 islands of all shapes imaginable, ranging in size from rocks to large landmasses—ninety-four of them, including Baffin Island, Ellesmere Island, Banks Island and Victoria Island, are classified as major islands. Combined with the deeply indented Arctic shoreline, the chaotic mass of islands presents a bewildering maze to sailing ships, one that is not equalled anywhere in the world. A snow-free summer can be shorter than two months and an ice-free sailing season even less (or perhaps not at all, in some regions); winter temperatures can fall as low as –50°C (–58°F). The conditions of this extreme climate make it easy to see why the discovery of a predictable and safe sea route through the archipelago had baffled passage-seekers for centuries. The land is mostly barren tundra, with occasional desolate mountain ranges; it offers little in the way of resources useful to European mariners for repairing ships, such as trees, and to the unknowledgeable it offers little food or other useful material for survival. Most of the region was and is uninhabited, apart from certain southern coastal regions that host a scattered population of hardy Inuit. Through ingenious technological adaptations these people had roamed the land for thousands of years. To survive, they needed a very specific set of technical skills and detailed local knowledge. Ignoring or discounting this knowledge had cost European explorers the destruction of dozens of ships and the deaths of countless sailors. The notable exception to the costly, large-scale expeditions that had proved disastrous in the Arctic were the journeys of the Scottish medical doctor and explorer John Rae. A proponent of small exploration parties and native survival techniques, Rae discovered the fate of the Franklin expedition half a century earlier and provided Amundsen with inspiration and a model for his own expeditions.

The many scientific voyages of the late eighteenth century, including several inland explorations north and west of Hudson Bay, laid to rest many of the myths that had led past mariners astray. In 1778, James Cook explored the North Pacific Ocean as far up the western coast of North America as the Bering Strait, where he was able to see North America and Asia simultaneously, but he was unable to penetrate north of that strait. Between 1791 and 1795, George Vancouver explored and charted the western shores of Canada and Alaska, finally ending the common but erroneous belief in a great inland sea. His charting of the Pacific coast produced an accurate geographical outline of western North America; the only region of the continent that remained obscure was the heart of the Arctic Archipelago in the far north.

Despite the understanding that a Northwest Passage no longer had any significant commercial viability, the British Royal Navy in the nineteenth century engaged in a concerted, politically motivated and organized assault on its discovery. The numbers of men and ships involved in the quest, and the money that was spent, were enormous. Even so, these expeditions were not entirely successful in mapping the Arctic Archipelago. By Amundsen's day, the location of a possible route through it from east to west could be more or less assumed, by linking the regions mapped by various expeditions, but none had ever put this geographical knowledge to the test by sailing through the Northwest Passage.

It was Amundsen's goal to put a period to this epic story of delusion and greed, to end it with the successful navigation of the treacherous waterways of the archipelago. His would be a symbolic victory rather than a practical one, but it would certainly fall within the mythology of the romantic quest that had characterized interest in the fabled waterway: a small ship of fearless adventurers, braving the unknown in a region that was a proven killer, returning with an uplifting moral victory—the conquest of an opponent with a first-rate pedigree of prior challengers. Surely such a feat would secure Amundsen's fame and launch his career.

⁓

Once free of land—and creditors—Amundsen steered the *Gjøa* across the North Sea and the Atlantic Ocean to Greenland. He was following a course with the best historical foundation. A sense of belonging to something larger and more powerful accompanied the seven mariners as their heavily laden ship sailed west, with dogs frisking about on deck. The dogs were more than useful; they were a great source of entertainment and amusement throughout the voyage. When the seas were rough and the *Gjøa* rolled ("and she can roll"), the beasts wandered about the ship trying to keep their balance and studying the faces of the men. Their ration was slim: a few pints of water and a dried cod daily, but still it must have been a chore to clean up after them on the crowded deck of the ship. Hungry and bored, they sneaked around looking for scraps to steal. Their relationships and hierarchy were well established before Amundsen had inherited them from Sverdrup—as was their propensity to quarrel, especially the "ladies—Kari and Silla. . . . Kari was the elder and exacted absolute obedience, which Silla, who was also a grown-up lady, found it difficult to put up with, so it often happened that they tore at each other's hair." The alpha male, Ola, tried to defuse the battles. "It was a rare sight to see old Ola, intelligent to an exceptional degree, jumping about with the other two, one on either side, trying to prevent them from fighting."

While the dogs fought as the *Gjøa* neared Greenland, the people worked harmoniously—an arrangement that would be reversed a year later. "Our daily routine was soon working smoothly," Amundsen reported, "and everyone gave the impression of being eminently fitted for his post. We constituted a little republic on board the *Gjøa*. We had no strict laws. I know myself how irksome this strict discipline is. Good work can be done without fear of the law. . . . My comrades also seemed to value it, and the voyage of the *Gjøa* was far more like a holiday trip of comrades than the prelude to a serious struggle lasting years." But it was still early in the voyage. Although Amundsen happily wrote of a republic where all shared the work equally and "were all captains and all crew," he himself was the first among equals; none were truly familiar with him, truly equal or truly friends. He did not need to order them about; he had selected well-qualified men, and they all knew their business. Of course, this did not preclude interpersonal conflict.

On July 25, 1903, the ship sailed into a small bay on the west coast of Greenland that was "beautifully situated with the lofty and mighty Disco [Disko Island] to the north and the sea to the south and west, from time to time filled with heavy icebergs." It was the site of the town Godhavn, population 108. The crew loaded additional supplies that Amundsen had ordered through Danish suppliers in Copenhagen, including petroleum, sledges, kayaks, skis and ten new sled dogs. Within a week the *Gjøa* was heading west into open water again, "vying with sea-gulls in dancing on the crests of the billows." The ship was riding low in the water, but the men were exultant and feeling free. "Surely the Arctic Seas have seldom seen such a spectacle as we presented," Amundsen recalled. The *Gjøa* was a single-masted sailing ship with a mainsail and a couple of jibs. The most unusual aspect of the ship, other than the yelping dogs, was its motor. "We had a good auxiliary motor, though in those days gasoline engines were still so uncertain that we had been gravely criticised for risking the dangers of explosion and fire when I had the motor installed." The *Gjøa* had a shallow draft, and the emergency engine was reserved to get it free from ice. Even the deck of the tiny ship was stowed with cargo, so that it "looked like a moving-van afloat" as it continued north along the Greenlandic coast.

For two weeks the *Gjøa* lumbered across the choppy waters of Melville Bay through fog, pushing its way into ever more remote and ice-infested waters, as the crew tested the engines and reorganized equipment for the ordeal ahead. The peace on board was ruined when the dogs became sick. Their mental state provided the first clue that something was wrong. "They went about in a stupid state," Amundsen wrote. "They never saw nor heard and had little relish for their food." Soon their rear legs became paralyzed, and many of them could only drag themselves across the deck in bewilderment as convulsions wracked their bodies. Two dogs became so debilitated that "we were glad to end their lives with a bullet." One they had to put down was the matriarch, Kari. The crew found the sickness and deaths to be disturbing, but Amundsen, always intrigued by canine psychology, observed that Silla, the quarrelsome underling who fought to escape the earlier browbeating of her companion, took this with "great satisfaction" and now "remained cock of the walk."

Amundsen's running commentary on the dogs provides a light-hearted counter-story to the expedition and in many ways mirrors the spirit of the expedition. Amundsen seemed to express his views on the crew through his details about the behaviour of the dogs. "Our surviving dogs meanwhile began to be manifestly bored," he wrote in good humour. "In the beginning they could study wind and weather and thus kill time; but now meteorological variations failed to interest them, and their thoughts sought new fields. Idleness is the root of all evil, it is said, and this applies just as well to beasts as to men." He then detailed the curious jockeying for position in the hierarchy and the subtle methods the dogs used to annoy, intimidate or frustrate each other.

One dog in particular, named Lurven, was "the most mischievous dog I ever knew. I can see him now with his head on one side, his little eyes blinking and tail cocked sideways, gliding along the deck meditating some new prank." Lurven learned to confine his pestering of the other dogs to occasions when no one could or was around to observe. "If, for instance, we were busy with the sails," Amundsen recalled, "we might be quite sure of a fight." When hunters brought in seals or other game and there was surplus meat, the dogs "stuffed themselves as tight as drums" and rolled in the viscera until they were "smeared all over with fat and blood." Amundsen took great pleasure in detailing all the dogs' numerous fights, particularly how often Silla "would jump round the combatants making the most deafening noise and, by way of variety, snapping at their legs."

The most dangerous stretch of the first season's journey was the crossing of Melville Bay on the way north. Following the navigational advice of whaling captains, the *Gjøa* worked through increasingly ice-choked waters, swerving around great frozen masses, blindly pushing through the fog, "ice's faithful attendant," and occasionally viewing jagged mountainous crags. When the crew spied the first enormous icebergs, they were amazed. Amundsen called them "solitary majestic masses." The ice surrounding the ship made working on deck unpleasant because of the cold. "Perhaps as an Arctic traveller, I ought not to admit this," Amundsen wrote, "but anyhow, I did feel perishing with cold. The fog settled down and drenched everything it came in contact with; it was sheer misery in the early morning."

The men hunted and fished whenever possible, bringing in many seals. Lindstrøm the cook "thought seal liver one of the greatest delicacies in existence, and he treated us to it morning and night. It must be noted, it does not taste badly at all." Though a bit of a tippler, Lindstrøm was an industrious man who took his job seriously; his pride was in preparing excellent and varied fare for the men. He frequently bragged "of his culinary exploits as chef" while regaling the others with mouth-watering tales of his bear sausages and steaks. Earlier, at Godhavn, Lindstrøm had traded some of the expedition's mouldy spice cakes for fresh salmon and birds. But in contrast to Lindstrøm's universally appreciated concoctions, the men also had to eat less-appreciated staples. When Amundsen noticed the ship's bread was getting soft, he ordered all the mouldy bread to be

brought from the hold and aired it on the deck, cutting off the ruined portions and saving the rest for later.

On August 13, after nearly two weeks of enduring drifting ice
and heavy winds, the crew spied land: "A gleam of light broke
through the fog, and, as if by enchantment, there opened up before
me a wide view out into the bright daylight; right in front of us, and
seemingly quite near, the wild, rugged landscape of Cape York appeared suddenly like a scene from fairyland." Amundsen ordered the
ship to set sail for Dalrymple Rock, where he planned to pick up
supplies that he had arranged to be deposited by Scottish whaling
ships earlier in the season. Dalrymple Rock was an imposing coni-
cal islet of dark stone that jutted from the sea. It was a common
meeting spot, a well-known feature for ships to use as a launching
spot for crossing the northern part of Baffin Bay and an easily rec-
ognizable landmark for those seeking to orient themselves after having made the crossing back east to Greenland. Used by European
whaling ships and by bands of Inuit cruising the coast of Greenland,
the famous rock was also near the place where the Inuit gathered
large quantities of eggs each year, Eider Duck Island.

As the *Gjøa* approached Dalrymple Rock, the crew were startled
by the sound of gunshots. Then, from an iceberg, two kayaks quickly
set a course for the ship. As they approached, "We were very anxious
to make the acquaintance of the North Greenland Eskimo, of whom
many strange things are reported," Amundsen wrote. "They were
extremely lively, jabbered both together, threw their arms about and
gesticulated. There was evidently something particular they wanted
to tell us, but we, of course, could not understand a syllable." Finally
Amundsen deduced that they wanted to know about other Norwegians. There was more gunfire, and six more kayaks cruised from
the iceberg, two flying a flag, one Danish and the other Norwegian.
Improbably, these kayakers were Mylius Erichsen and Knud Ras-
mussen of the Danish Greenland Literary Expedition, which was
then recording the customs of the Inuit before they were altered by

trade and outside customs and lost to history. The two groups enjoyed a harmonious and celebratory meeting of "joyous confusion" while the *Gjøa*'s crew loaded the contents of the supply cache onboard. The dogs were let ashore to run, and "the old *Fram* dogs and the new ones from Godhavn seized the opportunity to settle all the quarrels they had nursed on board, in a battle royal. Many of them bore dreadful marks of the battle."

When the work was done and they said their farewells, Amundsen set a course west across Baffin Bay to Beechey Island and Lancaster Sound, at the eastern edge of the Arctic Archipelago, on the Canadian side. Here the small ship stopped to conduct some magnetic measurements in order to gain an indication of the position of the magnetic North Pole, which they estimated to be roughly located on the western edge of Boothia Felix, near where James Clark Ross had positioned it decades earlier. They were now at the entrance to the Northwest Passage. There are in fact many possible northwest passages, any number of routes through the myriad channels and islands of Canada's north, but the one that seemed most promising in Amundsen's time, and remains so today, was a generally southerly route following Lancaster Sound west, past several other dead-end options, into Parry Channel until the west coast of Somerset Island, and then south down Peel Sound and Franklin Strait, turning slightly east along James Ross Strait into Rae Strait, rounding the southern coast of King William Island, before heading west again through Queen Maud Gulf, Dease Strait, Coronation Gulf and Dolphin and Union Strait before exiting into what is now known as Amundsen Gulf. As this account indicates, it is not an obvious or simple route, even when one has an accurate map to follow. One false turn could lead to the destruction of a ship and probable death, there being no one around to launch a rescue.

After days of sailing west into the barren, ice-ravaged terrain of the Northwest Passage, Amundsen steered the *Gjøa* into Erebus Bay on Beechey Island, a small island in Parry Channel that was the final known winter stopping point for Sir John Franklin's ships *Erebus* and *Terror* in 1845. It was also the place where several men from the doomed expedition were buried. The *Gjøa*'s crew had no reason to stop in this desolate spot, other than to have a quick rest and to appreciate the history of the site. Amundsen stayed up late into the brief night, sitting on the deck of the ship, imagining the British mariners coming ashore in their boats and setting up camp, already suffering from scurvy, and perhaps lead poisoning, and eventually succumbing to "darkness and death." He squinted, and the scene came alive for him: "The dark outlines of crosses marking graves inland are silent witnesses before my eyes as I sit here. . . . Franklin and all his men laid down their lives in the fight for the North West Passage. Let us raise a monument to them, more enduring than stone: the recognition that they were the first discoverers of the Passage." He and his men silently re-erected a fallen gravestone, noting that "the heaviness and sadness of death hung over Beechey Island."

After their brief stay and some time spent in meteorological observations and measurements, the *Gjøa* pushed west and then south, heading toward waters where "no keel had ever ploughed." As they silently sailed though Peel Sound and Franklin Strait, wending their way through the islands, the water remained calm, and storms did not materialize. Day after day the weather remained remarkably clear and the sailing was easy, although the distinction between days was somewhat academic under the midnight sun. Soon they reached the small cluster of the De La Roquette Islands. "Are we really going to get through so easily?" Amundsen wondered near the end of August.

Then the pleasant weather disappeared, to be replaced by storms and fog. A few days later, on August 31, the *Gjøa* was hit by the first element of a disastrous troika: it ran aground in the darkness of the short polar night. Godfred Hansen, the Danish naval commander, was at the wheel. Many of the men later believed that he was incompetent and therefore the cause of the accident. A couple of

Amundsen's men disliked him and called him a fool and a "mommy's boy" behind his back, and claimed he was a cowardly sailor in poor weather. But officially there were no real disagreements between the men, only grumbling. Amundsen called Hansen "cool and collected, a splendid fellow."

Later that night, when most of the men were asleep, a fire broke out in the engine room. A terrifying shriek for help roused the others and they instantly dashed below decks. Years later, during one of his lectures about the voyage, Amundsen chuckled about the incident and blithely noted that "I knew what this meant on board a small vessel carrying 7,000 gallons of petroleum, great quantities of gunpowder and explosives, and whose hull was, besides, saturated with tar." The fire was adjacent to storage drums containing 2,200 gallons of petroleum. There was little time to contemplate the situation. "We all ran like mad for vessel and life!" Working furiously and with great risk, the crew managed after several hours to extinguish the flames with water and fire retardant. It was a near thing. An explosion would have set off the other combustibles on the ship and doomed them all. Amundsen noted that they had avoided being "blown to atoms like an exploded bomb."

The following day the ship ran aground again, this time on submerged rocks near Matty Island, and more seriously. A storm blew in, and large waves buffeted the ship for two days while the men laboured to get it off the rocks. Furious winds "blew with unabated violence" against the rock-bound vessel while the waves tilted it, threatening to swamp it and then grind it apart. "The spray was dashing over the ship, and the wind came in gusts, howling through the rigging, but we struggled and toiled and got the sails set." The vessel pitched back and forth on the rocks, and pulverized chunks of wood floated to the water's surface as the false keel splintered. Amundsen climbed into the rigging, clinging desperately to it as the mast swung wildly about with the motion of the ship: "As a matter of fact, I cannot say I did feel calm," he admitted. "I had to hold fast with all my strength whenever the vessel, after being lifted, pitched down on to the rocks, or I should have been flung into the sea."

The ship remained stuck. Amundsen climbed down the mast and ordered the small boats to be loaded with provisions. They must abandon the ship before it broke up and they drowned or, worse, became stranded on a barren Arctic island without provisions just as winter was setting in. "On me rested every responsibility," Amundsen recalled, "and the moment came when I had to make my choice—to abandon the *Gjøa*, take to the boats and let her be smashed up . . . or go to meet death with all souls on board." At the urging of Anton Lund, the captain agreed to one final effort before abandoning the stricken vessel. In desperation, the men began to pitch overboard great bales of cargo, mostly pemmican intended for the dogs, to lighten the ship. The plan worked when their efforts coincided with a larger-than-usual wave, and the *Gjøa* was "lifted up high and flung bodily on to the bare rocks, bump, bump, bump—with terrific force. . . . In my distress I sent up (I honestly confess it) an ardent prayer to the Almighty." The *Gjøa*, battered but free, slid off the rocks and into the choppy waters.

Despite exhaustion and being soaked by freezing waves in the Arctic wind, and despite the men being "all pretty quiet and cool by nature," they "burst out unrestrained." Amundsen, self-critical as ever, admonished himself for not setting a watch in the crow's nest: if the ship had been crushed here, no one could have come to help and the entire crew would have perished miserably. His crew, however, didn't blame him; Helmer Hanssen later wrote that "no praise could be too much for Amundsen's conduct during all these trials. It was his first expedition, but he was just a born natural leader." Nevertheless, the captain vowed not to travel a single mile farther without a constant watch, though it would slow their progress and tire the men out.

The nights were getting longer and the weather colder, so Amundsen began searching for a place to overwinter, a safe harbour for the *Gjøa* to be frozen in for the season. The ship continued south along the desolate coastline of the eastern shore of King William Island until September 9, when the captain spied an enticing spot for overwintering in the vicinity of the magnetic North Pole. It was a snug, sheltered bay that would shield them from the grinding ice of the open waters, surrounded by a ring of low hills that would defend against the bitter polar wind. It even had fresh water sources. "If one had sat at home and thought out a winter harbour, it would have been impossible to conceive a better one," Amundsen said. He called the spot Gjøahavn and settled the little ship to be frozen in. There it would stay for nearly two years, amid a vast, treeless expanse of boulders and stunted grasses, soon to be entirely covered in snow. Coincidentally, the harbour, which is now a Canadian town, Gjoa Haven, was situated at nearly the same latitude north as Tromsø, the Norwegian home town of several of the crew. These men were accustomed to certain particularities of life in the high northern latitudes, such as the sun circling in a great arc in the sky, never dipping below the horizon in summer, counterbalanced in winter by a great, dark cap of stars and perpetual gloom. It was also close to the scene of Franklin's crew's demise more than sixty years earlier, when their enormous ships had been crushed in the ice on the western shore of the same island.

After finding a secure berth for the ship, where it could be frozen-in safely, the crew began to unload all their provisions and to construct a scientific observation hut on a nearby hill. For use as building materials, they shovelled sand from the beach into empty provision cases, digging them as far as possible into the rocky ground, for protection from the wind, and covered the hut with an old sail. They named the uninspiring structure "The Magnet"; Wiik and Ristvedt, who would be responsible for the magnetic and climatic measurements, would bunk there for the winter. They also later constructed an astronomical observatory out of hardened snow topped with a sailcloth roof that they playfully called "Uranienborg," after the famous astronomical observatory of Tycho Brahe. The dogs would also be living on land and, "of course, were highly affronted at being summarily ejected from the ship."

As the days grew darker and colder, the men tried to prepare themselves psychologically for the dreaded monotony of the long winter they faced living in the deserted, frozen expanse under a dome of perpetual dark. The daily routine, as far as anyone could predict, would consist of magnetic observations, hunting, taking care of the dogs and feeding themselves, with only a few extended excursions to pass the many months. The members of the small band had already grown tired of each others' company, and with little to occupy them once winter set in, the lack of new company proved to be the greatest challenge.

The first few weeks in their new home were, however, lively and exciting: a great herd of caribou was migrating nearby, and Amundsen, all too familiar with the ill-effects of salted and preserved foods eaten over prolonged periods, organized a hunt. Scurvy was a far greater danger than not getting a camp established right away. Amundsen knew that Dr. Cook had averted scurvy with his prescribed diet of lightly cooked seal meat on the *Belgica* and that the local Inuit did not suffer from the disease. All the fancy scientific theories that claimed to explain it and offer solutions were, as far as Amundsen was concerned, total foolishness.

Harald Sverdrup, who sailed with Amundsen in later years, wrote that Amundsen "cared little for [scientists'] conclusions and even less for their theories. When he talked about men of science he had met, he would stress their personal characteristics and not their scientific accomplishments." Amundsen liked to say during his lectures that the many scientific specialists who approached him before the *Gjøa*'s sailing pressed upon him their erroneous opinions on the location of the magnetic North Pole and that "they might as well have said the moon for all they knew." To Amundsen, science was a necessary evil that he put up with, much like seasickness. This perspective would become even more apparent in the coming years, as the tedium of the magnetic pole observations continued. For now, the men rushed out to hunt the caribou and brought in over one hundred carcasses in short order, easily enough meat to feed them and their dogs for the winter.

Amundsen and his crew had been discussing the possibility of meeting the local Inuit for some time, hoping for new companionship to relieve their own isolation, and Amundsen was desperate to learn Inuit techniques of polar travel and living. When the Inuit arrived, it was a great surprise, "exceedingly ridiculous, and one of our liveliest reminiscences." On October 29, the men of Gjøahavn noticed five strangers coming over a hill. Amundsen, Lund and Hansen, "armed to the teeth," started toward the strangers, who were clad in shaggy caribou furs, their brown, weather-worn faces peering from fur-lined hoods, and bows strung over their backs. The trio of Norwegians strode boldly forth with their guns at their shoulders and with "such a fierce expression on their faces that it alone would have been enough to put a warlike detachment to flight."

The five native men paused, as if wondering how to respond to this hostility, and then continued to advance, humming and smiling. When they saw that the Norwegians were apparently unarmed (they didn't recognize the guns as weapons), they started talking loudly in incomprehensible words. Amundsen recounted that as he and his companions approached and met the Inuit, the excitement and joy was mutual and the Norwegians "shouted and howled, patted and slapped, to the best of our ability."

The meeting was a grand success, the start of a multi-year alliance. As word of the friendly encounter spread throughout the region, various groups of Inuit came to Gjøahavn for short periods, departing as the urge or need arose. Meanwhile, Amundsen and his men met several other groups of people and found clusters of snow houses on their forays into the wintry wilds. Helmer Hanssen related that the learning process was slow on both sides, but that "as time went by we got more familiar with each other's languages. That is to say, when we talked Eskimo they thought we were talking Norwegian, and when they tried Norwegian, it sounded to us like Eskimo, but we understood each other quite well and carried on long conversations."

These meetings were not inconsequential. The greatest scientific accomplishments of that first expedition were not the magnetic data tediously collected in the two makeshift observatories, but Amundsen's detailed and unique collection of ethnographic artifacts and his accompanying descriptions of Inuit life and customs at the beginning of the twentieth century.

Roald Amundsen as
a boy in Christiania,
circa 1875.

Portrait of Amundsen as a
youth, showing how he
wanted to be known,
an intrepid adventurer,
rather than how he was.

Amundsen and Hanssen learning from the Inuit, preparing for their first dog sled foray in the winter of 1903/1904.

The remnants of practice snow houses litter the ground surrounding the Gjoa, the evidence of Amundsen's labor.

A Netsilingmiut Inuit family lounges inside a snow house, circa 1904.

A Netsilingmiut Inuit family readies for travel; note the baby carried on the woman's back.

Young visitors to Gjoa Haven. Amundsen encouraged the people to visit him at the Gjoa so that he could learn Arctic survival and travel skills.

The crew of the *Gjoa* pose in Nome, Alaska, after their successful navigation of the Northwest Passage, 1906.

9

Dancing with the dogs aboard the *Fram*, 1910. During the voyage south from Norway to Antarctica the dogs had the run of the ship and the attention of the crew. They all knew their failure or success would depend upon the health of the dogs.

10

Framheim snowed-in. The explorers dug tunnels through the snow and constructed several storage and workrooms from the snow. They also held contests to encourage each other to venture outside.

The *Fram* at the ice edge, ready to unload cargo for the expedition before sailing for Argentina.

Amundsen and crew working on equipment in the kitchen of Framheim, 1911.

Bjaaland, Prestrud, and Wisting packing sledges for the great trip in one of Framheim's underground snow rooms.

Four exhausted explorers stare at the flag they had planted at the South Pole, December 1911.

Helmer Hanssen and his dog team pose for a photo at the South Pole, an unremarkable patch of snow.

Amundsen and crew posing on the *Fram*'s deck in Hobart, March 1912, before announcing their news to the world.

5

An Education at Gjøahavn

*They waved long to us—probably a farewell for life;
and if some traveller, many years later, pays this place
a visit, the numerous tent-rings will remind him of
the many happy days the Gjøa expedition spent here
with their friends the Netsilik Eskimos.*

FOR THE NEXT two years, 1903 to 1905, the *Gjøa* did not move, nor did the observatory. The Norwegian adventurers used the occasion to venture into the tundra on many expeditions, in all seasons. They launched excursions to survey and chart the unknown portions of the nearby Arctic coastline. As the months rolled on, they made daily measurements of the wind and temperature, the duration of sunlight and darkness, the quantity of snow and rainfall, the number of frost-free days and the types of plants and animals to be found in each season. The seven men lived long enough at Gjøahavn to become acclimated to the region. Somewhat astonished, Amundsen noted that he preferred the Arctic winter to the summer; "when during the winter the temperature rose to merely −30°C [−22°F] it was a lovely day, and curious as it may sound, felt quite summer-like." Gjøahavn became the Norwegian adventurers' home.

They watched their dogs die and other dogs be born, they experienced relief at the end of the long, dark winter and witnessed the stunning transformation of the land during the thaw into a startlingly brilliant, intense but brief frenzy of life in high summer, with a profusion of flowers, animals and birds. Amundsen was delighted when a group of Inuit decided to set up camp right near the *Gjøa*: not only would the Europeans gain companionship but also opportunity to learn from the masters.

He also made several attempts to reach the magnetic North Pole on the Boothia Peninsula. At first he was not particularly successful, but then he learned new techniques from the Inuit, including their methods of driving dogsleds and of surviving in the north. To Amundsen, the true value of the two years spent at Gjøahavn was his exposure to the cultural knowledge of the Inuit, not the tedious magnetic and meteorological measurements.

Indeed, as time passed, Amundsen's lack of enthusiasm for scientific measurement became glaringly obvious. Ristvedt eventually noted with some resentment that "Wiik works continually on the magnetic north. The Governor [Amundsen] and the lieutenant read novels and smoke and go for walks from time to time. It is unbelievable that a man can change like the Governor has in the course of one year. Last year he worked constantly with his observations. This year he has done nothing and we achieved nothing on our sledge trip this spring that was sufficiently accurate." In fact, the expedition gathered a vast quantity of magnetic and meteorological data that was later distributed to specialists to help understand the climatology of the region and to provide a better understanding of the earth's magnetic fields. From a scientific perspective, the Northwest Passage expedition was far from a failure, but it wasn't Amundsen who did this work, and the men assigned to perform it could not help but resent his lack of interest.

Amundsen was an ethnographer by disposition, yet his interest was not only cultural but also practical. Even so, many of his men couldn't understand his preoccupation with the Inuit and disliked his hiring of local people as general labour and as instructors, thus encouraging several families to live near the *Gjøa* for months at a time. Second mate Helmer Hanssen, who felt that the Inuit "were lousy and smelled terribly," admitted to playing various tricks to get them out of his cabin, because "we couldn't chase them out . . . [and] we did not want them to go to Amundsen and say we had treated them unkindly." He added that "Amundsen had asked us to treat them with the greatest kindness, so that we could depend on them as friends if we ever needed their help." Wiik, who was the youngest member of the expedition and who least understood Amundsen, was most critical of his captain's interest in the Inuit. He complained in his journal that "there were always many of them. I cannot comprehend why on earth he needs them; they eat for three, but he can't afford to feed the dogs." The young man, and to a lesser extent several of the older adventurers, failed to understand that Amundsen was not planning merely this one trip and then retirement: he was keeping the locals around to learn from them for the future, in addition to satisfying his natural curiosity. Amundsen probably already had dreams for trips to the North and South Poles, and he knew the knowledge of the Inuit would be indispensable. For him, the true treasure of the Northwest Passage voyage was the knowledge and technology of local people. His open-mindedness toward different peoples and new ideas contributed in no small measure to his ultimate success in the Arctic and the Antarctic, as well as to his ability to reimagine or reinvent his career as technology and public interest evolved.

Amundsen had no intention of studying the Inuit in a condescending manner, as if they were subjects in an experiment. He accepted their culture on its own terms, without romanticizing the people themselves or their way of life, and he viewed them as cultural equals. Perhaps unusually, Amundsen was very interested in the Inuit as individuals and was not content with assigning the stereotypical idea of the "race" to each individual. In fact, judging from his writings and the transcripts of his lectures, he seems to have been more interested in his Inuit visitors than in his own crew; this should hardly be surprising, since he had just spent many tedious months with his handful of men and had long tired of them, their stories and peccadilloes. The locals, on the other hand, were fresh, exotic and intriguing, with different ways of looking at the world and different ways of living. And their temporarily intertwined lives were sort of a soap opera. All this so impressed him that later in life, Amundsen harboured the wish to return to Alaska or the Canadian Arctic and visit the Inuit again.

"It is often said that the Eskimo are lazy," he mused, "unwilling, and possessed of all other bad qualities under the sun. Certainly this was not true." A significant number of pages in his book *The North-West Passage* are devoted to anthropological observations of Inuit customs and material culture, and tales of his own interactions with them. Later in life he donated his collections of Inuit material culture to the Norwegian state, becoming the centrepieces of museum collections.

The band of Inuit that spent the most time near the *Gjøa* were the Netsilik, or Netsilingmiut, "the people of the ringed seal." Their main food sources were seals, reindeer, salmon, trout and cod. In the summer they caught birds as well: "swans, geese, loons, ducks, eiders, and many small birds." Amundsen's slide collections, which he used to accompany his lectures, include numerous images of these people in all manner of poses: fully clothed, holding long spears; standing near loaded sledges, with their dogs lolling about on the snow; children practising their bow-and-arrow shooting; men spearing fish; women lounging inside their snow houses or carrying babies on their backs; family groups posing in front of the ship with bundles of fur-covered goods for trade; hunters paddling in skin kayaks; the dead bundled for burial and laid out on the windswept barrens; men and women posing to display their clothing; and many of the Norwegians posing fully dressed in "Eskimo" style. But not all the people they encountered near Gjøahavn were friendly, and Amundsen does not shy from recording the negative attributes of other groups who occasionally were thieving, violent or untrustworthy. He met ten tribes during his sojourn and noted that although their material culture was identical, each group had its own distinct characteristics.

He spent many weeks in all seasons learning from the Netsilik visitors. After working with an elder teacher whom he had hired to teach snow-house building techniques to the Norwegians, the area around Gjøahavn was littered with dozens of snow houses of varying quality. Amundsen reported that "Old Teraiu, who could not understand what we were building all these huts for, shook his head pensively, evidently in the conviction that we had taken leave of our senses. Sometimes he would throw out his arms to indicate the overwhelming number of houses and exclaim, *'Iglu amichjui—amichjui— amichjui!'* Which means, 'This is a dreadful lot of houses.' But in this, too, we arrived at what we wanted: we became at last good snow builders."

On another occasion, during a sledding excursion, Amundsen wrote of his experience with Inuit clothing: "We were ready to leave on the first of March. The thermostat showed −55°C (−63°F). But through the months of February we had become so accustomed to the cold that it did not bother us much. We were also very well dressed. Some of us wore complete Eskimo costumes, others partly civilized clothing. My experience is that in these parts in winter the Eskimo dress is far superior to our European clothes. But one must either use it alone or not at all. Any combination is bad. Wool underwear gathers all perspiration and will soon make the outside clothing wet. Dressed entirely in reindeer skin, like the Eskimo, and with the clothing loose enough on the body to let the air circulate between the layers, one will as a rule keep the clothing dry. . . . Finally, skins are absolutely wind-proof, which is of course a very

important point." Within a short time after the arrival of the Netsilik during the first winter, all the crew had bartered for suits of the
finest caribou-skin clothing.

Amundsen also learned the finer points of polar sledge running.
During their first winter at Gjøahavn many of Amundsen's dogs
died from a mysterious disease. Rather than abort his plans to explore the surrounding territory, Amundsen decided to make an excursion using fewer dogs to haul the sleds. During this trip, the
sledges stuck in the snow, which was "like sand," and the animals
were exhausted. Amundsen and two companions took to hauling
one of the sledges themselves, which proved to be "terrible labour"
to cover a slight distance. "After ceaseless toil from morning to
evening, we managed to cover 3.5 miles. I realized now that this sort
of thing was not good enough." He soon learned to coat the sledge
runners with ice for smooth running, and set out to learn all he could
about the training and maintenance of dogs in the polar environment, which involved a different set of customs and practices from
those used for raising dogs as pets in Norway. To the Inuit, the use
of dogs was a matter of life and death, and they were working animals, not pets. Anyone accustomed to considering dogs as pets
would have been appalled by the rough treatment and heavy work
load of these animals.

Amundsen's interest in Inuit culture was not limited to aspects he
felt would improve his own career as a polar explorer. In *The North-
West Passage* he detailed, through story and anecdote, many aspects
of Inuit culture that were esoteric, spiritual or seemingly based only
on custom (although customs and beliefs have their foundations in
the environment and the need to survive). In addition to discussing
their material culture—their houses, clothing, hunting and food
preparation techniques and tools—he described Inuit religious practices, their songs, dances, stories and ceremonies. He was intrigued
by the changes in lifestyle from season to season, especially the winter practice of constructing a giant communal igloo where the tribe

gathered for dancing and drumming, and theatrical, spiritual and athletic displays. He also related events that were obviously disturbing and perhaps disgusting to him (to some of his men even more so), such as certain methods of food preparation. For example, Amundsen and Ristvedt joined a group of hunters one summer day. When a deer was shot, the blood was quickly collected and some of it was drunk by the hunters before they removed the animal's stomach. "The Eskimo partook of a portion of the contents by scooping it up with their hands. When the stomach was half empty, they put the blood into it and stirred it round with a thigh bone. The dish thus prepared was blood-pudding *á la Eskimo*, which even Ristvedt had refused to partake of."

In Amundsen's telling, the Inuit are fully realized multi-dimensional people whose customs, personality traits and emotions cover the entire spectrum open to the human race. Amundsen manages to convey a great deal of information and insight about them without being stereotypically judgmental or condescending. He notes that the culture could be harsh and unforgiving; some of the punishments for crimes, in particular, could be very violent and severe. One incident Amundsen witnessed has a prominent place in his book and includes a sketch of the event based on a poor-quality photograph. Two brothers, one a man's natural-born son and the other a foster son, were playing in a caribou-skin tent near the *Gjøa* during the first summer. The parents went visiting and left behind a gun, fully loaded and primed, in the tent. "Then followed what so often happens when boys play with weapons without having been shown how to use them properly; they were ignorant and the gun went off, and Umiktuallu's son, who was only seven years old, fell down dead." Hearing the shot, the father and a crowd of others rushed over. "At the sight of his own dead son, and the foster son sitting with the smoking weapon, he was seized with frenzy. He carried the horror-stricken boy out of the tent, stabbed him three times through the heart with his knife, then kicked him away."

Amundsen then related that the boys were buried, and the father, "with time and reflection," calmed down and "was seized with remorse." The family departed the next day, and Amundsen heard nothing more of them.

The Inuit women attracted a great deal of interest from the men of the *Gjøa* expedition. Amundsen wrote that "some of these women are absolute beauties. They are rather small but shapely." He also recorded the prevalence of wife swapping and bigamy, and that for a small price husbands would offer to sell sexual access to their wives: "a wife must obey but I doubt whether she does it of her own free will." Nevertheless, amorous liaisons between the crew and the local women were common, if not frequent, during their two-year stay, and the journals of several men make oblique references to this, although several published accounts of the voyage, including *The North-West Passage*, claim the contrary. In fact, Amundsen relates the story of how he discovered the open sores of syphilis on a sick boy in one of the tribes they encountered, a group that had had communication with European whalers. He then brought the crew together to "speak seriously. . . . I called the men together to inform them and added that I assumed the illness was probably rife in the tribe."

In the official account of the voyage, Amundsen writes in a somewhat lofty and prim tone that he discouraged his men from giving in to their "baser passions" and that "I therefore took the first opportunity to have a most serious talk with my companions and urge them not to yield to this kind of temptation." There was probably collusion among the men not to publicly discuss something of which all were aware, out of fear that it would ruffle the feathers of early-twentieth-century moralists. The issue is discussed, however, in an article in *Above and Beyond: Canada's Arctic Journal*: "Indeed, there are a few people in Gjoa Haven today who are proud to declare that they are Roald Amundsen's grandchildren, including Paul Iquallaq who is quoted as saying, 'My father was the son of Amundsen . . . I'm one of the proudest people in Gjoa Haven.'" According to local tradition, Amundsen's son, Luke Iquallaq, was born to a woman named Queleoq after the *Gjøa* departed, and his parentage was kept secret for fear of discrimination. Luke, who worked most of his life for the Hudson's Bay Company, revealed to his own children only in 1979 that his mother told him just before she died that his father was Amundsen. Recent DNA testing of Luke Iquallaq and the descendents of Amundsen's father, orchestrated by Norway's Fram Museum, show that Luke is not the genetic descendent of Amundsen. The tests do not, however, show that Amundsen has no descendants in Gjoa Haven or that Luke Iquallaq is not descended from another member of the *Gjøa*'s crew.

Amundsen's opinion of the Inuit was generally positive. "Evidently they enjoyed life," he reported, "but on the other hand, they had not the slightest fear of death. . . . I must state as my firm conviction that the . . . Eskimo living absolutely isolated from civilization, are undoubtedly the happiest, healthiest, most honourable and most contented among them. . . . My sincerest wish for our friends the Nechilli Eskimo is, that civilization may never find them." His attitude was unusual but not unique. Seven decades earlier, between 1829 and 1833, the British naval commander John Ross, captain of the expedition that first located the magnetic North Pole, wrote,

I believe that it is the Esquimaux alone who here knows the true secret of happiness and rational art of living. . . . He smells at no flowers, for there are none to smell at; but he prefers the odour of seal oil. . . . They could travel easier than we, could find delights where we experienced only suffering, could outdo us in killing the seal, could regale in abundant food where we should starve because we could not endure it. . . . The adaptation is perfect; his happiness is absolute. Had we been better educated, we should have done the same; but we were out of our element, as much in the philosophy of life as in the geography of it.

Amundsen was not an autocrat by nature—at least not a micro-managing autocrat. He wasn't interested in interfering in the daily routines or personal lives of his men. But in order to avoid the possible problems of a dispersed power structure, he formed a hierarchy in which all the major decision-making authority was vested in one individual: himself. This arrangement at times engendered some resentment among his men. It also raises the question of whether it is possible to achieve perfect harmony in any group engaged in a dangerous, stressful and at times monotonous and isolated endeavour—an expedition of exploration—without the spectre of personal disagreements arising. Even the famed master mariner James Cook during his three epochal voyages dealt with incidents that resulted in anger, resentment and violent punishment.

Inevitably, disagreements arose between the six crew members of the *Gjøa* and their captain as well as among each other, and they intensified during the two years the ship was stationary in the middle of the Northwest Passage. Some of the crew's private journals reveal irritation over Amundsen's apparently harsh treatment of the dogs and overly friendly relations with the Inuit, but these remained minor incidents of personal grumbling and never metastasized into anything bigger. There was never any serious public quarrelling, and the expedition was never in danger from it. The men grew sick of each other, bored with each others' jokes and stories, and irritated by each others' quirks and foibles. But this was nothing more than the friction to be expected in a small group living far from home, with only themselves for companionship for years at a time.

Lindstrøm the cook was the pillar of stability throughout the *Gjøa*'s stay in Gjøahavn. Always in a good mood, and a superior cook who took pride in excellent meals, he had no interest in the local peoples or polar survival techniques. Indeed, he seldom left the ship for those two years, except for infrequent short excursions to trade or to retrieve animals he had shot. But his kitchen continuously produced roasts, pies, pancakes, stews, cakes, breads—all delicious and of high quality. It is said that an army marches on its stomach—so too does a voyage of exploration. Lindstrøm kept everyone happy in that department with an ever-evolving diet for every palate: seals, walrus, polar bear, geese and various fish. The abundant supply of fresh meat also kept scurvy at bay. Amundsen recalled fondly that although Lindstrøm liked to indulge in not insignificant quantities of alcohol, "when he sets his mind on something he never gives up. The others laugh at him, but he just laughs back and continues on his way. He usually succeeds."

Lindstrøm was genuinely liked by all the crew, and was never the butt of criticism or the cause of quarrelling or frustration. "A funny chap," Ristvedt noted in his diary, "fat as a pig but always happy and in a good mood, in spite of having every reason to be bad tempered." Lindstrøm took great pleasure in hunting many of the animals for his meals and bartered with the Inuit to obtain others. On one occasion the other men played a practical joke on him. Two of them snuck across the snowy plain, perhaps 30 metres from the bow of the ship, and placed a frozen ptarmigan in the snow. "Lindstrøm! Lindstrøm!" yelled one, "there is a ptarmigan on the ice!" The cook rushed from the kitchen below deck with his gun loaded. "Where is it?" They pointed and he silently raised his gun, taking aim, and fired. The bird flopped over, and Lindstrøm scampered over the gunwales of the ship and trotted across the frozen plain to retrieve his quarry. He stooped to pick it up but then called out, bewildered, "Why, it is quite cold!" As he stood there, holding the frozen bird in his hand, the men on the deck of the ship laughingly let him in on the joke.

Lindstrøm was always working with a purpose and had daily responsibilities, which predisposed him for success in the Arctic winter, according to Amundsen's philosophy that idle time led to lethargy and depression. For the other men, filling the hours was not always easy. To counter this, Amundsen was constantly devising tasks for the men, keeping them on a daily schedule that otherwise would have disintegrated during the ever-shifting balance of day and night—from total light to none. Some of the men began to resent Amundsen for his enforced ski jaunts every morning, yet they also constructed a large hill and practised downhill techniques for fun. There were complaints that Amundsen was seldom on board the ship and was too often taking trips with the locals. But others went on excursions too, either with Amundsen or in other groups.

Furthermore, the men were being paid, while Amundsen was the one paying: surely he should have some leeway to do what he wanted. If the expedition failed, the thirty-two-year-old captain stood to lose all his investment, human and financial, and to see his reputation destroyed and his career ended. He had the strain of trying to be the indomitable optimist and leader, never faltering in his assessment of things and never appearing to waver in his belief in inevitable success. The crew's few disparaging journal entries were written in the moment, and reflect brief resentments—imagine working all day under difficult, stressful conditions and then eating dinner with your boss and sleeping in the same small ship with him, seeing all his sides, his temperamental episodes and moments of indecision. In such close quarters Amundsen could not conceal all his angers, frustrations, doubts and dilemmas. But Amundsen never had anything negative to say about his men; he always gave them credit and recognition, at least in public.

The second winter was the harder of the two, the novelty of the situation having worn off after they had experienced all four Arctic seasons. "It is extraordinary to see that already after only one year everyone has lost the desire to work and we all feel the need to get away from the vessel and camp out in the wilderness or even just to go to bed," Amundsen wrote. John Ross had also begun to despair during his expedition's second winter, and by the end of the third winter he was downright depressed about the climate of northern lands: "Amid all its brilliancy, this land, the land of ice and snow, has ever been and ever will be a dull, dreary, heart-sinking, monotonous waste, under the influence of which the very mind is paralyzed, ceasing to care or think." Ross later wrote: "The sameness of everything weighed on our spirits, and the mind itself flagged under the want of excitement. In such a life as ours, even the capture of an Arctic mouse was an event. Everywhere was suffocated and paralyzed by the endless, wearysome, heartsinking, uniform, cold load of ice and snow."

The crew of the *Gjøa* must have had similar moments. For them, the sole source of wonder and amusement was their dogs, who were the kernel of numerous amusing anecdotes. The dogs, Amundsen noted during the second winter, were "now turning their noses up at pemmican. They consider old pieces of fur a delicacy. 'The menu of the Polar dog is comprehensive,' said Ristvedt. 'I think I can manage many dishes, but I don't think I could have managed your old underpants.' The dogs smacked their lips over them like a bear with honey."

Amundsen perfected his polar survival techniques during the two years he spent in the Northwest Passage, including skills such as the prevention of frostbite by the use of proper clothing. The skills for which he lacked experience he had now mastered and adapted to his own life and plans. He was now in possession of a remarkable and unique blend of skills that would be the foundation of his success. Perhaps there was no other person on the planet better educated for geographical exploration and survival in its polar regions.

On August 13, 1905, when the sea ice was sufficiently melted, the obligatory scientific measurements completed, and Amundsen was confident that he had learned what he could from the Inuit, there was nothing left but to head west into the unknown. The *Gjøa's* engines fired up, smoke blew from the exhaust pipes and the silence was shattered as the little ship pushed slowly westward through the ice. The Norwegian visitors left their local hosts priceless gifts, including the wood and materials from their on-shore huts. "I am not sure that the little brown-eyed people on the beach were quite cheerful that morning," Amundsen related. "They waved long to us—probably a farewell for life; and if some traveller, many years later, pays this place a visit, the numerous tent-rings will remind him of the many happy days the *Gjøa* expedition spent here with their friends the Netsilik Eskimos."

Simpson Strait is the narrow, labyrinthine ice-choked channel separating the northern part of Canada's mainland from the innumerable islands of the Arctic Archipelago. Uncharted in Amundsen's time—parts of it never before navigated—the strait is littered with hidden shoals and icebergs. After four days of slowly picking its way through the treacherous channel, the *Gjøa* passed Cape Colborne, the point beyond which no one had ever sailed east through Simpson Strait. Amundsen wrote in his memoirs that "time and time again it seemed certain we should be defeated by the shallowness of these tortuous channels. Day after day, for three weeks—the longest three weeks of my life—we crept along, sounding our depth with the lead, trying here, there and everywhere to nose into a channel that would carry us clear through to the known waters to the west." They were saved by the motor that Amundsen had had installed in the ship, for with the erratic winds and currents, sail power alone would not have provided the manoeuvrability needed to clear the obstacles. On one particularly stressful day, the ship slipped over some jagged rocks with barely a few centimetres of water beneath the keel. Another time, they spent three days anchored behind barren islands, waiting for fog to lift.

The strain on Amundsen was enormous as the ship inched through the deadly waters. Here the voyage would either utterly fail or grandly succeed. "I could not get rid of the possibility of returning home with the task unperformed. The thought was anything but cheering." He spent hours brooding in the bowels of the ship when he should have been sleeping. He craved food with "a devouring hunger," but at mealtimes the food stuck in his throat. He was sick with worry. Afterward his appetite returned, and he later reported in *The North-West Passage* that "I would rather not mention what I managed to dispose of." In his memoirs, however, written decades afterward, he was less concerned with propriety and ready to entertain his readers with a lurid tale. "Instantly, my nerve-racking strain of the last three weeks was over. And with its passing, my appetite returned. I felt ravenous. Hanging from the shrouds were carcasses of caribou. I rushed up the rigging, knife in hand. Furiously I slashed off slice after slice of the raw meat, thrusting it down my throat in chunks and ribbons, like a famished animal, until I could contain no more." His stomach rejected this "barbarous" feast and he had to "feed the fishes," but "my appetite would not be denied and again I ate my fill of raw, half-frozen meat." This time his rude meal stayed down and his usual "sense of calm and well being" returned. The strain, however, left its "mark upon me in such a way that my age was guessed to be between fifty-nine and seventy-five years, although I was only thirty-three!"

Not until August 26 did the *Gjøa* slip into the safer waters of what has become known as Amundsen Gulf, where the crew spied the distant outlines of a sail in the hazy distance. The sail was flying the Stars and Stripes. It was the *Charles Hansson*, a whaling schooner from San Francisco. The Norwegians rushed below deck to change from their ragged working outfits into their best clothes—they had been saving them for years, for just this purpose. As the two ships neared, the *Gjøa* lowered a small boat and Amundsen and three others rowed across the icy sea to board the *Charles Hansson*. "How surprised was I not, when Captain McKenna wrapped his fist round mine and congratulated me on a brilliant success." McKenna had been on the lookout for the *Gjøa*. After a couple of hours chatting and gathering information on ice conditions and exchanging sailing tips, the Norwegians bid farewell to the Americans and returned to the *Gjøa* with an armful of old newspapers as a precious parting gift. One of the newspapers contained a vague and unnerving article under the headline "War between Norway and Sweden." The world had changed during the adventurers' sojourn with the Inuit.

Amundsen still hoped to cruise west as far as Herschel Island near the Alaska-Yukon border and then, if ice conditions permitted, push further west along the Alaskan coast before turning south through the Bering Strait. But it was not to be. The little ship was iced in for a third winter about 65 kilometres east of Herschel Island at King Point in the Yukon. Nearby there was a wrecked schooner and its Norwegian second mate, some American crew and a cluster of Inuit. Several whaling ships were also iced in within sight of Herschel Island. The *Gjøa*'s crew began hammering together an on-shore shed to provide shelter for the winter and making the *Gjøa* ready to do some more magnetic measurements during the frozen months ahead. By September 7, 1905, the ice was thick enough to cross, and the small community of ship-bound men could visit each other and exchange news. It didn't take long before they all knew about Amundsen's historic feat.

Amundsen was filled with frustration and impatience—if he didn't get out the news himself, he would risk losing the money to be earned from the first publication of his story. In late October, when two Inuit and a whaling captain said they would set off for a distant Alaskan outpost, Amundsen decided to go with them through the trackless wilderness of the Yukon and Alaska. The small community of Eagle City, about 800 kilometres south over a mountain range, was a fur-trading settlement along the Yukon River that boasted a telegraph link. Amundsen was bursting with excitement to relay his historic news to the world and let his family and the families of his crew know that they had succeeded and were safe.

Amundsen and Captain William Mogg brought one sled and five dogs, while the Inuit travellers, Jimmy and Kappa (husband and wife), worked a second sled with seven dogs. Mogg brought along supplies such as pork and beans, buns, butter, sugar, tea, chocolate, dried milk and raisins. "It was certainly a much richer list of stores than I was accustomed to, but I had my doubts as to whether in solidity this variety would compare with the simpler stores used for our sledge trips," Amundsen fretted. He had proposed pemmican as the natural and best food for the journey but was rebuffed by Mogg, and he could barely conceal his contempt: "Even the most unskilled dweller in the Temperate Zone can imagine how much needless waste of water content in the beans we should be dragging over the weary miles of snow."

The four travellers journeyed through a landscape that "suddenly appeared like a piece of genuine Norwegian scenery, timbered and rocky." This brought on a bout of homesickness in the young captain, who hadn't seen a tree since leaving Norway. As they reached increasingly more populated territory, they stopped each night in small cabins and "road-houses" that were spaced out along the shores of the Yukon River every 30 kilometres or so. Amundsen later related an incident that reveals a great deal about his character. The provisions they carried were inadequate for all but Mogg, who "sat on one of the sleds all day" while Amundsen "grew hungrier and thinner with every mile." By then they had split up with their two Inuit companions, and Mogg informed Amundsen that they would now travel all day without stopping for lunch. Amundsen protested, pointing out the difference in their levels of exertion and his own greater need for food. "The captain angrily dismissed my protest and pointed out that as he was the commander of the expedition, and had all the money, his orders would prevail." Amundsen said nothing, but "like the Irishman's parrot, 'I kept up a devil of a thinking.'" The next day about lunchtime, Amundsen stopped and told Mogg that he would continue only if he had three meals a day. He would hike back to the previous shelter on foot and let Mogg continue on by himself. The terrified Mogg, who was in no physical shape to do anything so strenuous and had no idea how to handle dogs, "piteously claimed that I was leaving him to perish in the wilderness." Amundsen coolly informed him that his survival was his own responsibility and agreed to accompany the captain only after they had agreed on the increased food allotment.

On December 5 Amundsen and Mogg arrived at Eagle City, its rude log houses fronting the frozen river and "its blue smoke standing out darkly against the bright sky." The gold mining town had sprung up in the wake of the Klondike gold rush a few years earlier. Amundsen went straight to the telegraph office and sent his famous telegraph announcing that the Northwest Passage had finally been navigated after centuries of fatal striving. As he had no money, he sent off his lengthy telegram collect, to Nansen in Norway. His rambling telegram cost Nansen a small fortune, the equivalent of thousands of dollars today, but Amundsen hoped to recoup the expense from the exclusive sale of the story to newspapers, including *The Times* of London. Unfortunately, the story was leaked to the press. The information passed through Seattle on its way to Norway, and by the time Nansen read the note, the news was already several days old in the United States and was no longer a scoop. Many American papers pirated the story, and *The Times* refused to pay—a severe financial blow to the indebted Amundsen. The theft of his intellectual property contributed to Amundsen's penchant for secrecy and distrust of the press, as well as the realization that news was a commodity to be handled and sold like any other. He would not make this mistake again.

Nansen was nevertheless delighted with the news, and responded a few days later, informing Amundsen that Norway had achieved independence from Sweden. He offered Amundsen some advice on how to handle the politics of the situation, for Amundsen's feat had become intertwined with Norway's independence celebrations: Amundsen was the first hero of the newly independent nation.

The penniless but now famous explorer spent the next several months in Eagle City as the guest of Frank Smith and his family.

Smith was the resident manager of the Alaska Commercial Company, and Amundsen wrote that "I shall ever be grateful for his hospitality." So began Amundsen's lifelong association with and love of Alaska: these months in Eagle City gave him "every opportunity to become acquainted with the generous hospitality of Alaska" while waiting for mail to arrive from Europe so that he could bring it back to his men, before the final push out of the Arctic. On February 3, 1906, Amundsen put on his skis again and set out on an uneventful return to the *Gjøa* at King Point. An encounter on the return journey is revealing of Amundsen's character. Heading north, he encountered a solitary traveller hauling a toboggan without any dogs. It turned out to be Mr. Darrell, a Scot, who was hauling the mail alone through the wilderness "with not a soul to aid him in case of illness or accident, cheerfully trudging through the Arctic winter across an unblazed wilderness, and thinking nothing at all of his exploit. I was lost in admiration of this hearty and cheerful Scotsman." Amundsen had a genuine respect for remarkable individuals who were quiet and unpretentious, and he was generous in acknowledging the skills and talents that he admired in others. Darrell and Amundsen became friends and kept in touch, and only Darrell's accidental death prevented him from joining Amundsen's South Pole expedition years later.

Amundsen arrived on March 12, having skied over 1,500 kilometres, to a "heartfelt welcome." He was a hero again, delivering mail and news to his "splendid lads." In a letter to his brother Leon, Amundsen commented with understatement that "I walked every inch of the way, so I am quite fit at the moment." Then misfortune struck. Gustav Wiik, the young magnetic measurer, began to feel ill. He soon was stricken with severe abdominal pain. By the end of March, he was confined to bed with an erratic and racing pulse and soaring temperature. He died before Amundsen could transport him to Herschel Island. Perhaps it was a burst appendix; it happened so quickly and without any apparent reason that it stunned everyone.

"Death must always be a gruesome guest, but to us, in our position far away from friends and relations, it was if possible, more depressing than it would otherwise have been," Amundsen wrote. Some writers have implied that Wiik's death was somehow Amundsen's fault, because his medical skills were inferior and there was no physician on board. But it is hard to see what anyone could have done about a burst appendix in the isolated channels of the Northwest Passage, even if they had been able to diagnose the problem.

Its crew eager to move on, the *Gjøa* broke free of the ice on July 11, 1906, and slowly cruised the final stretch of coastline of the Northwest Passage. The ship passed Point Barrow, the northernmost part of Alaska, on August 21, when the coast was hemmed in by pack ice to the north, sailing through the Bering Strait during a storm on August 30. "I thought to celebrate our passage through the Bering Strait rather formally—but all we managed was to raise a quick glass on the deck; a flag up the mast was out of the question. . . . It was with great joy that we drained our cup. Whatever we might now encounter—we have carried the Norwegian flag through the North West Passage, on *one* boat." On August 31, the ship slid silently into Nome, Alaska, a gold rush town that housed many Norwegian expatriates. The crew were received with enthusiastic cheers and the singing of the Norwegian anthem, followed by a raucous party. Before the *Gjøa* departed for the south, Amundsen had already received his first invitation for a speaking engagement—from the Geographical Society of Philadelphia. But Nansen urged him to return to Norway.

70°S

Victoria Land

Ross Sea

Ross Island

Bay of
Whales

Ross Ice Shelf

Amundsen Expedition

Axel Heiberg
Glacier

Beardmore
Glacier

80°S

Amundsen
(12/14/1911)

SOUTH POLE

PART TWO
SOUTH

6

"I Resolved Upon a Coup"

*You cannot pick up a bag and start for the North Pole
as you would go to Philadelphia. . . . It will take all of
two years to get ready. . . . [T]he food has to be especially carefully prepared, otherwise the men get scurvy,
and it is no use to be an explorer unless you live to
come back.*

AFTER A FEW DAYS celebrating in Nome and a tour of the
nearby gold mines, the company of Norwegian adventurers
split up. Amundsen boarded the steamship *Victoria* on September 5,
1906, bound south for San Francisco, while first lieutenant Godfred Hansen took command of the battered *Gjøa* and prepared to
follow. When Amundsen arrived in the city, San Francisco was a
mess of crumbled, burned buildings and sprawling tent communities. It had been devastated by its now-famous earthquake in April,
and the sounds of frenetic construction rose from the ruins. Under-
standably, its residents were preoccupied with their task, and
Amundsen was not met by cheering crowds, nor indeed by anyone
but a small contingent from the local Norwegian community. Nevertheless he remained in San Francisco, speaking and touring around
the region, until the *Gjøa* arrived.

When Amundsen and his crew were reunited, second lieutenant Helmer Hanssen noted that "there were celebrations one after the other, both given by Norwegians and Americans, until finally we could not distinguish night from day . . . ladies, dancing, good food, and quite a lot of good drinks, too." In mid-October the crew made arrangements to return home and to leave the ship in the hands of the Norwegian American community in California. The *Gjøa* was unable to sail home in its worn-out condition, and Amundsen couldn't afford to keep the crew on salary any longer.*

Amundsen was now a famous man, and he was in great demand as a speaker in the United States. He spent most of October and November riding the train east across the country, lecturing and presenting his story, photographs and artefacts. In the early twentieth century, before the invention of radio, Americans went out to seek entertainment. All their forms of entertainment—theatre, musical performances, circuses and lectures—were live. Amundsen's hastily organized lecture tour was highly anticipated, and halls were sold out in cities across the country. He made stops in Seattle, Minneapolis, Chicago, Milwaukee, Cambridge, Philadelphia and New York, among countless others. But the novelty of celebrity wore off quickly. By November he was tired of the daily grind, the rounds of public speaking in a language in which he was not yet fully fluent. In a letter to his brother, he complained of being exhausted from the endless celebrations and the constant retelling of his story: "I'll be glad when the 8th arrives and we can turn our back on it all and leave with the *Hellig Olav* [a Norwegian luxury liner departing from New York]." Many years later, his friend Harald Sverdrup wrote of Amundsen's dislike of the lecture circuit. "He hated the lecture trips on which he had to place himself in the hands of a manager and sell

---

*The *Gjøa* was later presented as a gift to the city of San Francisco, remaining on display in Golden Gate Park until 1972, when it was returned to Norway. It now resides in Oslo harbour, next to two other famous Norwegian ships, Fridtjof Nansen's *Fram* and Thor Heyerdahl's *Kon-Tiki*.

his freedom of action to a person whose publicity schemes he disliked but could not avoid." But speaking engagements were a vital source of income for a man destined not to enjoy stable government funding or institutional support, yet possessed of an expansive imagination and a determination to explore the remotest frozen regions of the globe.

The final stop on Amundsen's first whirlwind American lecture tour was at the Norwegian Club in New York, where the tables were festooned with Norwegian and American flags and he and his crew were placed at tables of honour. After a toast was proposed to President Theodore Roosevelt and Norway's newly elected King Haakon VII, the president's letter of compliments was read aloud, congratulating Amundsen "on the notable feat he has accomplished." Amundsen stood to begin his speech, starting in English and then with a sigh pushing on in Norwegian, a language understood by most of his audience that night. A giant map of the Arctic hung on the wall behind him. He turned to highlight the route of the *Gjøa*, but could not seem to locate it. Finally he turned and announced, "I found the Northwest Passage, but I cannot find it on this map!" Evidently this was taken as a joke, since it was met with "roars of laughter." Later that night, the explorer and his crew boarded the *Hellig Olav*, bound for Norway.

The adventurers were met by a Norwegian battleship and escorted into Christiania, where they were feted with banquets and public ceremonies. It must have been strange for them to return as the first internationally recognized heroes of a newly independent nation. On May 17, the Norwegian national day, Amundsen delivered the keynote speech from the balcony of the National Hotel in Christiania. Then, after a brief tour of the larger Norwegian towns, he began preparing for something he had long dreamed of: presenting a paper to the venerable Royal Geographical Society in London. He had been exchanging letters with the society's secretary, J. Scott Keltie, about the particulars of the prestigious invitation: the length and content of his paper, the issue of his lack of proficiency in English and the support of his compatriot Fridtjof Nansen, now the Norwegian ambassador to Britain. The first letter from Keltie, sent before Amundsen sailed into San Francisco, had been waiting for him when he arrived there. Keltie heartily congratulated Amundsen on his "great feat" and then advised him on how to manage his financial affairs to obtain the most money from his exploits, having been in close discussions with Nansen: "I am sure that you will be careful not to give away any information about your work, and about your adventures to Newspaper Interviewers for nothing. If things are properly managed you ought to make a considerable sum out of Articles for Newspapers, out of Lectures, and also out of the book which I have no doubt you will publish as soon as possible." Keltie recommended that Amundsen get all agreements in writing and even suggested the amounts Amundsen should receive for his lectures. But he also wanted to ensure that Amundsen, then on the west coast of the United States, would sail directly to England, preferably around South America: "there is no doubt that if you came home round Cape Horn with your ship, and so practically circumnavigated America and then came straight across the Atlantic and came up the River Thames to London, it would produce a very great effect upon the British Public"—and thereby increase his earnings. Come to London first, before the United States, Keltie urged him, "and give your account of the Expedition to our Society." He suggested that "in order to please the Americans," Amundsen might have to give a talk to one or two of their societies, but that he should make his arrangements to tour America after his triumphant presentation in London.

Britain and the Northwest Passage had been linked for centuries. There are countless stories of British mariners who struggled and perished in their search for incremental pieces of the geographical puzzle, and in the post-Napoleonic world the quest for the Northwest Passage had become a playing field for displaying the talents and perseverance of the Royal Navy. That quest was the source of more than a few of Britain's national myths. If a Norwegian was fated to be the one who claimed the laurels of victory in the epic struggle, then at least the celebrations should take place in London, rather than in the United States. "Hoping to see you soon," Keltie signed off. He was disappointed that Amundsen spent so much time in the United States and then followed that with a brief tour of Norway, thereby preventing the Royal Geographical Society from hosting the premiere of the explorer's publicity tour. Nevertheless, a date was set for Amundsen's lecture—February 11, 1907—and Keltie offered to "be of any service to you with regard to the English Edition of your book, or for Articles in English Papers." Keltie planned the address to be a prominent affair, featuring not only Amundsen but a roster of additional speakers, including distinguished politicians, admirals and scientists, blowups of up to one hundred photographs, to be "mounted on screens in the Reception Room," and a giant map, specially made for the occasion. He urged Amundsen to wait until after his lecture before signing any book, article or lecture deals, because he was sure the publicity would "attract a great deal of attention" and elevate Amundsen's fees.

Keltie also addressed the concern that Amundsen didn't speak English fluently enough for such an august congregation. "If you find that you could not make yourself quite intelligible, perhaps you could read a portion of the paper at the meeting, and allow Dr. Nansen if he is willing, to read the remainder." Nansen acted as Amundsen's spokesman and gave a speech at his lecture, which fell within his professional duties as ambassador; Amundsen was, after all, the unofficial representative of his new nation. The sombre lecture, followed by serious questions and discussion, was not the casual affair that would have suited Amundsen, who was not really familiar with or comfortable in these class-dominated British surroundings. He was more at ease with the Inuit or the working-class society of his crew, even though he always remained the first among equals.

And Nansen, with his aristocratic air, was "too kingly, he will not hobnob with the common herd." But in Britain Nansen was accorded a great deal of respect, more than Amundsen would ever receive. Keltie was even concerned that Amundsen's "secretary"—his brother Leon, who planned to stay with Amundsen in the Royal Society's Club—would not be up to the social standards of the establishment. He sent Amundsen a note that contained a barely disguised warning: "I have no doubt he would be a quite suitable person for the Club, I shall be glad to arrange a room for him there." It would be Amundsen's job to make sure that his secretary was, in fact, "quite suitable."

Despite Amundsen's misgivings, the lecture was a great success. But even though Amundsen had hired Nansen's lecture agent to organize a tour, the public interest was not enough to make it profitable. Amundsen was offered various explanations, including that he had gone to the United States first and that he hadn't sailed up the Thames in his ship, thus failing to provide a newsworthy event upon which to report. But it is more likely that the mediocre interest was due to his lack of proficiency in English (he concluded his speech with the comment "I speak English so badly that I hope you will excuse me if I thank you in only a few words") and the fact that no Briton was interested in celebrating a foreigner's victory over what had traditionally been seen as a British quest. As a result, he and his expedition were essentially ignored by the British press. After the warm reception he had received in the United States, Amundsen had every reason to imagine that the conquest of the Northwest Passage would be heralded as a historic achievement in Britain as well, and its conqueror afforded a hero's welcome. But he was disappointed and hurt by the apparent snub he received in Britain.

After his muted reception in Britain, a disillusioned Amundsen turned to Europe. For several months trains carried him to the major cities from Copenhagen to Rome, where theatres were packed and dignitaries hosted receptions in his honour. He addressed the Geographical Society in Paris, and he addressed the Berlin Geographical Society, with Kaiser Willhelm II in attendance. He did not bother to return to Britain, even when he was invited to receive King Edward's Gold Medal "for his work in connection with the magnetic North Pole," since his continental lecture tour kept him fully occupied in profitable appearances—exceedingly important for a man with debts to pay. He also penned articles for various American periodicals, such as *Harper's Monthly Magazine.* On April 20, 1907, at Nansen's urging, the Norwegian parliament voted to award Amundsen a sum large enough to clear all his remaining debts from the *Gjøa* expedition.

His massive European tour ended in August. Soon he was dreaming of "new worlds to conquer," as he put it in his autobiography, and needed new financing. He returned to Norway for a few months, but in the fall was back in the United States, continuing his Herculean lecture and publicity tour in order to raise funds. He can hardly be said to have lived in Norway during these years, so often was he on the road. It was the start of a pattern that would shape the rest of his life: his home was on rail cars, in hotels and aboard ships.

While in America, Amundsen floated the possibility of his next adventure. In a frank discussion with a *New York Times* reporter on October 27, he announced his plans to "discover" the North Pole. The reporter, expressing amazement at the extreme cold and the social isolation, was shocked by the number of years Amundsen claimed the expedition would take. Amundsen replied, "You cannot pick up a bag and start for the North Pole as you would go to Philadelphia. . . . It will take all of two years to get ready, to provision the ship, and five years rations. You see, the food has to be especially carefully prepared, otherwise the men get scurvy, and it is no use to be an explorer unless you live to come back." The reporter, quite taken with Amundsen's charming ways, enthusiastically reported Amundsen's claims about the comfort of snow huts, the

friendliness of Arctic peoples, the dangers of frostbite and his fondness for ice: "'I have some pictures of fine ice,' Amundsen said, feel-
ingly, and one could almost see his eyes kindle with pleasure at the
memory of some particularly artistic iceberg. . . . Your arctic explorer
revels in a field of ice, as a farmer delights in a wheat field."

Icebergs, people who dwell in snow houses, windswept lands of
perpetual darkness lying in the uncharted wastes at the globe's poles:
in the early twentieth century, these exotic scenes were finally being
revealed to "civilized" people by the intrepid actions of seemingly
fearless adventurers who were impervious to hardship. Newspapers
craved this sort of never-before-known content for their papers and
spun a variety of angles on the experience to enliven their news reporting. Another article in the *New York Times* that year reported
Amundsen's speculation that he might have polar bears haul his
sledges to the pole ("they'll be cheap to feed") under the control of a
bear trainer who "guarantees they won't eat the explorer." This apparently was something Amundsen was seriously considering but
eventually dropped as impractical, not to mention dangerous.

On December 14, Amundsen was in Washington, D.C., attending a dinner at a posh hotel, where he was honoured to receive
the Hubbard Gold Medal from "the largest organization of its kind
in the world," the National Geographical Society. The illustrious
guests included Vice President Charles W. Fairbanks, the French
and British ambassadors and "a host of other members of the Diplomatic Corps, Senators, Representatives, prominent officials, [and]
distinguished scientists," according to a newspaper story covering
the event. It was a signal honour, not to mention that the medal was
a large and valuable piece of gold. Soon after, at a well-attended lecture at Carnegie Hall, Amundsen "horrified the audience" with tales
of how the Inuit occasionally committed suicide. He explained how
a hide string was placed across the snowy ground of an igloo and
"all the members of the family solemnly retire to the outside, leaving
the sick person within. But there are peep holes, and through these

they watch him. He gets up and bends down over the string, trying to force his throat so hard upon that he is strangled." If the family outside spying through the holes thought the man was not "getting along as fast as he should they kindly go in and help him strangle himself." Despite spinning amusing or shocking stories for the press, Amundsen continued claiming that he despised the lecture tour after the initial excitement wore off. Certainly, he was making money; but, as he later wrote, he felt he was "merely part of a lecture machine set in motion between New York through intermediate stops to San Francisco." He earned every penny on his "journey full of work and strain."

Amundsen returned briefly to Norway in early 1908 and purchased a chalet-style house perched on some rocks above Bunde Fjord outside of Christiania. He named it "Uranienborg" after the primitive observatory at Gjøahavn, and decorated it in the style of a ship's cabin with etchings of scenes from his adventures in the Arctic on doors and walls. He moved his old family housekeeper, Betty, into a nearby cottage. In photographs of the home taken from the decks of ships anchored at its dock, it can be seen peeking through the forest upon a rocky promontory; it was easier to reach by water than by land. But all was not perfect. Amundsen's fame and relative wealth had allowed him to help friends and family, but he was having problems with two of his brothers, Gustav and Jens, whose failed business ventures, resentments and demands for money were bad for the family name. Amundsen provided them with some money to help out, but he soon realized that whatever he supplied would never be enough.

Amundsen's journals from the *Gjøa*'s three-year cruise through the Northwest Passage were heavily edited and published as a book, which came out in the summer of 1908. Originally written in Norwegian, it was translated into English and appeared in the United States as *The North-West Passage*. Amundsen dedicated the book to Nansen, the man to whom he owed so much. Generous in victory, he devoted the book's first sentence to his crew, offering his "warmest and most heartfelt thanks to the small party of brave men who risked their lives to ensure the success of my undertaking" and a solemn mention of the young Gustav Juel Wiik. A review in the *New York Times* pronounced the account "a notable contribution to science and literature" and revealed that "the fascination of the book lies in just this wholehearted kind of simplicity, the sort of sincerity that goes with the doing of great deeds." *The North-West Passage* was a modestly successful endeavour rather than a bestseller, but its proceeds, combined with the profits from the American lectures and articles, meant that Amundsen was now reasonably well off. In his autobiography he summed up the two years after emerging from the Northwest Passage rather perfunctorily: "I devoted 1906 and 1907 to lecturing in Europe and the United States, and returned to Norway with enough funds to repay all my creditors, including the one who had nearly prevented the voyage, and I was now free to make other plans." Now in his mid-thirties, Amundsen could not settle down. He was already dreaming of his next adventure.

When Amundsen was in San Francisco in early 1908, he inspected the *Gjøa*, noticed its condition and decided to sell it. He would need a new ship for his next expedition—a polar ice drift, similar to Nansen's original voyage on the *Fram*, except this one would succeed in reaching the North Pole.

For some time, Nansen had been toying with the idea of taking the *Fram* on another voyage. Antarctica was his preferred destination, for a quick ski dash to the geographical South Pole. The *Fram*, now officially owned by the Norwegian state, was specially designed to withstand the pressures of being pinched in the ice. Nansen was eleven years older than Amundsen and running out of time for embarking on a multi-year expedition that demanded stamina. He was also preoccupied with his responsibilities as Norway's ambassador to Great Britain. But in late 1907, Amundsen had sent a letter to Nansen from the United States asking if he could borrow the *Fram*, which of course would end Nansen's dreams of attaining the South Pole. Since he was not working toward this objective, and after much inner debate, Nansen relinquished his claim to his old ship and offered it to Amundsen, along with his support. Amundsen was Nansen's protégé, but Nansen was also pragmatic, appreciating the political benefit to Norway of Amundsen's conspicuous achievement.

Amundsen's fame had made securing the financing for this expedition a much simpler task than the wheedling and begging that had occupied him before he sailed for the Northwest Passage. He presented his plans to the Norwegian Geographical Society in the fall of 1908. His plan was to take the *Fram* and repeat Nansen's famous drift, ramming the ship into pack ice and being carried by the currents in the Arctic Ocean, which would allow him to continue the scientific work that Nansen had begun—of mapping the currents and measuring the temperatures at varying depths and seasons—but using better-designed and more sophisticated instruments. These tedious, perpetual measurements, undertaken as his ship sat immobile for years, drifting with the ice, were not the type of thing to inspire Amundsen. But the expedition would offer him the opportunity to do something he found far more exciting: dash on skis toward the North Pole, also using dogsleds—although this was not how the expedition would be sold to the public, at least not in Europe. Amundsen knew that science (and respectability) would still be the necessary frame upon which to hang the cloak that concealed his true intention. King Haakon and Queen Maud immediately forwarded a large donation in support of the expedition, and the resulting publicity sparked fundraising throughout Norway.

The plan was to enter the Arctic Basin through the Bering Strait and sail northwest until the *Fram* was immobilized in the plateau of grinding ice. The ship would drift with the undulating fields of ice, and the crew would take soundings to determine water depth in order to map a rough outline of the sea floor, measuring air temperature, water salinity, winds and tides, as well as, according to a London *Times* article, "the modifying effects of the flaming, shooting boreal aurora." It would emerge from this seemingly unpleasant polar tour perhaps four years later, somewhere between Greenland and Spitsbergen. The Arctic ice, according to the *Times*, was the ideal place from which to conduct oceanographic observations and measurements: "This is due to the peculiar conditions there—a sea of 2,200 fathoms deep, or more, upon the surface of which one can move about almost as on dry land. One can live and build upon the ice, and from it lower all one's instruments into the sea, and reach down to the greatest depths, without all the difficulties with which one has to contend in storm and rough water on the open sea. There is no more ideal place to be found for oceanic investigation."

Amundsen sailed to London, and on January 25, 1909, presented a detailed paper outlining his goals to the Royal Geographical Society. The important scientific questions that the expedition would try to answer included the mystery of the aurora borealis: "We all know the magnificent auroras up there in the deep, gloomy polar night . . . those strange, flaming, shooting movements across the sky on calm winter nights—we know them all so well, and have so often admired the mysterious spectacle. No one can doubt that a remarkable force is the back of this, a force that we human beings are determined to find, bind, and utilize." Nansen wrote a short postscript for the proposal in which he lavished praise on Amundsen as a friend, "a scientific explorer of the right stuff and also as a leader of men, and my confidence in him makes me believe that he is one of those that carry through successfully, in one way or another, whatever they undertake." He was enthusiastic about the expedition from the start, giving Amundsen his wholehearted support both publicly and privately, and helping with the planning and fundraising.

Nansen's support, combined with the support of the Royal Geographical Society, was instrumental in persuading the Norwegian parliament to approve 75,000 kroner in February for the repair and special outfitting of the *Fram* to meet its new challenges. Although the ship's main propulsion would remain wind power, as part of the refitting Amundsen had a new diesel motor installed to replace the bulky steam engine. The *Fram* would not be ploughing through the pack ice; it needed to be manoeuvrable and nimble, to take advantage of momentary openings in the ice and respond quickly to changing conditions. Although steam could be powerful, it needed time to build up the pressure required for that power. Another important consideration was that steam engines wasted fuel—a scarce commodity in the Arctic—because the boilers had to be kept at a slow burn. But using diesel engines for marine propulsion also meant taking a chance: the "direct reversible Marine-Polar-Motor," built by the Diesel Motor Co. of Stockholm for the *Fram*'s upcoming voyage, had been designed only a few years earlier. The *Fram* was one of the first ocean-going vessels—and the first polar exploration vessel—to be fitted with a marine diesel engine, which was much safer and fuel efficient than the small gas motor on board the *Gjøa* and produced about fifteen times the horsepower. No polar exploration ship had ever had the advantage of a diesel engine, but it was one new piece of technology that Amundsen immediately recognized as being of inestimable advantage. The work on the *Fram* at the shipyards also included improving the ventilation of the engine room, insulating the beams, remodelling the propeller shaft, adding bilge pumps, repairing the exterior of the hull and replacing the motors for the windlass, as well as installing new anchors and new floors in the galley. Many other minor improvements would update the aging vessel and prepare it for the rigours of at least four years in the Arctic.

Although he had raised only a quarter of the funds he needed—despite appeals to the nation's pride—Amundsen, with his characteristic boldness, was already happily launched into the planning and logistical details, taking on more debt, making promises and deals for a voyage that could last for seven years. Despite the mountain of work, he was enjoying a measure of happiness in an aspect of life that had so far eluded him. His relationships with women had been of the clandestinely arranged variety familiar to the travelling mariner, in brothels or with courtesans, or inside an igloo. But in Norway Amundsen met a woman who captured his attention— Sigrid Castberg, the wife of a well-known Christiania lawyer. At the time that they began their secret affair, the city had a population of around 250,000—small enough that within certain circles secrets were bound to escape. Despite his plans for an imminent and lengthy polar expedition, Amundsen urged Castberg to get a divorce and marry him. She wisely put him off, suggesting they be united after his return and remaining his companion until his departure.

In November 1909, Amundsen boarded a ship bound for New York, on another tour that combined advance publicity for his forthcoming venture with arrangements for some of its practical aspects. He arrived in New York in the centre of a controversy. While he was in the quarantine zone awaiting clearance to enter the United States, a yacht carrying reporters from the *New York Herald* cruised close by to try to get a quote from him. He declined. Stepping off the gangplank onto the wharf, however, he was beset by dozens of reporters. They were seeking his opinions on a matter that had not been much in the news in Europe but undoubtedly weighed heavily on Amundsen's thoughts: the claims of Robert Edwin Peary and Amundsen's old friend Dr. Frederick Cook to have been the first to reach the North Pole—separately.

Their rival claims had become public on September 1, mere weeks before Amundsen had sailed from Europe. The *New York Times* reported on its front page at the time: "Peary Discovers the North Pole after Eight Trials in 23 Years." Peary claimed to have reached the Pole on April 6, 1909. Cook countered that he had reached the Pole nearly a year earlier, on April 21, 1908. Both American explorers had been striving to reach this elusive goal for many years in many expeditions, some of them together. At one point Cook had even led a voyage that rescued Peary from the ice near Greenland. The evidence supporting their rival successes was vague and inconclusive—some perhaps even fraudulent, as later analysis revealed. But at the time the claims had yet to be scrutinized. Peary was the favourite of the establishment; he had many powerful friends and the backing of the National Geographic Society. One of these friends, Rear Admiral Colby M. Chester, had cast doubt on the accuracy of Cook's claims, and the press not surprisingly encouraged the battle. It would be advantageous to them for Amundsen to take sides, to stir up additional controversy.

The reporters pestered him with questions. Taken aback by the vigorous questioning, he "reaffirmed his belief in Dr. Cook." Amundsen made this potentially damaging statement even though he had been warned not to do so by the Norwegian consul in Chicago, Fredrik Herman Gade, a well-connected lawyer and old friend from Amunsen's school days, who would be helping him contract for supplies. Amundsen didn't realize the extent of the controversy in the United States, nor did he appreciate that Peary was the man with the greatest institutional support. Before sailing to New York, he had made a quick trip to Copenhagen to meet Cook. They stayed at the same hotel, and the two explorers were constantly seen about town together. While in Europe, Amundsen declared that he believed Cook's claim was credible: "Peary's behavior [in denouncing Cook] fills me with the deepest anger and I want to proclaim publicly that Dr. Cook is the most reliable Arctic traveler I know and it is simply unreasonable to doubt him and believe Peary."

Amundsen had greatly admired Cook from his days on board the *Belgica* and fondly remembered the older man's friendship and willingness to share what he knew about the techniques of polar survival. Cook had gone out of his way to befriend and mentor

Amundsen. In his narrative account of the *Belgica* voyage, published as *Through the First Antarctic Night*, Cook wrote of Amundsen that he was "the biggest, the strongest, the bravest, and generally the best dressed man for sudden emergencies." No wonder that Amundsen's innate sense of loyalty kicked in. This loyalty, once given, was solid; some of his friends claimed that he was in fact too trusting. Amundsen would go out of his way to help and support anyone he considered to have helped him in the past. It was an admirable character trait, but it would get him into trouble in the coming years.

In the American press, it was Cook who was being challenged. The balance of evidence, however selective, and public sentiment joined the institutional tilt toward Peary. Amundsen, belatedly sensing trouble while still on the wharf, became evasive with the reporters, who badgered him with questions: What did Scandinavian explorers in general feel about the controversy? Were Inuit boys who had travelled with Cook capable of lying about their destination? Did Cook have the necessary scientific training to make proper measurements? Had Amundsen seen Cook's records or proof?

"You don't hear very much about it," Amundsen responded to a *New York Times* reporter. "They [the European press] are very quiet. . . . Perhaps they do not feel justified in rendering their verdict until after Dr. Cook has presented his proofs, as he has agreed to do." Amundsen mentioned his and Cook's voyage aboard the *Belgica* to suggest that Cook had written about that voyage accurately and honestly—so he could not be entirely untrustworthy. He displayed considerable tact in his reply, deflecting the pointed questions while refusing to endorse either of the claimants. "It may be," he hedged, "that they differed by several geographical minutes. It is not important if the exact mathematical pole was reached or not, but it is important that the geographical conditions of the spot were observed."

By this time Amundsen had clearly learned a great deal about managing his public image and playing the press for his own benefit. Gone were the awkward, stuttered sentences in broken English and the uncomfortable responses. The Norwegian adventurer now looked and acted the part of a famous explorer—tall, erect, stately and clear in his opinions and in expressing them. He could be direct or obfuscating. He could spin a tale of the sort he now instinctively knew reporters wanted to hear and people wanted to read.

American reporters were not interested only in Amundsen's expeditions and opinions on exploration. The adventurer was already beginning the slow transformation into that particularly American creation, the celebrity, that would reach its apogee a decade later. What did Amundsen think about American football, one reporter wanted to know, and Amundsen had an answer: he "liked American football" and would be recommending it to the Norwegians when he returned. He had taken in a Yale-Harvard game in Cambridge and was impressed with the action, noting that "Yale's team was superior in every way to the one that represented Harvard" and that "I will talk to the university Presidents [in Norway] and shall attempt to persuade them to adopt the American college rules. . . . [I]f [Norwegians] could see an American game I am sure that this change would be made."

Amundsen also mused about the feasibility of and interest in an auto race from New York to Paris, via the Bering Strait. "The crossing of the Bering Straits on the ice will probably be the most difficult stretch of the journey," he casually remarked; "the eventuality of the loss of a machine at that point should be considered by the contestants." He was learning to play to the media, getting a sense of how to enthrall people with his exploits and stories, to endear himself to people and to have his opinions reported. He now spoke English well but with a strong accent, and with the occasional distinctive turn of phrase that is evident in his writing and his speeches—an uncommon blend of the casual and the formal, underplayed with a mischievous grin, as if the world was an amusing place and everyone was participating in a shared joke.

During Christmas 1909, Amundsen stayed at the consul Gade's estate outside Chicago. Gade was an influential man who had many contacts among other wealthy families, not only in Chicago but in New York and Boston as well. In Chicago, Amundsen was arranging for the shipment of pemmican and canned goods, but he didn't want to pay full price for these items. Gade helped to arrange for "official supplier status," much in the way that many companies become brand sponsors of publicity-generating spectacles today. The manufacturer would give Amundsen free or discounted product, which he would then publicly endorse as the best tinned meat, shoe polish, boots or toothpaste, and so on, used in the Arctic by the famous polar explorer. He also sought to arrange deals with suppliers to have their products appear in a photograph taken at the North Pole. Amundsen's fame, complemented by Gade's money, ensured that they remained close until the end of Amundsen's life—each lending the other something he lacked.

The unexpected conquest of the North Pole, whether by Peary or by Cook, was not good for Amundsen and his latest expedition. Although the controversy got him into the papers again, and reporters dutifully mentioned his next planned voyage in the *Fram* in the spring of 1910, his expedition was now overshadowed—the North Pole had already been reached. Amundsen, thinking quickly, suggested that perhaps he could verify Cook and Peary's rival claims on his own journey. But still his fundraising took a precipitous dive. The hook of the expedition, the expedition to the North Pole, had been taken by another, or others, and he needed a new plan. "Will you stop long enough to explore the land Dr. Cook says he observed on his way to the pole?" asked one reporter. "A ghost of a smile flitted across the face of the Norwegian explorer. After a moment's hesitation he said, in all seriousness: 'If we strike it—yes.'" He already knew that he wouldn't be anywhere near the North Pole; he was already contemplating a new objective before he had even departed Norway for New York. During his tour of the United States in the fall of 1909, Amundsen had secretly been planning an expedition to the South Pole, even while talking up the benefits to science of his now-pointless north polar drift. "Everything was prepared quietly and calmly," he wrote in his book *The South Pole.*

The British explorer Ernest Shackleton had just returned from a daring Antarctic adventure, and another British explorer, Robert Falcon Scott, announced in September that he was planning to travel to Antarctica in the summer or fall of 1910, to reach the South Pole. Nansen had been interested in this same geographical prize, but had passed it over to allow Amundsen to use the *Fram* for his north polar drift. The two Norwegians had earlier discussed the difficulties likely to be encountered on a dash to the South Pole, concluding that a ski and dogsled expedition would be just the method to succeed in Antarctica.

Years later, Cook wrote that it was he who suggested to Amundsen that he change his plans and go south, when the two men had met in Copenhagen. Wherever the idea had its genesis, the change of destination occurred with remarkable rapidity. Amundsen was fluid with his plans, never backing down and admitting defeat but pushing on in defiance of daunting odds. Faced with similar setbacks, most people would have returned whatever money had been raised and made their apologies. They would have accepted the vagaries of fate or ill luck. Amundsen, however, just changed his goal and continued in secret. The fact that Scott's British expedition would be departing in the same season as his was an unexpected bonus as far as Amundsen was concerned. What better way for an independently financed explorer to gain publicity than with the public spectacle of a race?

7

The Napoleon of the Poles

Only one challenge remains in the Polar Regions that can be guaranteed to awaken the public's interest, and that is to reach the South Pole. I knew that if I could do this, the funds for my planned expedition would be assured.

ANTARCTICA IS AN uninhabited mass of rock and ice covering the South Pole. The fifth largest continent, falling nearly completely within the Antarctic Circle, it is surrounded by the turbulent, icy waters of the Southern Ocean—the southern portion of the Atlantic, Pacific and Indian Oceans—known for its enormous waves, ferocious winds and treacherous obstacles. It is the coldest land on the planet, with temperatures as low as −90°C (−130°F) in the interior during winter. During summer, along the coast, the thermometer sometimes rises as high as 15°C (59°F), but it usually remains below 10°C (50°F). It is also the windiest and driest continent, whose interior is a desert receiving as little as 10 centimetres of snow a year. The Antarctic ice sheet smothers nearly 98 per cent of the continent's land, having an average thickness of 1.6 kilometres and locking up around 70 per cent of the world's fresh water. It is, of course, entirely dark in winter and endlessly sunny during the summer, making sunburn a serious risk for explorers.

The continent's howling waste of permanently frozen, almost uniformly white terrain is punctuated by jagged rock outcroppings—mountain peaks. It has no permanent human population, and it has never had one. Only along the coast does life flourish. There, various species of penguins, fur seals, blue whales, orcas, squids and various fish thrive. Other fauna include such less-than-charismatic creatures as midges, mites, lice and krill. Plant life in this land of rock and ice and seasonal darkness is sparse and consists of lichens and mosses. No animals live in the interior.

For centuries before ships probed the fringes of this desolate landmass, images of a great southern land appeared on charts. Claudius Ptolemy's map of the world from the first century C.E. portrays it in order to support the idea that a landmass existed in the south of sufficient size to counterbalance the weight of the continental land in the north, lest the world wobble lopsided and spin out of control. This was one of the key theories motivating Captain James Cook's second epic voyage of discovery between 1772 and 1775. Cook made several attempts to push south through the ice toward the mysterious, never-before-visited region. His ships *Resolution* and *Adventure* fought their way to within 120 kilometres of land before being pushed back by pack ice and storms.

The first documented sighting of the continent came in 1820, when three separate expeditions voyaged within 30 kilometres of the coast and reported a vast expanse of ice fields. In 1839, the United States Exploring Expedition, led by Lieutenant Charles Wilkes under the auspices of the U.S. Navy, also spied the continent but did not land. A decade later, a British expedition led by James Clark Ross in the *Erebus* and the *Terror* sailed into what is now known as the Ross Sea, without charts and entirely under wind power, cruising along the mighty ice wall for several hundred kilometres.

Amundsen was enthralled by these old adventure seekers, particularly Ross. He wrote in his account of his own Antarctic expedition that the long-dead British captain had "plunged into the heart of a pack which all previous polar explorers regarded as certain death. . . . It is difficult for us to understand[,] . . . we who only need a signal to start the propeller, and wriggle out of the first difficulty we meet." This observation is an example of Amundsen's characteristic understatement, humility and appreciation for the achievements of others who had gone before—certainly the primitive diesel-driven propeller on the *Fram* could not have been expected to be this effective.

Throughout the nineteenth century, various areas near Antarctica, especially South Georgia Island, were used as the semi-permanent bases of American, Norwegian and British sealers and whalers. These mariners confined their activities to the plentiful hunting grounds, devoting little time to surveying the coast and no time to exploring the interior of the continent. It was not until the 1890s that interest in exploration drove several expeditions to probe the coastline for a means of accessing the interior and the South Pole. There was, of course, the *Belgica* expedition, with Amundsen as second mate, and the British Southern Cross Expedition, led by Norwegian mariner Carsten Borchgrevink between 1898 and 1900. Robert Falcon Scott also led an expedition between 1901 and 1904.

Most important was Ernest Shackleton's expedition in the *Nimrod* between 1907 and 1909. Men from Shackleton's expedition had located the magnetic South Pole, climbed several famous mountains near their McMurdo Sound base, crossed the ice shelf, traversed the daunting and gloomy peaks of the Transantarctic Mountain Range, entered the South Polar Plateau, and with ponies and by man-hauling sledges had come within 150 kilometres of reaching the geographic South Pole, before being forced back, suffering from scurvy. Shackleton returned to Britain in the spring of 1909 a national hero.

Everyone knew that with Shackleton's near success, the South Pole, the last remaining great symbol of geographical conquest, would be claimed soon. This was the last chance for fame and glory for the handful of polar hopefuls who had been probing the extremities of the earth for the past generation. Other expeditions to Antarctica were imminent: Robert Edwin Peary mused about going south, now that he had claimed the North Pole, and so did Dr. Frederick Cook. A French doctor, Jean-Baptiste Charcot, had just returned from his second Antarctic expedition and was pondering a third. A German expedition under Wilhelm Filcher was soon to depart for Antarctica, and a Japanese expedition led by Nobu Shirase would set out in December 1910. A scramble to the pole seemed inevitable.

Amundsen knew there was little time for delay. He was in a race with more than just Scott and the British Antarctic Expedition, though they were his immediate competition. If Amundsen failed, others would be close behind. He believed that this was his final chance to achieve fame as an explorer, to build a reputation that could be leveraged to undertake other projects in the future. Around the world, members of the budding community of adventurers who wanted to be professional explorers all knew it. For many, an expedition to the South Pole was tied to nationalistic ambitions and prestige, and enjoyed institutional financial support. Certainly this was the underlying assumption behind Scott's expedition: that the discovery of the South Pole should be reserved for the world's greatest empire, an empire with a history of thus-far doomed but fascinating expeditions in the far-flung corners of the earth, particularly in the Arctic. An American had a competing claim to the North Pole; a Swede, Baron Erik Adolf Nordenskiöld, had navigated the Siberian coast of the Northeast Passage in 1878–1879; and Amundsen, a Norwegian, had claimed the Northwest Passage. The South Pole was to be Britain's prize.

Although Amundsen's ship, the *Fram*, was owned by the Norwegian state and was only on loan to him, the loan was for an expedition to the North Pole; Amundsen's desultory efforts to emphasize nationalism were a calculated strategy in his and his brothers' otherwise private schemes. His expedition did not begin as a "Norwegian" expedition; it would only become more closely tied to the nation after it was successful. The adventurer's motivations were less nationalistic, more personal. Even most of the *Fram*'s crew were kept in the dark about the expedition's ultimate objective. "At all costs we had to be first at the finish," he wrote. "Everything had to be concentrated on that." The stated motive of science was likewise merely part of a calculated marketing plan for the expedition. The voyage's scientific veneer, thin as it was, was scrubbed away entirely when the *Fram* changed course from north to south without warning. Amundsen later wrote, with a self-deprecating smile, one can imagine, that "on this little detour, science would have to look after itself."

As early as the fall of 1909 Amundsen had been planning to contrive a race between himself and Scott that he was sure would appeal to the American public in particular. Americans seemed less preoccupied with the objects of science and more accepting of conspicuous achievement, especially in a sporting event. In the United States, if not in Europe, the race itself, coupled with the symbolic if utterly valueless destination of the South Pole, would be enough. Adventure was a form of entertainment, and Amundsen was increasingly aware of his role in satisfying the demand for vicarious competition in a dangerous and little-known region. A race would give the geographical conquest of the pole a human element: something for the press to talk about, to make predictions and wagers over, and to take sides on. In this way Amundsen would be able to sell books and articles, charge for his lectures and gain lucrative product endorsements; he could make a career out of his quest for adventure.

As far as the public knew, however, he was still pushing on to the Arctic with plans for a north polar drift. Much of the equipment required for expeditions at opposite ends of the planet was the same, so Amundsen's true intentions could easily be concealed. It was a lot of work to gather everything the *Fram* would need to sail around the world and to arrange for everything the crew might conceivably need for several years once they were in Antarctica. They would not be able to obtain any supplies once they departed. Nineteen people and about a hundred dogs eat a lot of food over several years. Everything conceivable had to be itemized, quantities calculated and stores obtained beforehand.

For months only a handful of people knew Amundsen's true destination. Among them were his brother and business manager, Leon; his wealthy American friend Fredrik Herman Gade; his friend from Tromsø Fritz Zapffe, who had planned to join the expedition but pulled out for personal reasons; the oceanographer Bjorn Helland-Hansen; and the commander of the ship, Thorvald Nilsen. Some, if not all, of the expedition's major financiers probably knew of the public deception as well, particularly the ones whom Amundsen had met through Gade in America. He alluded to the fact that despite his funding for the north polar float drying up, "something had to be done to attract the attention and interest of the public in order to procure the relatively large amount of money still lacking."

In a letter to Fridtjof Nansen, Amundsen wrote: "The question became how I could raise the necessary funds. Something had to be done to increase the public's interest. Only one challenge remains in the Polar Regions that can be guaranteed to awaken the public's interest, and that is to reach the South Pole. I knew that if I could do this, the funds for my planned expedition would be assured." If the expedition was still in the future, how then did the funds arrive, if their arrival was based upon exciting public interest in an expedition that was supposed to be entirely secret? It is more than likely that key investors were aware of the expedition's true destination and had provided financing based on this updated but suppressed knowledge.

Luckily, Uranienborg was a secluded spot, ideal for keeping secrets. By June 1910, however, even some of the eighteen crew members were becoming suspicious, particularly about a prefabricated hut that was being stored in Amundsen's garden. It was a large structure, complete with a kitchen range, a linoleum floor and separate sleeping quarters for nine people—a hut that would have been completely out of place on an Arctic drift. The hut had obviously been a long time in the making. Helmer Hanssen, the second mate on the *Gjøa* voyage, who would also be aboard the *Fram*, expressed his confusion: "The house was to be an observatory I was told. But I was very doubtful whether such a large elaborate building would be of any use in the drift ice. I thought our plan was to drift across the Arctic Ocean and I told Captain Nilsen that no power on earth would get me to sleep in that house, built on drift ice. But Captain Nilsen suddenly disappeared and after that he did not seem to want to talk any more about this house." Some of the other cargo also raised eyebrows: why load piles of timber in Norway, when it could be obtained easily in San Francisco? And why kennel nearly a hundred sled dogs on the deck and cart them around the world to the Bering Strait, when they could be obtained cheaply and without difficulty in Alaska? Amundsen admitted that the faces of many of his men "began to resemble notes of interrogation."

He felt, however, that secrecy was paramount to his success. Not only was he heavily in debt to his financial backers and morally in debt to his scientific supporters in both the government and scientific societies, but also he knew his career as an explorer would come crashing down if the plans for his voyage, already years in the making, were to collapse. "If at that juncture I had made my intention public, it would only have given occasion for a lot of newspaper discussion, and possibly have ended in the project being stifled at its birth." He clearly remembered the result of his earlier slip-up with the media, immediately following his Northwest Passage success, when his story was leaked and essentially stolen, costing him a fair amount of lost money in fees and royalties. Never again would he be forthright with the press about his plans. He also recalled the previous year, when he had almost been tripped up by the press's incessant attempts to get him to take sides in the Cook-Peary controversy in the hope of linking him to the discredited claims of his old friend Dr. Cook. Following the advice and direction of his brother Leon and his friend Gade, Amundsen would feed the press information only as he saw fit—when it was useful to promote his cause. Amundsen the strategist was increasingly aware of how the media worked and how to make it work for him, not against him. The media and publicity were just another detail of the expedition to be planned and controlled.

Amundsen maintained a furtive and reclusive lifestyle. He never answered the telephone; he was rarely ready to receive visitors; and he seldom ventured out in public during the winter of 1910. When not overseeing the acquisition of supplies and provisions, he spent a great deal of time in Uranienborg poring over both old and recent maps, and reading historical accounts of mariners and explorers who had visited Antarctica. He studied all the literature he could obtain, seeking any information that would give him an edge, an advantage over his rivals that might sway the race in his favour or increase his chances of survival. It had worked for him in the Northwest Passage, and he intended that it should work for him at the South Pole.

From his reading, Amundsen determined the precise location to which he wanted to sail the *Fram* and begin skiing to the South Pole. It was something that had never before been attempted: landing the ship and making a base atop the imposing 30-metre ice wall now known as the Ross Ice Shelf. Amundsen compared the charts of the region made by Ross in 1841 with those made sixty years later by Borchgrevink of the British Southern Cross Expedition (the first to overwinter on the Antarctic mainland), which confirmed that the ice barrier was an almost insurmountable length of cliff that, as Amundsen later said in his lecture to the Royal Geographical Society, was "broken at intervals by bights and small inlets. . . . [The Southern Cross Expedition] found this bay in the same place, where Ross saw it in 1841—sixty years earlier. It is interesting that this expedition succeeded in landing in a little bay—Baloon Bight—some miles to the eastward of the big one, and from here climbed up on the barrier, which up to this time had been considered an inaccessible and invincible hindrance for an advance toward the south."

The explorer also noted that the *Discovery* expedition led by Scott in 1901 had steamed along the edge of the ice barrier and confirmed the location of the small bay. In the course of the *Nimrod* expedition in 1908, Shackleton had observed that the ice had only minimal breaks, and had named the inlet the Bay of Whales, but he did not make a landing because it looked too dangerous. Amundsen concluded that "though some few pieces [of ice] had broken off here and there, this bay had remained constant for about seventy years. It was an obvious conclusion that the bay was no casual formation, but owed its existence to substantial land, banks, etc." Though he had never set eyes upon it, Amundsen chose this never-before-used bay to launch his land parties. It was about 650 kilometres from Scott's planned base at McMurdo Sound, and "therefore seemed to us that we were at sufficient distance from the English sphere, and need not fear that we should come in their way."

Once he had settled on using the Bay of Whales as his base, Amundsen proceeded with his plan of attack. If successful, it would be a logistical triumph that would see him and his chosen men begin the race to the South Pole an entire degree of latitude closer than Scott's base at McMurdo Sound, at the far western end of the ice shelf. The plan was a closely guarded secret; any leak might give advantage to Scott, who might decide to use the same base before the Norwegians. Amundsen had the advantage of having decided on his expedition before hearing the confirmation of Scott's expedition, yet being able to read the details of Scott's plans in the newspapers while refining his own plan.

In April 1910, Scott visited Norway to test the new motorized sleds he planned on taking to Antarctica. The northern plains between Oslo and Bergen would provide a mild version of what to expect in Antarctica. Scott and his wife, Kathleen, met with Nansen and discussed their plans for the South Pole. He also tried to meet with Amundsen, but without success. Certainly Amundsen was busy, but furthermore it is unlikely that he could have met the English naval officer whom he planned to race to the South Pole and still have kept his plans secret.

Amundsen has been criticized for keeping Scott in the dark about his true intentions. It is important, however, to point out that Amundsen and others were already planning their South Pole expeditions when they read Scott's announcement, and this detailed and highly public proclamation by Scott was little other than an effort to forestall others from heading south until he had had his chance at the pole. Scott's tactics were to use publicity to clear the field, to cause any potential rivals to back down, and in effect to lay claim to the pole as his and Britain's property. His actions were no more honourable or dishonourable than Amundsen's keeping his plans secret. Amundsen had many reasons for secrecy, not the least of which was his financing and that his ship had been borrowed for a different purpose. He had already been in the Antarctic and knew what the conditions were like. No one on the planet had his set of skills and knowledge, practical and theoretical, learned first-hand from the people who had the most to teach others on the subject— the Inuit. Although Amundsen had learned some of the details of Scott's expedition, such as Scott's plan to use motor sledges and ponies, he knew they would not fare well in the harsh conditions of the Antarctic. He found it nearly inconceivable that Scott would not be using dogs and skis for transport. Amundsen knew his business; he was confident of victory and did not fear that Scott would, or could, beat him and his team, which was equipped lightly and efficiently for speed.

At the same time, there was no advantage in keeping the details of his expedition secret from Scott, Amundsen reasoned, since Scott would not have done anything differently in any event. "Scott's plan and equipment," Amundsen noted in his autobiography, "were so widely different from my own that I regarded the telegram that I sent him later, with the information that we were bound for the Antarctic regions, rather as a mark of courtesy than as a communication which might cause him to alter his programme in the slightest degree." This is probably true—it's hard to imagine the naval officer Scott using dogs and learning to ski. However, if Scott had known he was in a race, he might have set sail earlier; or perhaps the excitement of a race would have helped Scott with his own fundraising.

As things stood, Amundsen could mull over his plan without public scrutiny while Scott had to disclose his plans to the newspapers before he departed—which is how Amundsen knew that Scott would be using McMurdo Sound as his base. He could develop a counter-plan to avoid the British expedition while using his superior skills in dog driving and skiing. In addition, the momentum of Scott's expedition depended not merely on his desire to attain the South Pole but on a host of other cultural and political foundations that precluded secrecy. As a private adventurer, Amundsen could go wherever he wanted and do whatever he wanted. Not so Scott, who was weighed down by the rigid traditions of the world's then-greatest empire.

In the spring of 1910, after debating the news of Peary's and Cook's competing claims to have reached the North Pole, the Norwegian parliament did what Amundsen had expected: it voted not to provide the *Fram* polar drift expedition with additional funds. In the wake of this decision, private donations were cancelled as well, promises of free supplies were withdrawn and offers for newspaper rights to the exclusive story were declined. Faced with a shortage of funds, Amundsen put up all his remaining money, mortgaged his home and took on debt wherever possible. Tired and frustrated with the tedium of fundraising—begging, as he thought of it—he signed over the responsibility for all money matters to his brother Leon and devoted himself exclusively to the logistics of the operation. He assumed a financial solution would be found. If he could only get to sea with the *Fram* and his crew, he would be successful; and if he was successful, he would be forgiven his minor deception, and wide acclaim would be forthcoming.

Cancelling the expedition would result in astronomical financial loss: its provisions, supplies, equipment—nautical and personal— had been ordered and paid for, the crew had been hired and other financial commitments made. It would bankrupt Amundsen, and hurt his friends and family. The loss of financial support from businesses and government agencies also meant that he could easily lose the use of the *Fram*. It had been refurbished at great expense by the Norwegian government and provided for his proposed serious and scientific endeavour, which would presumably bring respectability and prestige to the new nation; without the *Fram* Amundsen would be unable to launch a significant expedition. At the same time he knew that the newly independent Norwegian government would take a dim view of any attempt to directly compete with Great Britain in its goal of claiming the South Pole. The diplomatic ramifications were not a small matter, and Amundsen agonized over his secrecy for months.

As a result, even a month before Amundsen's departure for the South—or the North, as it was still generally believed—he was short a substantial amount of money and had no credible plan to obtain it. Even Nansen was concerned; the money would be needed to keep the ship in repair during the many years of the voyage. Amundsen, while nearly sick with stress, calmly maintained that the money would surely be forthcoming once he arrived in San Francisco. The financial shortfall was his greatest secret: if his many creditors ever found out, they would surely call in their loans and impound the ship. The money was not needed immediately, as Amundsen knew, but it was vital to the success of the expedition; indeed, it was vital to his survival. Once it had navigated the treacherous waters of Antarctica, the *Fram* was to drop off the polar party and then sail to Argentina to refit, repair, refuel and reprovision before returning to the Bay of Whales to pick them up. The money was essential for the relief expedition; otherwise, the adventurers would be stuck on Antarctica. Certainly a third-party rescue operation could be organized, but it would be an embarrassment and would jeopardize any attempt to capitalize on their success, should they win the race but be unable to return.

A preliminary test of the *Fram* to gain some experience for the crew was planned for June 7, the fifth anniversary of Norway's independence from Sweden. The two Amundsens, Roald and Leon, planned to link the voyage to Norway's independence to defuse any anger from the government or disgruntled creditors. Roald had to reveal his secret plans to two more of his officers; after all, they would be commanding the ship and needed to know where they were going. Fortunately, as was the case with everyone else in whom Amundsen confided, the officers were enthusiastic about the scheme and happy to be taken into his confidence, and they readily agreed to keep the grand secret. Before casting off, Amundsen held a party in the yard at Uranienborg. After a simple supper, the men cleared their throats and "united in [singing] 'God preserve the King and fatherland.'" Then they climbed into small boats and ferried themselves out to the *Fram*, which was anchored in the fjord.

One of the officers brought a horseshoe aboard and nailed it to the mast in the ship's saloon. "In his opinion it is quite incredible what luck an old horseshoe can bring. Possibly he is right," Amundsen mused. They hauled in the anchor, got the diesel engine running and then, "at precisely midnight," they set off.

Twice already had a band of stout-hearted men brought this ship back with honor after years of service. Would it be vouchsafed to us to uphold this honorable tradition? Such were, no doubt, the thoughts with which most of us were occupied as our vessel glided over the motionless fjord in the light summer night. . . . [A]mong our bright and confident hopes there crept a shadow of melancholy. The hillsides, the woods, the fjord all were so be-witchingly fair and so dear to us. They called to us with their al-lurement, but the Diesel motor knew no pity. Its tuff-tuff went on brutally through the stillness.

While making last-minute preparations, including loading the dogs and carrying out some final tweaks to the diesel engine, Amundsen still had to keep some of his creditors in the dark and at bay, just as on the *Gjøa* expedition, until he was at sea and be-yond their reach. Leon maintained a straight face and a calm de-meanour, though he privately noted that "the position is no better, and maybe even worse, than when *Gjøa* sailed." Neither Leon nor Roald had found a solution to the pressing problem of how to pay for the work done on the *Fram* in Argentina. Not even the men they had taken into their confidence knew about this looming, show-stopping problem.

Then, with little more than a week remaining before the final departure for Antarctica, Amundsen received a telegram from the Norwegian Foreign Ministry. It contained happy news: a wealthy and respected businessman in Buenos Aires named Peter Christo-phersen had offered to provide the *Fram* with coal and supplies. A Norwegian who had been living in Argentina for decades, where he had made a fortune, Christophersen had heard of Amundsen's public request for donations—one of his brothers knew Nansen, and another was the Norwegian minister in Buenos Aires. Amund-sen must have chuckled with relief: he had always forged ahead on the assumption that things would work out, even when others shook their heads and advised caution. With great relief, he replied right away, requesting oil rather than coal, and was assured that he would have all he needed in Buenos Aires. Fortune again was smiling on him.

After its test voyage from Bergen to Scotland and back, the *Fram* was shipshape. The real voyage began on August 9, eight weeks after Scott's expedition had departed from Cardiff. On the voyage south the dogs crowded everywhere, barking and fighting, even on the bridge. Thorvald Nilsen, the captain of the ship, wrote in his brief account of the voyage, "The number of living creatures on board when we left Norway was nineteen men, ninety-seven dogs, four pigs, six carrier pigeons, and one canary." In photographs of the *Fram* at sea, the dogs are ubiquitous; they lounge against the railing, sleep on the open deck, look curiously toward the camera, take shelter under awnings and collapse panting in the equatorial heat. The pups play with the men and generally appear to have the run of the ship. The hopes of the expedition depended upon them, and their antics provided respite from the monotony of the voyage. Although all on board were responsible for the welfare of the "four-footed friends," crew member Oscar Wisting became the official dogkeeper.

Amundsen loved the dogs: "There can hardly be an animal that is capable of expressing its feelings to the same extent as the dog," he mused.

Joy, sorrow, gratitude, scruples of conscience, are all reflected as plainly as could be desired in his behavior, and above all in his eyes. . . . [T]ake a look at a dog's eyes, study them attentively. How often do we see something "human" in their expression, the same variations we meet with in human eyes. This, at all events, is something that strikingly resembles "soul." We will leave the question open for those who are interested in its solution, and will only mention another point, which seems to show that a dog is something more than a mere machine of flesh and blood.

~⌐~

In a scheme that more than any other earned for Amundsen the honorific "the Napoleon of the Poles," he and Leon timed the public announcement of the change in destination with a precision more common in a military operation. While the *Fram* was at sea, Leon had boarded a steamer and cruised south to Funchal on Madeira. He was waiting there when the *Fram* arrived on September 6, 1910, having made arrangements for taking on provisions such as fruit, vegetables, fresh water and any items that had been missed earlier. Most of the crew spent several days relaxing in the sun, but Amundsen dismissed one man for his seeming inability to get along with the others.

Amundsen selected his crew carefully and knew from instinct and experience that one sour or unmotivated man could poison the voyage's atmosphere and endanger the entire expedition. He had been in no hurry to make his selections; after his success in navigating the Northwest Passage, men had been approaching him for years before the *Fram* sailed. He did not have to seek them out. His discussion with a *New York Times* reporter on October 27, 1908, is revealing: "I never read the references a man brings to me, when he applies for a position with us in an exploring trip. I can generally tell, after observing him closely and talking to him a while, if he will be equal to the strain, and I have never been mistaken. It is important to get the right sort of men, for one weak man will disorganize the rest. The main thing is always to keep busy, to keep the men at work all the time, and to keep at work yourself." Two of Amundsen's companions from the *Gjøa* expedition had joined the South Pole expedition: Helmer Hanssen and the cook, Adolf Lindstrøm.

Amundsen was reasonably confident that the men he selected were sufficiently adventurous to be willing to challenge the South

Pole, and he had already secured the support of most of the leaders, but he couldn't know for sure. In the afternoon on September 9, 1910, mere hours before the ship sailed, ostensibly on a route around South America to San Francisco, Amundsen called a meeting of the entire company. He and Leon and Nilsen stood shoulder to shoulder in front of a large chart that prominently displayed Antarctica. Amundsen spoke directly and firmly to the gathered men: "It is my intention to sail southwards, land a party on the Southern continent and try to reach the South Pole." The men—most of them, at any rate—just stood there with their mouths agape.

Hanssen, recalling the scene years later, wrote that "he said that he had deceived us and also the Norwegian nation. But that could not be helped. He suggested that we should all be released from our contracts . . . and be given free passage home. Anyone on board who didn't want to go south was at liberty to leave the ship right away and go back to Norway with Amundsen's brother." It was a reasonable offer, and Amundsen spoke to each man personally to determine his true opinion.

The crew's assent was vigorous and unanimous, and the pressure was off. "Before I had finished," Amundsen related in *The South Pole,* "they were all bright with smiles. I was now sure of the answer I should get when I finally asked each man whether he was willing to go on."

One of the men, on hearing that they would be racing the British to the Pole, exclaimed: "Hurrah, that means we'll get there first!" For Amundsen it was "difficult to express the joy I felt at seeing how promptly my comrades placed themselves at my service on this momentous occasion." Why not exchange one pole for another? Both were equally cold and dreary, but the southern one offered a greater chance for glory and fame. The men were up for a race. Although it has been suggested that Amundsen's tactic placed unacceptable pressure on his crew to accept the new terms, when one considers his philosophy of leadership it becomes clear that he really did want any dissenters to leave at the outset rather than cause trouble later.

As soon as the *Fram* cleared Funchal and set a course south, Leon boarded a steamer back to Norway with a collection of the men's final letters and other communications that would soon be made public. Amundsen wrote in his journal that "my brother has taken it upon himself to convey the news as to where we are headed. I do not envy him the task." News of the *Fram*'s startling change of course would be hand-delivered to the palace and to Nansen on October 1, a day before the news would be made public with a statement to the newspapers. Amundsen wanted to explain himself candidly and more personally both to his king and to his friend and mentor, so that they wouldn't first discover his deception in the morning newspapers.

In a sincere and heartfelt letter to Nansen, who Amundsen had kept completely in the dark about his change of plans despite their close working relationship, he wrote:

> There have been many times I have almost confided this secret to you, but then turned away, afraid that you would stop me. I have often wished that Scott could have known my decision, so that it did not look like I tried to get ahead of him without his knowledge. But I have been afraid that any public announcement would stop me. . . . Once more I beg you. Do not judge me too harshly. I am no hypocrite, but rather was forced by distress to make this decision. And so, I ask you to forgive me for what I have done. May my future work make amends for it.

He further explained, "I understood that it would be impossible for me to obtain the necessary funds for my enterprise," and gave the example of the Norwegian parliament cancelling his funding in the spring.

Amundsen emphasized to Nansen that the race to the South Pole would merely be an additional objective for the *Fram*, not the entire expedition, and he promised to continue with the scientific voyage in the Arctic once he had attained the pole. The money that would come from victory at the South Pole, he maintained, was the only way to pay for the valuable scientific voyage to the North Pole. The public announcement, which would be reprinted in countless newspapers around the world, read: "You can count on hearing from us again in February-March 1912. . . . We will then continue to San Francisco, where the last preparations for the drift across the Polar Basin will be made."

The next day, October 2, the papers announced the sensational news: Amundsen and the *Fram* had changed course and now were heading south "to battle for the South Pole." Amundsen downplayed his competition with Scott and the British expedition. "It is my intention not to get in the way of the English. They, of course, have priority. We will have to make do with what they discard." Of course he had already made his detailed plans for the attack on the pole, and he knew exactly where he intended to set up base in Antarctica. Oddly, the news was not picked up in any detail by the British press. On October 3, Leon released the final letters to the men's families. They detailed the men's new roles and their thoughts on the expedition, including the observation of at least one that Amundsen was astonished that Nansen hadn't guessed his true intentions when he observed the pack of nearly one hundred baying dogs being loaded aboard the *Fram*, and that the details of the scheme hadn't been leaked. Leon also posted the now-famous telegram to Scott: "Captain Scott Terra Nova Christ Church Beg inform you *Fram* Proceeding Antarctic. Amundsen."

Amundsen had elected not to take the recently developed wireless communication technology aboard the *Fram*. When Leon departed Madeira, taking the mail bag with him, it was the last time the men on board the *Fram* would be in communication with the outside world for the duration of the South Pole expedition. Amundsen had explained his decision during his presentation to the

Royal Geographic Society the previous year. He claimed to reject the wireless not because of its weight or expense or doubts about its functionality, but because of its potential effects on his leadership. He had spent a great deal of time weighing the arguments in favour and against, and had concluded that wireless communication might only add to the crew's feelings of anxiety and helplessness while offering no solution to the problems it generated. "Imagine that we have spent two years in the drifting pack, and still have three more years to spend—imagine that we suddenly get a dispatch stating that some of our dears are seriously ill or dying, or whatever it may be. What would then be the result?"

Of course, in the circumstances in which Amundsen now found himself, being incommunicado had the additional benefit of ensuring that no one could call him back to Norway.

8

Dogs and Skis

*If one is tired and slack, it may easily happen that one
puts off for tomorrow what ought to be done today;
especially when it is bitter and cold . . . and that plays
a not unimportant role on a long journey.*

"OUR LONG VOYAGE was entered upon as though it
were a dance," Amundsen wrote in *The South Pole*. "Here
was not a trace of the more or less melancholy feeling that usually
accompanies any parting. The men joked and laughed, while witti-
cisms, both good and bad, were bandied about on the subject of our
original situation. . . . [W]e had the satisfaction of seeing every sail
filled with the fresh and cooling north-east trade." The *Fram*'s route
to distant Antarctica followed the time-honoured route of sailing
ships: south and west from Madeira across the Atlantic to the coast
of Brazil, following the trade winds, and then re-crossing the Atlantic to the waters south of Africa.

As the *Fram* approached the uninhabited outcropping of South
Trinidad Island (now Trindade) off the coast of Brazil, Amundsen
corrected the expedition's chronometers by comparing the known
longitude of the island against Greenwich time before pressing on
south and east through the vast expanse of ocean, around the Cape

of Good Hope and toward the terrifying waters of the Roaring Forties, the powerful winds of the Southern Hemisphere south of 40 degrees. Ever south the *Fram* pressed, into "the foggy fifties, and the icy sixties." A photo of the *Fram* from this time shows its sails spread and tarps covering everything, tied down, as two men in waterproof coats and hats grapple with the wheel. Meanwhile, dogs lounge in every protected corner they can find. Monstrous waves threaten to swamp the ship; it would be at sea for several months before reaching the Bay of Whales.

The *Fram* was not a sleek or swift sailer, but a rounded, tough vessel that would resist being crushed by grinding pack ice. This made sailing rougher, as the tubby ship wallowed and rolled in the troughs and bucked among the waves. Through rough storms and waves, it slowly but steadily worked its way ever southward into colder and more unforgiving waters. When they were not on duty sailing the ship or tending to the dogs—feeding, cleaning and exercising them, or playing with the pups—the crew were busy sewing and altering their tents and garments to prepare for even rougher weather. The dogs caused "trouble and inconvenience" and "our patience was severely tested many a time," Amundsen noted, but "I am certainly right in saying that these months of sea voyage would have seemed far more monotonous and tedious if we had been without our passengers." The crew also occupied themselves with other pastimes during the tedious voyage. Several of the men offered musical performances on their violins, mandolins and other instruments; the ship's captain, Nilsen, gave refresher courses in English; and the men read Amundsen's library of works on polar exploration.

When the *Fram* approached the Ross Sea, off the coast of Antarctica, the ice had just broken up, forming a ring around the southern continent. Amundsen chose this location to break through the ring of pack ice based upon his reading of other explorers' journals. The writings suggested that the pack was at its weakest at this time of year and that in this particular spot it would the thinnest. "We have now found the sea free of ice further south than anyone else," Amundsen wrote in his diary. "But—we will meet it in the end." The expedition's ice pilot, Andreas Beck, a quiet, burly man with a mighty moustache and a facility with the violin, was experienced in getting ships through pack ice, knowing how it shifted with tides and wind. His work in the Arctic waters north of Norway gave him knowledge and experience that would be useful in Antarctica.

The *Fram* cruised through the Ross Sea without encountering significant ice congestion en route to the Bay of Whales. There was, however, still enough to allow several of the men to go out onto the ice to hunt seals, giving Lindstrøm the chance to show off his culinary flair: the crew feasted on seal steak and seal stew, which were "favourably received." The dogs too had a feast. They gorged themselves on the blubber and scraps, "til their legs would no longer carry them. . . . As to ourselves it may doubtless be taken for granted that we observed some degree of moderation, but dinner was polished off very quickly." They were very aware that fresh meat would always be available, while the quality of their rations was likely to decline in the coming year in Antarctica.

The *Fram*, equipped with a custom-installed diesel engine, had an additional short-term power supply unusual for a sailing ship, and it was here, in the congestion of the ice that the benefits of the new engine were apparent. Rather than depend on the wind, as the earliest explorers had done, or on inefficient power from a steam boiler, the *Fram* was able to nimbly manoeuvre through the chunks of ice and worm its way through channels to the open water beyond. On January 14, 1911, about four months after departing Madeira, the ship had squeezed through the morass of ice and entered the Bay of Whales—within one day of the date Amundsen and Nilsen had calculated, and with only three days of battling through the pack ice. The ship had sailed approximately 25,000 kilometres from Norway, and nearly 22,000 kilometres since Madeira without touching land.

The men stared from the deck, their breath visible in the cold, and beheld the frightening spectacle. "At 2.30 p.m. we came in sight of the Great Ice Barrier," Amundsen wrote.

> Slowly it rose up out of the sea until we were face to face with it in all its imposing majesty. It is difficult with the help of the pen to give any idea of the impression this mighty wall of ice makes on the observer who is confronted with it for the first time. It is altogether a thing which can hardly be described; but one can understand very well that this wall of 100 feet in height was regarded for a generation as an insuperable obstacle to further southward progress. . . . We knew that the theory of the Barrier's impregnability had long ago been overthrown; there was an opening to the unknown realm beyond it. This opening—the Bay of Whales—ought to lie, according to the descriptions before us, about a hundred miles to the east of the position in which we were. Our course was altered to true east, and during a cruise of twenty-four hours along the Barrier we had every opportunity of marvelling at this gigantic work of Nature. It was not without a certain feeling of suspense that we looked forward to our arrival at the harbour we were seeking. What state should we find it in? Would it prove impossible to land at all conveniently?

Other members of the crew were equally impressed. Olav Bjaaland, a professional skier from Telemark, Norway, wrote in his diary: "At long last, the ice barrier hove into sight today. It is a strange feeling that grips one as the sight now reveals itself. The sea is still as a pool, and before one stands this Great Wall of China and glitters. Far off, it is like a photograph that has just been developed on the plate."

In his diary, without the need to write for an audience, Amundsen was a little more pragmatic: "There it lay, this infamous 200 ft. high snow wall—wall of ice one cannot call it—and gleamed at us. I had expected it to impress me more than it does, but the excellent reproductions in Shackleton's book meant that I had got used to it and looked on it as an old acquaintance. So here we are." On a certain level Amundsen may have been in awe, but he was also already planning his next move, evaluating the terrain and assessing the danger. He scanned the bay looking for the perfect spot to approach the ice. Soon he spied a spot where the wall "sloped very gently down to the sea ice [giving] us the best ground for sledging." The *Fram* sailed right up to the sloping wall and was tethered to the ice. Speckled grey seals lay on the ice, and curious penguins drew near to observe the proceedings, while a chill wind blew silently over the deck of the ship. Disembarking would be a simple process, because the ice came only halfway up the hull. Several men scrambled overboard onto the ice and climbed up the slope until they were high above the water, where they had a commanding view of the desolate bay and its jagged features made entirely of snow and ice. Inspecting the ice, Amundsen noted that it was old and buckled, with "steep hills and crests, with intervening dales, filled with huge hummocks and pressure ridges" that showed no sign of movement since "far beyond the days of father Ross." The stability of the ice was a welcome confirmation of Amundsen's ideas about the suitability of the Bay of Whales as a base. In a small valley about 3 kilometres from the ship, the crew chose a spot for their winter quarters, where they would be "sheltered against all winds," and set to work in the south polar summer.

Now the *Fram* had to be unloaded. Off the ship came materials for the construction of a permanent base: a hut, equipment, food and sundry supplies to enable nine men to live there for up to two years, as well as all the supplies for the dogs. Photographs of the off-loading reveal the extent of the quantity of goods, showing mountains of boxes and tarp-covered sledges. Fortunately, it was easy to load supplies directly from the ship onto the ice and then onto the sledges, which were hauled up the incline to the top of the ice ridge by dogsleds and men on skis. Hauling the supplies inland gave the men critical dog-driving experience.

The adventurers nostalgically named the ramshackle camp that was taking shape on the ice ridge "Framheim." The carpenters began work on the prefabricated house, assembling components that had been marked and coded like pieces in a large three-dimensional puzzle. This also involved digging more than a metre into the ice "for stability and insulation." All this work, done at "a dizzy speed," was substantially completed within two weeks, by January 28. The result was a bizarre-looking wooden house, but "what a snug, cosy, and cleanly impression it gave us when we entered the door," Amundsen wrote. Framheim was surrounded by tents, dogs and mounds of cased provisions and equipment, each case boldly numbered to correspond to a list that identified the case's contents.

Amundsen had calculated that they had several months to become fully established at their base and to run three expeditions to deposit supplies at depots along his proposed route to the South Pole. Everything needed to be completed by the end of April, before the onset of the perpetual dark of winter, in order to be ready for the dash to the South Pole when spring returned in September or October 1911.

Several hundred kilometres away, at the western edge of the ice wall, at McMurdo Sound, Scott and the British Antarctic Expedition were busy with similar activities: unloading their ship and preparing for their expedition. Amundsen had never met Scott or any of his men, and although they were both camped in on the Ross Ice Shelf, they would never meet. Amundsen proceeded with his own plans without any further knowledge or communication of Scott's plans, and he would hear nothing of the fate of the British Antarctic Expedition until nearly two years later, long after he had toured the world giving lectures and published his book on the race. Before departing England, Scott had written in a letter his famous boast that "I don't hold that anyone but an Englishman should get to the S. Pole." It is worth noting, however, that in contrast to Amundsen, who had been preparing for a polar expedition for about two years, Scott had done little other than test his motor sledges. He had never lived in the Arctic, and did not ski or know how to drive sled dogs; in fact, he had rarely dealt with snow.

Amundsen suspected that Scott would essentially follow in Shackleton's footsteps from McMurdo Sound to the pole—the conventional approach, mostly pioneered already, its dangers, advantages and disadvantages already known. He had studied Shackleton's account of his polar trip, which was published in early 1910, and had learned much from it, especially much about what not to do, how not to proceed. Shackleton's hair-raising tale is a litany of near-disasters: food was scarce, the supply depots too far apart, the equipment not quite suited to the task. Interestingly, Shackleton himself noted afterward that if only he had used skis instead of walking, hauling sledges across the continent in man-harnesses, he would have made it to the South Pole.

Oddly, Shackleton's admission that his failure to reach the South Pole was mostly a failure of equipment and planning didn't affect the plans of his countryman Scott. Amundsen rightly concluded that one minor delay or malfunction in Shackleton's expedition—from an unexpected storm, for example—would probably have doomed them all. As an intellectual man of action, Amundsen had been working on logistics and obsessing over the details of his equipment for two years, ever since he had returned from the Northwest Passage: how much food, and of what type, would each man need per kilometre travelled? How far apart should the food and supply depots be placed for optimum efficiency? What type of skis would work best in the conditions of Antarctica? What bindings, what clothing, what sleds, what food for the dogs?

He had spent countless hours in his study, doing the paperwork, sketching various scenarios, adding the figures, all the while attempting to account for erratic weather and other potential delays. Amundsen had enough imagination and experience to take into account all the possible setbacks that he might encounter. By studying the successes and failures of previous expeditions, scrutinizing their use of equipment and drawing heavily on his own Arctic experiences, he gained expertise and confidence. If the devil is truly in the details, as the saying goes, then Amundsen could indeed have been said to be besting the devil; every conceivable detail had been pondered, multiple calculations performed and solutions decided upon. He had left little to chance.

During his years of preparation, Amundsen had been perfecting his polar travel gear, clothing and equipment to adapt the traditional designs and materials of the Netsilingmiut to modern materials for his specific purpose of speedy ski and dog travel in Antarctica. During the Norwegian winters, he had been testing and comparing designs and materials for nearly everything he would need on a polar trip. He had concluded, for example, that clothing made of reindeer hide, sealskin and other loose skins with built-in hoods trapped heat far better than any other design; footwear made extra large, in the Inuit style, and insulated with dry natural materials kept the feet from freezing.

He had custom-designed the expedition's snow goggles and skis. The skis were designed to be very long, almost 3 metres, to span crevasses and to distribute weight in order to avoid breaking through the snow crust. They were made of hickory, a wood Amundsen concluded was best for cold temperatures. Although these skis were very hard to turn and control, this was a problem only for a small part of the expedition. During the many months on the *Fram* sailing south from Madeira, Bjaaland had adjusted and perfected the design of the skis to prevent warping and to shave weight. The ski champion also worked on perfecting the custom bindings and the ice crampons, and on making the sledge frames lighter with a special strapping mechanism that also made loading and unloading easier.

Amundsen had also had the expedition's food prepared specifically for his crew's needs, including vast quantities of pemmican made with oats and peas. "If one is tired and slack," he mused, "it may easily happen that one puts off for tomorrow what ought to be done today; especially when it is bitter and cold." Light and simple were his benchmarks, "and that plays a not unimportant role on a long journey."

Amundsen was obsessive and finicky to an extent that under other circumstances would seem ridiculous. He had the expedition's paraffin tins specially soldered to prevent them from leaking, a problem he first encountered while navigating the Northwest Passage. He felt he could not trust this sort of detailed work to a commercial outfitter working to meet standard specifications—conditions in Antarctica, he knew, were unusually harsh and would create unusual problems. His life, and the lives of his men, might depend on his obsessive attention to detail. The men, for the most part, trusted his leadership and worked toward these unusual goals without complaint. They all had their roles in meeting the ultimate objective: it was a team effort, with Amundsen as the first among equals. In the main cabin of the *Fram*, Amundsen had hung a great map of Antarctica on which the planned route to the South Pole had been sketched in, as well as an outline of his plan. It was labelled: "For everybody's use."

Amundsen's plan for reaching the South Pole was simple and clear: "Our method of attacking the Pole was to make repeated trips from the permanent camp southward, setting up shelters and making caches of provisions one after the other at several days' travel apart, so that we should be able to make the return trip from the Pole without having to carry all our supplies there and back." He organized these initial forays also to perfect the working of the dog teams and the men's ski techniques, for this was the centrepiece of his South Pole plan: the combined effort of dog teams hauling sleds, with men skiing alongside—a unique combination that would ensure the efficiency and speed needed to cover such an enormous distance through dangerous, uncharted and extreme terrain.

The use of dogs and skiers, first tested and proven successful by Fridtjof Nansen in Greenland, was later perfected by Otto Sverdrup on the second *Fram* expedition. Sverdrup, who gave Amundsen his first set of dogs, those he took to the Northwest Passage, boldly stated that "Polar exploration has two natural requirements: skis and dogs." A loaded dog sled and a moderately paced cross-country skier travel at about the same speed. A runner is too slow and tires sooner than a skier, and if men ride on the sleds they get too cold, the dogs tire more quickly with the added weight and fewer supplies can be carried. In proper terrain, dog teams and skiers eat up the miles, saving energy and carrying a large quantity of equipment and supplies.

As soon as the *Fram* had arrived in Antarctica, Amundsen had informed the men of their roles in the coming adventure, in either the Polar Party or the Ship Party, based mostly on their skills and temperaments. Nine men under the command of Nilsen would "navigate the *Fram* out of the ice," sail to Buenos Aires for re-provisioning and return to retrieve their comrades. The shore party, also consisting of nine men, would remain on Antarctica and ski to the pole. Although several were disappointed to not be included in the Polar Party, Amundsen was firm in his choices. The only consolation he offered was that the Ship Party would receive additional pay. Among the men Amundsen selected for the Polar Party were several who had dog-driving and skiing skills. Helmer Hanssen, who had been on the *Gjøa* expedition, was the best dog driver, having learned his skills from the Inuit. Sverre Hassel, a former customs officer, also a skilled dog driver, had sailed with Sverdrup aboard the second *Fram* expedition. Hjalmar Johansen, a former world champion gymnast and captain in the Norwegian army, had been Nansen's companion on his attempt to reach the North Pole during the *Fram*'s first voyage. Oscar Wisting, a young gunner in the Norwegian navy, was also selected for the Polar Party, because of his general competence in working in cold weather and his steady demeanour. Kristian Prestrud, a lieutenant in the Norwegian navy, was also the first mate on the *Fram*. The final member of the Polar Party was Olav Bjaaland, for whom the race to the South Pole was like a ski race, only on a larger scale. The Polar Party's cook was the indefatigable Adolf Lindstrøm, who was also, incidentally, the first person to sail completely around the American continent. All these quietly competent men were around the same age as Amundsen, in their late thirties and early forties.

Their leader was pleased to note that the dogs, the key to his whole plan, had weathered the voyage well—in fact, their numbers had increased during the months at sea. "One of the most difficult problems of the expedition was solved," he wrote: "that of conveying our draught animals in sound condition to the field of operations." The 97 dogs with which they had begun the voyage had now increased to 116, and all were ready for the rigours of "the final march to the South," he noted, a little smugly.

> Before we sailed there was no lack of all kinds of prophecies of the evil that would befall us with our dogs. We heard a number of these predictions; presumably a great many more were whispered about, but did not reach our ears. The unfortunate beasts were to fare terribly badly. The heat of the tropics would make short work of the greater part of them. If any were left, they

would have but a miserable respite before being washed overboard or drowned in the seas that would come on deck in the west wind belt. To keep them alive with a few bites of dried fish was an impossibility, etc.

It is in writing about the expedition's hundred dogs that Amundsen's book takes on its most poetic tones, just as he celebrated the dogs in his account of the Northwest Passage. He muses philosophically about their motivations, waxes poetic about their personal attributes and personalities. "If we had any watchword at this time it was: 'Dogs first, and dogs all the time.'" In some cases the dogs are more alive than the men, and Amundsen revels in the details of their antics. He and his men gave them names such as The Corpse, The Scalp and The Pimp, and referred to them as "our children." Amundsen wrote about the dogs nearly as often as he wrote about his crew, using them as metaphors to introduce philosophical musings. In one of these unexpectedly lucid and insightful observations he commented, "What a commotion at feeding time. It was like a howl from the depths of Hell. What love these animals conceive for those who look after them. Of course it is cupboard love—but so it is often the case with our own love; look carefully, and you'll see!"

On February 4, as the final provisions were being hauled up to the campsite by dogsled, Amundsen prepared to lead a small group of men on a ski reconnaissance of the region. But before they set off, a sailing ship unexpectedly cruised into the Bay of Whales. The lookout "rubbed his eyes, pinched his leg, and tried other means of convincing himself that he was asleep, but it was no good." The vessel was the *Terra Nova*, Scott's ship, out from McMurdo Sound under the command of Lieutenant Victor Campbell to explore the nearby King Edward VII Land, along the ice wall. The two groups were equally astonished to encounter each other in the vast expanse. Amundsen and several men, who had spied the ship from their inland base, came rushing down to meet the British, urging the dogsleds to great speed in an effort to impress the Englishmen, who had never imagined that dogs could run so fast before a sledge.

As the two groups dined together and toured each other's ships, each found something to fear in the plans of the other. The English were impressed not only by the speed of the dogs but with the efficiency and cleanliness of the *Fram* and the inland base camp. The Norwegians were appalled at conditions aboard the *Terra Nova.* They were told of the unsanitary conditions created by the ponies, which had been housed above the mess room during the voyage from England, allowing their excrement to form a foul "mustard" on their dining table. On the other hand, the lunch served aboard the *Terra Nova* contained far more luxurious food than the Norwegians had eaten for months. It was news of the motor sledges, though, that worried Amundsen: Campbell told him that they had already been landed at McMurdo Sound, yet offered no more information. Amundsen did note, with relief, that the *Terra Nova* had no wireless communication equipment aboard and that therefore he would not be at a disadvantage in getting the news out first after the race—Scott would have to sail to a port before communicating the news, just as he would. "We made a strange discovery after this visit," he wrote. "Nearly all of us caught cold. It did not last long, only a few hours and then it was over. The form it took was sneezing and cold in the head."

On February 10, with the *Terra Nova* gone, Amundsen resumed his plans and set off from Framheim with three men, three fully laden sledges and eighteen dogs. The weather was calm and the skies slightly overcast, "ahead of us the vast, endless snow plain; behind us the Bay of Whales with the great prominent icecaps." The *Fram* lay peacefully in the bay, but Amundsen knew that he might not return from this first foray before the ship departed for the season. Once the men got all the heavy loads onto the ice shelf on February 11, they said their goodbyes. The *Fram* needed to escape the ice before winter set in, sail to Buenos Aires for a refit and repairs, perform some oceanographic measurements of the polar seas and then return through the pack ice. The shore party would be stranded in Antarctica until early 1912.

The first foray lasted only six days, but it covered about 170 kilometres across "the smooth, flat snow plain" hauling about 550 kilograms to the first depot. Amundsen was pleased to find that "the dogs pull magnificently, and the going on the barrier is ideal. Cannot understand what the English mean when they say dogs cannot be used here." When the party returned to Framheim, the *Fram* was gone and the "bay looked dreary and desolate. Seals and penguins had taken over the place."

During the next few weeks all members of the Polar Party, with the exception of Lindstrøm the cook, made two additional forays across the ice plain, depositing food and equipment caches weighing approximately 3,400 kilograms in three depots along the route they planned to take to the South Pole. They also put into the snow two-and-a-half-metre posts with numbered black flags to mark the route and keep them from getting lost in a featureless white plain during conditions of blowing snow and blizzards. Amundsen wanted to avoid any life-threatening mistakes on the return from the pole, when he and his men would be exhausted. It was again the experience from the Northwest Passage that led Amundsen to implement his flag-marking system. For each depot there were twenty numbered flags, with half a mile between each flag. The flags were placed at right angles to the depot rather than along the travel route so that if the explorers veered off course they would intersect the line of flags and know by the number where they were in relation to the depot. "The plan proved to be absolutely reliable, and even in the densest fog we succeeded in finding our depots," Amundsen recalled with some pride.

The skis, dogs and sledges were all working better than Amundsen had hoped, and the expedition found the travelling easier than was the case in the Northwest Passage. The ski boots caused problems and needed adjustments, and the small two-man tents were re-sewn to accommodate four or five men. The dogs, though generally healthy and in good spirits, had on the *Fram* grown unaccustomed to harsh winter conditions and heavy work. The initial sledging journeys had left their paws bloody, and the dogs were losing weight. In order to preserve them for the race to the pole the following spring, Amundsen shortened the distance between depots, although the third depot was still placed at 82 degrees south, within 800 kilometres of the South Pole. Laying the depots and marking the route had perfected the men's skiing techniques and the dog-sledding skills they would need in their assault on the South Pole the following spring.

By the end of their depot work, the men were exhausted and suffering from frostbitten fingers and cracked faces. Eight dogs had died. "The lowest temperature observed on these depot trips was –50°F (–46°C). Considering that it was still summer when this temperature was observed, it was a serious warning to us that we must have our equipment in good order," Amundsen wrote with characteristic understatement. He himself was unable to complete the third depot expedition because he was suffering from a rectal complaint, probably hemorrhoids, that made skiing and walking excruciatingly painful. Instead he remained at Framheim with the jocular Lindstrøm, to clean and prepare the camp for the winter. The camp now included ten huge tents to house the dogs, with a 2-metre pit dug beneath them to give the dogs a feeling of more space and reduce the hoarfrost that was "so annoying to the dogs." Each tent had twelve dogs and a man assigned to tend to their needs.

When they were not on depot journeys, the men hunted on the ice. They processed hundreds of seals and penguins, storing them up as food both for the dogs and for themselves in the long, dark winter to come. In a few months, they stocked an incredible 55,000 kilograms of meat. Nearly a tonne of seal meat for the dogs had been hauled toward the South Pole and placed in the depots.

The Norwegians felt confident: with a trail marked to within 800 kilometres of the South Pole and vast quantities of provisions securely stashed along their route, they could settle into their snug quarters at Framheim and wait out the punishing Antarctic winter.

9

A Featureless
Expanse of Snow

*Victory awaits him who has everything in order—
luck, we call it. Defeat is definitely due for him who
has neglected to take the necessary precautions—bad
luck, we call it.*

"THE SUN LEFT us today," Amundsen wrote, "and we did not see it again for four months . . . and then began the longest night ever experienced by men in the Antarctic." By late April, winter had closed around Framheim and the explorers hunkered down for the long wait. The snow quickly piled up, covering most of the house, so that only the tip of the roof was visible. The men dug snow tunnels between the handful of destinations that formed their dark, submerged community: the storage rooms, the forge, the sewing room, the packing room, the general workshops and the dog pits. The rooms had been all dug out of the accumulated snow. "Thus we got large and spacious rooms without buying or fetching materials," Amundsen noted with evident pleasure. Photos of Framheim before and after the April snows show the huge difference. Once the tunnels were dug, the men and dogs seldom had to venture outside. Although the mean temperature was −14°F (−26°C), on many occasions it dropped to −58°F (−50°C) and as low as −74°F (−59°C) on the coldest day, August 13.

Amundsen and his men spent this time perfecting their equipment, packing and repacking the sledges, measuring and testing them for maximum weight and ease of loading. Photos from that winter variously show the men sitting down to eat at the table, Lindstrøm preparing his latest culinary treat, the crew experimenting with their custom-designed goggles and in their rooms packing, sewing, working on skis and tweaking bindings, rigging up a steam bath, venturing out for meteorological observations and tending to the dogs. Kristian Prestrud, the only of the *Fram*'s officers to join the Polar Party, gave refresher courses on navigation and English. "Everyone had his hands full all the time; our house was warm and dry, light and airy, consequently the health of everybody was excellent. We had no physician, and we didn't need one."

Following Amundsen's lead, there were no social distinctions between the men, everyone contributing equally to the common goal and participating in discussions of importance. There was no head of the table, nor overt superiority or bossing. The daily routine involved waking at 7:30 a.m., when Lindstrøm laid out the table for the first of the day's communal meals. "Nothing wakes one up so well as the noise of knives, plates and forks," Amundsen wrote in his diary. The favourite was breakfast "hot cakes," freshly baked with yeast to get vitamin B in the men's diet, and smothered in preserved berries. Helmer Hanssen recalled that "to the end of my days I shall see before me Lindstrøm standing at the end of the table, comfortable and round, while four of us at each side of the table sat expectant like hungry young birds in a nest."

Lindstrøm also served seal meat undercooked to preserve its vitamin C content, to prevent scurvy. Because the daily rations for the sledging journeys consisted only of pemmican, biscuits, chocolate and powdered milk—high in calories but lacking in many nutrients and vitamins—Amundsen and Lindstrøm planned meals carefully to ensure adequate amounts of vitamins B and C throughout the winter. If the men subsisted on a diet lacking these nutrients, they would never be in the physical condition necessary to survive a race to the South Pole in the spring.

After breakfast, the men departed for their separate work stations until the next meal, at noon, and then worked again in their separate rooms until 5:15 p.m., when they cleaned up for dinner. Because they worked alone for most of the day, the men had something to talk about at the communal meals. The routine was part of Amundsen's strategy to keep everyone busy, with a sense of purpose, to prevent melancholic brooding and quarrelling and to make all the men feel important and vital to the expedition's success. He wanted them to feel that they were their own overseers, the masters of their respective tasks. He also instigated a contest to guess the temperature each day, offering a prize each month. It got the men out in the morning to start the day and sharpened their ability to detect changes in the weather. They also had dart competitions, storytelling and a weekly sauna night. Liquor was served at intervals, as a celebration—something to look forward to on birthdays, holidays and Saturdays.

There really was a lot of work to do, besides shovelling out the snow tunnels and snow rooms and repairing clothing and equipment. The men enlarged the ski boots to accommodate many layers of socks and further planed the wood to reduce the weight of the sledges. There were two models of sledges, one for speed over level ground, and the other, slightly heavier, for more rugged terrain. Bjaaland eventually shaved an incredible 50 pounds from the heavier 150-pound sledges and up to half the total weight off of the lighter ones. And they practised igloo building, according to the style Amundsen learned from the Inuit. Make, test, remake, repeat, until the design was perfect. Even a barely noticeable flaw or something that caused minor irritation on a short excursion of a day or two was unacceptable because these minor issues would become magnified into serious, perhaps life threatening, problems over the course of a month or more of hard travel on difficult terrain. As he expressed it later in life: "Victory awaits him who has everything in order—luck, we call it. Defeat is definitely due for him who has neglected to take the necessary precautions—bad luck, we call it."

The most peculiar aspect of Framheim was, oddly, the latrine. Like most of the other buildings, it too was dug in the snow, but with a special corridor to the dog tents, so that the dogs could go for a short walk and scavenge for excrement. Amundsen, following his generally curious and accepting approach to life, an approach augmented by his time in the Arctic with the Inuit, didn't feel the need to bend the natural environment to his will or to uphold preconceived notions of propriety. With respect to the dogs, he shrugged and accepted the fact that they were different from humans, letting them do what he had seen them do in the past, even if others regarded it as disgusting. This roll-with-the-punches approach made him flexible in dealing with the challenges of an unforgiving and rigid environment. It was the same lesson he had been taught by his father when he was a boy: don't fight unless you have to; and when you do have to, approach your battles wisely so that the outcome is not in question.

Most of his men were better than Amundsen at something, particularly skiing, dog running and dog tending. But he didn't mind. The prime skill he had was his ability to recognize the strengths and weaknesses of others. This was furthered by an instinctive understanding of how to motivate people and keep them content and optimistic, an innate appreciation of their psychology and interpersonal relations, and the knowledge of how to keep things running smoothly and reduce grumbling and discontent.

Amundsen also took responsibility for tough decisions. The only interpersonal issues that could have endangered the expedition arose between Amundsen and Hjalmar Johansen, the one person on the crew he had taken on against his instincts, as a favour to Nansen. Amundsen notes that Johansen frequently challenged his leadership, boldly questioning him in front of the other men, with the implication that Johansen was a better polar explorer than Amundsen. Amundsen could sense in him an underlying resentment and a sense of repressed superiority. Johansen was already a source of mild muttering and complaining. He was inclined to quarrel with some of the other men as well. He did have skill, or Amundsen would never have taken him on: he had been with Nansen on the famous polar drift, struggling across jagged ice on skis in their ultimately failed attempt to reach the North Pole. But Johansen had not weathered well the return to regular life after this monumental journey. Once the expedition's fame had subsided, he slipped into erratic employment and bouts of heavy drinking. He was an alcoholic and struggled with the restricted access to alcohol at Framheim. If there was to be a nucleus of discontent when things became tense, Amundsen knew it would likely start with Johansen challenging his decisions.

The sun returned in August, but the weather remained turbulent, with wildly fluctuating temperatures throughout the month. "The days went by and the temperature would give no sign of spring; now and again it would make a jump of about thirty degrees, but only to sink just as rapidly back to −58°F. It is not at all pleasant to hang about waiting like this; I always have the idea that I am the only one who is left behind." The conversations at the dinner table kept turning over the same theme: Scott and the British expedition, and the weather conditions at the other end of the ice wall. "The uncertainty was worrying many of us—and personally, I felt it a great deal."

The original date scheduled for a departure to the South Pole was November 1, but Amundsen was growing nervous. He put to his men two earlier dates for departing, but he was voted down both times by secret ballot. Amundsen was not a military officer who could command blind obedience from his men—he didn't want that

role, and the men weren't raised or trained to feel at ease with it either. If he wanted an earlier date, he would have to persuade them
when the time was right. The men didn't want to get caught in winter weather no matter how well prepared they were, though fear of the
English expedition preyed on their minds. But Amundsen persevered and when there was a brief respite from the winds and cold, he
finally persuaded the men to an early start on September 8. At this
time of year, the weak rays of the sun only lingered on the horizon,
providing little light and no warmth. The men loaded the sledges in
the under-snow caverns, and then hoisted them to the wind-lashed
ice surface by block and tackle. Comically huge quantities of boxes,
bales and other equipment were strapped onto them. After fitting a
little wheel on the rear of one of the sleds to measure distance, the
eight men set off, leaving only Lindstrøm behind at the base.

For the first couple of days the travel was "glorious," but on the
third day the weather turned while they were on their way to the
first depot. The temperature dropped to a bitter −70°F (−56°C), and
the men spent a near-sleepless night trying to stay warm. The dogs
were miserable, whimpering and shivering. "They rolled up as
tightly as possible, with their noses under their tails, and from time
to time one could see a shiver run through their bodies." Amundsen
decided to press on, but only as far as the first depot. The next night
the men built an igloo, as the weather remained deadly cold. "God
help me it was just shit and best forgotten," Bjaaland wrote in his
diary. Amundsen mused philosophically about their predicament,
as he often did: "To risk men and animals out of sheer obstinacy
and continue, just because we have started on our way—that would
never occur to me. If we are to win this game, the pieces must be
moved carefully—one false move, and everything can be lost." They
dumped their load at the first depot, at 80 degrees, and turned back
for Framheim. "It is grim to get going in such weather—but it has
to be done," wrote Amundsen; "God help me miserably cold,"
wrote Bjaaland.

On the return journey the going was slow in the face of raging winds and punishing temperatures. Several of the dogs froze to death, while others were "in agony with frostbitten paws." Men got frostbitten heels while they slept. The final day of travel to Framheim was a miserable and dangerous dash. Amundsen, Hanssen and Oscar Wisting pulled ahead with their dogs, frantic to return to shelter. But the other men had a much more difficult time, nearly getting lost, and were unable to move fast with their frostbitten feet. Somehow, due to poor planning, no one in the slower contingent had packed a tent or a stove. The final two, Johansen and Prestrud, couldn't ski properly and did not reach the base until after midnight, nearly collapsing from exhaustion. This trial run was the tipping point that exposed the festering personality clash between Amundsen and Johansen.

Around the breakfast table the next morning, Johansen unleashed a wild burst of anger at Amundsen, uttering "scarcely flattering opinions of me [Amundsen] in my capacity as leader of the proceeding here." Amundsen noted in his diary that the worst thing about Johansen's outburst was not that he was angry, but that he had spoken in front of the entire crew. Amundsen knew that to avoid risking his authority to lead the assault on the pole, "the bull must be taken by the horns; I must make an example immediately." Amundsen first tried to explain and justify rushing ahead with Hanssen and Wisting by claiming that Hanssen and Wisting were also complaining of frostbite and that he didn't know about Prestrud's frostbite. Amundsen had no way of knowing that Johansen and Prestrud were so far behind, or that they hadn't packed a tent. He kept expecting them to arrive at any moment throughout the night, knowing it was pointless to go out into the blizzard to locate them. In fact, the distance between the men should never have grown so great. But while the men were mollified by his explanation at what had obviously been a rare lapse in judgment (in allowing the men to lose contact with each other on the wind-lashed plain),

Amundsen knew that he needed to do more or risk losing the group's trust and focus, perhaps even leading to a mutiny.

Amundsen was so put out by Johansen's challenge to his authority that he refused to speak directly to Johansen, apart from making simple requests like passing the salt. At lunch he announced that Johansen, Prestrud and the carpenter Jørgen Stubberud would not be going to the South Pole. They would instead explore the nearby King Edward VII Land. Bjaaland summarized Amundsen's reasons in his diary: "Johansen could intrigue with the others during the journey and everything would grind to a halt." Johansen protested the decision until he received written orders from Amundsen, who was still his employer, and he was further humiliated by having the inexperienced Prestrud placed in command, even though Prestrud was a naval officer with navigation and chart-making experience. Although Prestrud realized that he wasn't in any condition to go the full distance to the pole, the "splendid unity" was over: only five men would be making the final dash to the South Pole.

Amundsen knew it was safer to wait for milder weather to head for the South Pole, but he was in a race with Scott. No one at Framheim knew the conditions at McMurdo Sound, and they all— especially Amundsen—feared losing everything they had striven for. "It seems that many have criticized our early departure," he wrote. "Well, it is easy to do so afterwards. Looking back, when I headed South as early as the beginning of September, the reason was that I assumed that we might possibly find more reasonable temperatures further in the Barrier than here. . . . To sit without doing anything would never occur to me, criticize me who will. With the exception of the three frostbitten heels, and some dogs, our little journey has not caused us any loss. It was a good trial run." Hanssen corroborated this feeling when he wrote that the reasons for attempting an early departure were strong: "our goal, and our only goal, was to reach the South Pole. If we did not manage that our whole expedition and much more than that was completely wasted."

Several writers have implied that Amundsen contrived the entire scenario to weed out the men that he judged were unable to meet the challenge of the South Pole. Men seldom recognize their own weaknesses, and it certainly would have been an admission of weakness to voluntarily remove oneself from the Polar Party. But although Amundsen was a schemer, this goes too far. He may have suspected that Johansen was too unstable to let him make the group decisions, and he may have known that Prestrud was not hardy enough, but it doesn't seem credible that Amundsen manipulated events to achieve this objective. It left Johansen an outcast; he had already quarrelled with some of the other men, and now he no longer enjoyed any respect as second-in-command, despite his considerable knowledge. The camaraderie of the group as they worked toward their single goal was shattered. Yet Johansen knew that this was his fault, a result of being unable to contain his public outburst. As Bjaaland commented in his diary, Johansen's were "words that would have been best left unsaid," and Johansen regretted them as soon as his temper subsided.

Amundsen glosses over these events in his published version of the epic race, with its jocular, smooth and entertaining style. "We sat in the tent cooking and chatting," he wrote, and "Hanssen exclaimed 'Why, I believe my heel's gone!' Off came his stockings, and there was a big, dead heel, like a lump of tallow. It did not look well. He rubbed it until he thought he 'could feel something again,' and then put his feet back in his stockings and got into his bag." Clearly, though he could write with self-deprecating humour and a ready acknowledgement of the skills and abilities of his comrades, he was also disingenuous in describing what was real desperation during the return trip and the heated words it provoked. He wrote: "Heaven knows what they had been doing along the way!" The passage's jaunty tone conceals the dark underbelly of the events and of Amundsen's personality. Amundsen was capable of holding a grudge, and never forgot or forgave a challenge to his leadership while on an expedition—the time for challenge was before, not during, the event. Every man had the option of not coming along, he reasoned, and disunity could lead to the splintering of the group and ultimately failure or death.

Amundsen believed Johansen's "demotion" was for the good of all, and perhaps it was: he had read dozens of accounts of failed expeditions, of breakdowns in leadership, of the infighting and suffering that followed. He was not inventing scenarios to justify being an autocrat. He didn't like pulling rank and in fact resented it, which may have been the source of his rigid refusal to forgive and forget: he didn't like being compelled to behave in a way that ran counter his generally easygoing nature. It challenged his perception of himself as the guiding hand among experts who were united behind his vision.

During the following weeks, the men slowly recovered from their frostbite. Several lay in bed, bathing their damaged extremities in warm water and boric acid poultices. Lindstrøm had no sympathy for the invalids, offering the enigmatic observation, "now you can sit there like a lot of vermin. You should always look out of the window, when the old dog barks." They also applied the antiseptic to the dogs' feet.

The first real signs of spring didn't come until September 29, when the seals returned to the ice and a flight of Antarctic petrels flew overhead, sending the dogs into a frenzy as they ran out onto the ice to give chase. But not until near the end of October, after another gale and periods of billowing fog, did the weather seem stable enough to start for the South Pole. Now the sun was constantly in the sky and the temperature was at −20°C (−4°F). The men made several small ski excursions while they waited for the skin on their feet to heal, all the while worrying about Scott and his presumed departure. The stress was growing and adding to tensions again. Bjaaland wrote in his diary that "if I emerge from this journey, I must see that I get out of polar exploration. It's hardly worth the trouble."

October 20 was the day. As the five trekkers readied their sledges and dogs, Amundsen had a quiet reconciliation with Johansen; they shook hands and bid each other good fortune. The disappointed man, full of regrets, lonely and nagged by self-doubt, stood apart and watched as the chosen four made their final preparations with Amundsen, their dogs frolicking and eager. They started off. According to Amundsen it was an uneventful departure, with Lindstrøm not even bothering to come out of the kitchen to bid farewell. "Such an everyday affair: What's the use in making a fuss about it?" he imagined Lindstrøm thinking. The Polar Party now consisted of four sledges with thirteen dogs each, the best of the pack. While viewing the little cavalcade of mounded sledges tethered to the wildly excited, almost uncontrollable dogs, who were "on the verge of exploding," Amundsen had a moment of introspection about this final dash to the pole. "I tried to work up a little poetry," he wrote, "the ever restless spirit of man, the mysterious, awe inspiring wilderness of ice—but it was no good; I suppose it was too early in the morning. I abandoned my effort, after coming to the conclusion that each sledge gave one more the idea of a coffin than anything else, all the cases being painted black."

Fast and uneventful cruising along the now-familiar snow road brought them to the first depot on October 23. That day presented some challenges, with fog and wind limiting visibility and the men temporarily lost among some crevasses. Navigating blind through the thick fog proved the value of the numbered flag system, as the men were led quickly to the otherwise hidden depot. The pattern was set early on: they would try and cover about 30 kilometres a day, but during blizzards they would rest. During most days the travel time would be limited to five or six hours, the better to sleep and retain their energy. Anything more "could not be risked for the sake of the dogs." They knew their British rivals would be starting for the South Pole at around the same time, but Amundsen also was aware that wearing out the men early would not get them safely to the South Pole and back. And the dogs could easily grow exhausted hauling the sledges, which weighed an incredible 350 kilograms each. Without the dogs, the men would probably all die.

There were some very difficult days. In early November, during a particularly thick fog, the troupe was driven off course and entered the realm of the Steers Head crevasses. For 20 kilometres they slowly crossed a series of small crevasses about a metre wide that lay across their path. Both Hanssen and Sverre Hassel cracked through snow bridges and fell into crevasses, luckily not too far to be hauled out. Two weeks after their departure from Framheim, on November 4, the group reached the third and final depot that they had created the previous fall, at 82 degrees, about 770 kilometres from the pole, and rested for two days under unexpectedly sunny skies. The men were in good spirits, having reached the third depot without any serious setbacks. It was like an extended ski trip; by now, they were in great physical condition, and the dogs were "in better shape than when we left. All the sore feet have healed, and a little of the superfluous obesity has gone." After every day's travel, the dogs, who had no tents, were turned loose after each being given a pound of frozen pemmican to gnaw on.

The journey would now traverse deadly terrain that had never before been trodden or skied. The expedition pushed on, skiing behind the sledges, with a lead skier breaking trail for the dogs. Amundsen argued in favour of leaving a new depot every degree on the way to the pole, both to lighten the load for the dogs and to leave something for the return journey, on the assumption that the men could easily find them on the return trip. Every 5 kilometres they stopped the sledges to rest the dogs and to construct a human-sized cairn of snow chunks containing records that stated the date and their location. After several days they saw a range of mountains, clearly in view in the cold crisp sun, and named it the Queen Maud

Range, a large range of the Transantarctic Mountains. "Glittering white, shining blue, raven black, the land looks like a fairytale," Amundsen wrote. "Pinnacle after pinnacle, peak after peak—crevassed, wild as any land on our globe, it lies, unseen and untrodden. It is a wonderful feeling to travel along it." Amundsen's account is often characterized by this type of not-quite purple prose, a style that conveys the childlike glee he experienced in beholding nature's most hidden and chaotic manifestations, lands of mystery that were not suited for human habitation. Nature with a capital "N" appears frequently in Amundsen's writing as something in which he takes spiritual delight, particularly in connection with rugged, inhospitable and wild regions.

The appearance of the mighty mountain range directly in their path to the South Pole was not unpredicted—Shackleton had written of seeing mountains in the distance—but it was a daunting obstacle. Time was always the issue—it was not just a race against Scott, but also a race against diminishing food supplies. On November 17 they ascended from the ice at the end of the Ross Ice Shelf onto the land plateau and skied toward the Transantarctic Mountains—monstrous, jagged peaks soaring to 4,900 metres that extend across Antarctica for nearly 2,000 kilometres. For all they knew it might not be possible to cross these mountains, or it could take months to find a safe pass.

Amundsen pressed on, but the stress must have been great. There was no time for the men to scout for a pass or weigh alternatives. They probably had about a week to find a way through the mountains before a food shortage would make the dash to the pole an impossible prospect. The explorers left their next depot at the base of the mountains rather than push on up. The skiing became steep and treacherous on the long skis with leather-strap bindings. Somehow the skiers controlled their own speed while steering their sledges and managing the dogs on 600-metre descents to ice plateaus. Sometimes the dogs had to be tethered to a single sledge just to get it up a steep incline, and ropes had to be wrapped around the runners to slow the descent. The trek was a remarkable and heroic conquest of their personal fear.

Amundsen was busy naming land features for friends and patrons in the time-honoured tradition of European explorers stamping their culture and history onto the world's landmarks. At least in this case the Norwegians did not supplant the names given by indigenous peoples. As well as naming the Queen Maud Mountains, Amundsen named Mount Don Pedro Christophersen, Mount Ruth Gade, Betty's Knoll, Mount Bjaaland, Nilsen Plateau, Amundsen Glacier, Mount Fridtjof Nansen, Axel Heiberg Glacier and other features.

Fortunately the temperature remained at a relatively balmy −20°C (−4°F), so the snow was in stable condition, making avalanches less likely. "As usual," Amundsen recorded, "the weather has been clear, calm and boiling hot." This feeling of boiling heat amidst snow and ice is a phenomenon anyone who has spent time on a sheltered ski slope in the spring can appreciate. As the explorers slogged up the incline into the mountains, the silence was occasionally interrupted by the ominous rumbling of distant avalanches.

One night they camped in the shadow of the mountains on the edge of the Axel Heiberg Glacier, which was "huge, mighty . . . [and] absolutely fjord-like." From this vantage point Amundsen spied an alternate pass and ruefully noted that a lot of time and danger could have been avoided by merely following the glacier as it oozed back toward the ice shelf, making a relatively easy path up to their current camp. Had they had more time, they could have scouted a better route.

On November 20, one month after starting their trek, they faced another treacherous climb. It was a clear day, and the sun heated up the glacier so much that they again felt "boiling hot." Yet the conditions were perfect for skiing uphill. Bjaaland led the way up the steep incline, the dogs following, sometimes using double teams to get the sledges up the incline while swerving around "crevasses and chasms." The men pitched tents for a second night on the glacier amid the "enormous blocks of ice, mighty abysses and huge crevasses" that blocked their progress in all directions. It was only mid-afternoon and Amundsen set off with Bjaaland and Hanssen to search for a route through the chaotic ice field while the others tended to the dogs and made camp. After exploring several possible routes that were unstable, they found a relatively smooth route to a pass at the head of the glacier that would lead to the Antarctic Plateau. About skiing back down to camp, Amundsen wrote, "It was a beautiful and impressive view we had. . . . The wilderness of the landscape from above is indescribable. Pit after pit, crevasse after crevasse, and huge ice blocks scattered helter skelter. It was easy to see that here, Nature was at her mightiest."

The next day was a brutal twelve-hour slog up to the crest, where the exhausted team did little more than eat and then crawl into their sleeping bags. It had taken the team four dangerous days to pick their way through 70 kilometres of mountain range, climbing more than 3,000 metres to reach the edge of the Antarctic Plateau. Now they had a clear run to the pole. But both the men and the dogs were exhausted, and Amundsen called for several days of rest. On November 24, Amundsen called the men together to carry out a plan that had been avoided so far: the slaughtering of the dogs.

The dogs were a tough breed, "cunning and resourceful in the extreme." Amundsen had seen them fight and kill each other, steal food from each other, attack newborn pups and eat them. Sometimes the men had had to kill dogs when they were locked in deadly fights with each other. Dogs had fallen down crevasses or wandered away into the polar winter and were never seen again. Many had succumbed to disease, and some had to be killed to end their suffering. "The dogs were quite mad today and went on the rampage," Bjaaland wrote one day, expressing a frequent sentiment. These dogs were not pets; they were fierce. On one occasion, Amundsen had wrestled to the ground a dog that had stolen food and had torn the meat from the animal's snarling mouth. Each night the men had to bring their leather ski bindings into the tent or the dogs would have devoured them.

All of this was familiar to Amundsen and Hanssen from their time with the Inuit in the Canadian Arctic. In those regions, life was harsh for dogs and people alike, and the dogs generally ran free when not harnessed to sledges. Perhaps knowing it would be their epitaph, Amundsen wrote many dog stories in his book: "Thus Jaala, a lady belonging to Bjaaland, took it into her head to go off with three attendant cavaliers. We came upon them later; they were then lying quietly behind a hummock down on the ice, and seemed quite happy. They had been away for about eight days without food, and during that time the temperature had seldom been above –58°F." At the end of the final day of climbing to the crest of the Arctic Plateau, Amundsen recorded: "It was a sheer marvel . . . what the dogs accomplished today . . . 17 miles with a 5000 ft climb. Come and say that dogs cannot be used here," he concluded, a direct reference to Scott's claim that dogs were unsuitable.

But the pace and the conditions had worn the dogs out, and they were sickly and thin, despite being fed a pound of pemmican a day. Less than a month earlier, Amundsen had described them as "bursting with health" and Bjaaland had claimed they were "hale and hearty." Now they were barely capable of carrying on. It had long been part of Amundsen's plan to kill the ones who were too weak or sick, but it was still a hard job. On the night of November 21, each man shot selected members of his dog team. Amundsen, who had no team directly under his control, prepared dinner in the tent. In total, twenty-three dogs were killed and gutted, leaving eighteen, who appeared the healthiest and strongest. The men named this camp "The Butcher's Shop."

The next day they were hit by a sudden storm—one that might have proved disastrous on the glacier, had it come a day earlier. But their forced inactivity allowed the men and their remaining dogs to recover and feast on dog meat. Amundsen knew the dogs would eat each other because he had seen them do it in the Arctic. He explained in *The South Pole* that by eating some of the sled dogs, the expedition required both less human food and less dog food, thus lightening its load. Comparing sled dogs with ponies as draught animals, Amundsen noted the

> obvious advantage that dog can be fed on dog. One can reduce one's pack little by little, slaughtering the feebler ones and feeding the chosen with them. In this way they get fresh meat. Our dogs lived on dog's flesh and pemmican the whole way, and this enabled them to do splendid work. And if we ourselves wanted a piece of fresh meat we could cut off a delicate little fillet; it tasted to us as good as the best beef. The dogs do not object at all; as long as they get their share they do not mind what part of their comrade's carcass it comes from. All that was left after one of these canine meals was the teeth of the victim—and if it had been a really hard day, these also disappeared.

Bjaaland also noted that "we have now had three splendid dinners out of our good Greenland dogs, and I must say that they tasted good, a little tough perhaps, though they were not boiled enough." The fresh meat, in addition to providing calories, was also an extra protection against scurvy.

The killing and eating of dogs certainly raises the issue that they were being used for the sole purpose of one person's desire—and society's desire—to reach the South Pole, a symbolic though unnecessary destination. It is a moral question that equally applies to Scott's use of ponies, which surely could not have been expected to survive the journey. In traditional Inuit societies the life of a dog would frequently be terminated, but this seems more acceptable in traditional societies, doing what they need to do to survive in harsh and unforgiving environments, rather than using them for the sport or entertainment of their handlers and the public. In the early twentieth century, however, the killing of Amundsen's dogs apparently wasn't of any particular concern. Stories written at that time about the South Pole related lurid details about the eating of the dogs, but never questioned the issue of deliberately planning the deaths of animals to further what was in essence a sensational sporting event. Nevertheless, Amundsen wrote, "It is my only dark memory from down there, that my lovely animals were destroyed. I demanded more of them than they could manage. My consolation is that I did not spare myself either."

The blizzard kept the men in their tents while the remaining dogs huddled together against the wind. It was still a "heavy gale with thick drift" on November 26, when they crawled out of their tents to set off down the hills to the Arctic Plateau. "We were all fed up with this long lie-in at home," Amundsen wrote. Bjaaland was more vivid: "Bloody horrible lying still, you can hardly breathe at this altitude." Despite the weather, they set off through conditions that were "extremely bad—sticky as glue." Visibility was so poor in the driving snow that they couldn't see the dogs running ahead of the sleds. And the dogs' energy was also low: "They had overeaten of their comrades," Amundsen observed. When the hill turned steeply down, the trekkers stopped and set up camp midslope, on the flattest spot available.

The next day, the blizzard continued to lash the open plains. The explorers nevertheless continued their relentless trek south, running on compass bearings through the fog and wind as they slowly crossed what Amundsen had named the Nilsen Plateau, after the *Fram*'s captain. Their march toward the South Pole was frustratingly slow. For days they laboured through innumerable small crevasses that were concealed by the fog. At rest times, they had barely enough room to pitch a tent between the crevasses. At one point they crept forward roped together, as they passed through a jumbled mass of ice crags, pits, hummocks and buckled terrain, where "one has to move two miles to advance one. Chasm after chasm, abyss after abyss has to be circumnavigated." Amundsen called the deadly region "the Devil's Ballroom," and when the fog lifted the explorers saw they could have just gone around it, if only the fog hadn't blinded them.

On December 2, with a temperature of –24°C (–11°F), in a "raging gale," they encountered wind-polished ice on which the dogs' paws couldn't get a grip. The crampons had been left at the Butcher's Shop to save weight. Bjaaland recorded that "we couldn't see in front of our nose tips and our faces were white and hard as wax candles. The Chief's nose is like that of a country bumpkin, Wisting's jaw looks like the snout of a Jersey cow. Helmer has thick scabs and skin as rough as a file. It was a bloody hard day." The only thing keeping them from freezing to death was the quality of their Inuit-style clothing.

After a day of rest and a few more days of slogging through gale-force winds, travelling blind most of the way, they passed the previous furthest-south record point, set by Shackleton—about 160 kilometres from the South Pole. The terrain eased, becoming "completely flat and fine everywhere." But the dogs were "horribly worn," according to Bjaaland, and they needed a rest after the brutal haul. The sun appeared again, the wind dropped and the turn of events was celebrated with extra rations of chocolate. Amundsen was in "a shining humour." On December 9, the men rested in their tents "to prepare for the final onslaught." The South Pole was now less than 10 kilometres distant and the skiing looked fine. They cached a final depot of goods to lighten their loads and set off the next day. Despite the good weather they were all now suffering from frostbite, feeling "sore, pain and scabs the whole of our left sides." Amundsen again noted the poor condition of the dogs, who were being ground down by the crushing job of hauling the sledges through seemingly endless storms. Hunger too was making them dangerously violent and uncontrollable, and the dogs "must be considered as mortal enemies when one leaves the sledges," he wrote. "Oddly enough they have not tried to break in." Although they were getting plenty of food, it wasn't enough.

The journey's final days were noteworthy for the mostly clear skies. The pole was straight ahead, but they zigzagged across the plain. "It is no easy matter to go strait in terrain where one has no distinguishing marks," Amundsen noted. "An Eskimo can manage but none of us." The dogs remained weak and slow, even with the reduced weight of the sledges. Mad with hunger, they were eating their own excrement, searching for leather straps and bindings and gnawing on the wooden sledge frames even after they had eaten a full meal. One wandered off and died, but the rest plodded on to their close but elusive destination. It was, Amundsen noted laconically, "nothing to make a song about."

In camp on December 14, Bjaaland wrote that they "can now lie and look toward the Pole. . . . The excitement is great. Shall we see the English flag?" The next day the explorers woke early and set off with trepidation and mounting excitement. Hanssen's eyes were glued to the compass as he yelled out slight direction changes. Amundsen skied ahead, leading and guiding the sledges in their erratic pattern across the featureless expanse of snow. Then one of the men called out "Halt!" at around three o'clock in the afternoon: they had reached the South Pole. (Amundsen thought the date was December 15, but it was actually December 14—he had forgotten to subtract a day as the *Fram* crossed the International Date Line.)

The moment that had dominated the desire and dreams of the men for a year and a half was strangely anticlimactic. They quietly gathered in a group—five fur-clad men on skis, with seventeen exhausted dogs and three wooden sledges—in the midst of a vast wilderness of ice and snow, the farthest possible point from any human habitation on the planet, and shook hands. Amundsen un-wrapped the Norwegian flag they had brought for the occasion. "[F]ive roughened, frostbitten fists it was that gripped the post, lifted the fluttering flag on high and planted it together as the very first at the Geographic South Pole." Amundsen wrote that planting the flag "was not the privilege of one man, it was the privilege of all those who had risked their lives in the fight and stood together through thick and thin. It was the only way I could show my com-panions my gratitude here at this desolate and forlorn place."

Bjaaland later scrawled in his diary: "Today, tired and hungry, thank God we have enough food for the return journey." In their tent, the explorers in weary satisfaction feasted on a special meal of seal steaks, biscuits, pemmican and chocolate. Wisting then rum-maged through his pack, produced a plug of tobacco and quietly handed it to Amundsen. "Can anyone grasp what such an offer meant at such a spot, made to a man who, to tell the truth, is very fond of a smoke after meals?"

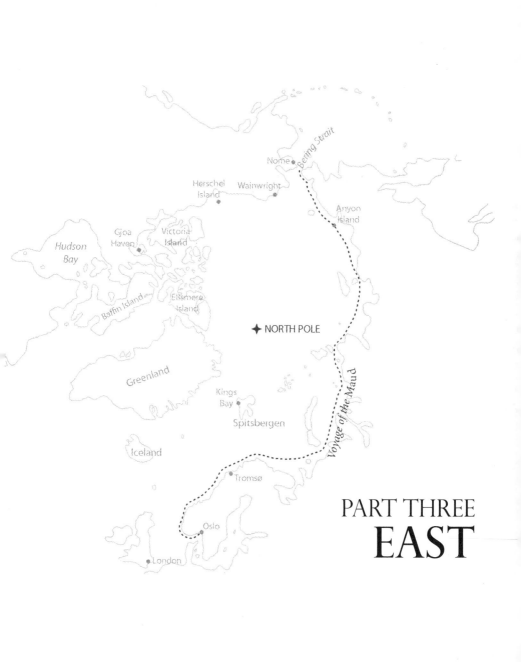

PART THREE
EAST

10

A Hero Returns

Good morning, my dear Lindstrøm. Have you any coffee for us?

"OUR FACES SHONE in rivalry with the sun," Amundsen wrote as his ship neared the port of Hobart, Tasmania, "and soon the *Fram*, too, began to shine." The men scrubbed the decks with soap and water, washed the sails and tidied everything to make a good impression when they docked. They exchanged their worn and filthy work clothes for their "shore clothes," which had been packed away for "a two years' rest," and "razors and scissors had a rich harvest." Amundsen recorded that "even Lindstrøm, who had up to that date held the position among the land party of being its heaviest, fattest, and blackest member, showed unmistakable signs of having been in close contact with water." As a motor launch putt-putted alongside, the men donned matching Burberry caps and snapped to attention. A brisk old man called up "Want a pilot, captain?" startling them with the sound of a new voice. The old pilot clambered up onto *Fram*'s deck and glanced around in perplexed silence for a while before exclaiming "I should never have imagined things were so clean and bright on board a Polar ship. Nor should I have thought from the look of you that

you had come from Antarctica. You look as if you had had nothing but a good time."

They eagerly chatted and shared news with the pilot, but
Amundsen remained tight-lipped about their exploits. The Tas-
manian pilot declined his invitation to remain for breakfast: "Presumably he was afraid of being treated to dog's flesh or similar
original dishes," Amundsen surmised. The *Fram* was led through
Storm Bay to the quiet town of Hobart, which was then surrounded
by dry meadows and woods. Although the region was suffering from
a heavy drought, the gently undulating terrain was an "unmixed delight." It wasn't ocean, ice or rock, and therefore held considerable
novelty. "The Custom-house officers were easily convinced that we
had no contraband goods," Amundsen reported, as he and his men
disembarked with the secret of their voyage held close. It was March
7, 1912, and there was still no news of Scott's expedition. Amundsen knew that it would have been nearly impossible for Scott to have
beat them in the race back to civilization; he and his men were indeed the first humans to have reached the South Pole.

He booked into the Orient Hotel. Dressed more shabbily than
the other patrons and completely silent about his exploits, he
recorded tersely in his diary that he was "treated as a tramp" and
"given a miserable little room." The next day, he visited the Norwegian consul and the telegram office and sent off coded messages to
King Haakon, Nansen and Leon. Then he tried to relax while re-
buffing the advances of local reporters, hungry for a scoop. Boats
cruised out to the *Fram* to snoop, but his men also revealed nothing.

Amundsen believed that silence would be his key to success; he
remembered well how his news had been stolen in Alaska after his
Northwest Passage voyage, and he had made great efforts to avoid
any financial loss this time. Earlier, he had announced to Nansen
and others that the *Fram* would be putting into Lyttelton, New
Zealand, after their voyage, even though he planned on Tasmania all
along. No doubt the cable operators and reporters in Lyttelton were

primed and waiting to profit from Amundsen's valuable news, but no one was waiting in Hobart. Although the local reporters knew something was up, they couldn't get the story, and Leon telegrammed his brother in Hobart, instructing him to cable his story directly to the *Daily Chronicle* in London and the *New York Times* in the United States. These papers had agreed to pay 2,000 British pounds for the exclusive rights (the equivalent of roughly several hundred thousand U.S. dollars today). On Friday, March 8, 1912, the papers' front pages featured a photo of Amundsen, looking jaunty in a dark hat and with a well-coiffed moustache, next to the headline "The South Pole Discovered: Norwegian Explorer Reaches Coveted Goal." These were accompanied by a map of the polar region and articles such as "Amundsen's Career of Adventure," "Amundsen vs. Scott: Mystery of Yesterday's Press Messages" and "How the News Came to *The Daily Chronicle*." The news was republished in Norwegian newspapers, and others around the world followed. Although Amundsen and his men could now relax and begin to enjoy their celebrity, he still didn't give away too much information—Leon had sold the announcement of the feat, not the details. The feature rights still had to be guarded. For the next week, the *Fram* was deluged with visitors and well-wishers who wanted to see the famous ship, shake hands with the heroes of the day and perhaps get more information out of them. What was it like at the South Pole?

Before the five conquerors had departed the South Pole on December 17, 1911, they had set up a spare tent there and with some humour named it "Polheim," "home of the pole." A Norwegian flag hung limply from the tent's central pole. Inside the tent were notes for Scott and King Haakon and some superfluous equipment. In case they should not make it back, Amundsen asked Scott to forward his letter to the Norwegian king as additional proof that he had reached the pole. Amundsen debated whether or not to leave a few cans of extra fuel oil, but in the end he decided to take them with him, just in case. He and his men then staged a photo shoot. The classic image shows four men arrayed in front of Polheim, dressed in their bulky furs with their hats off, staring up at the flag, while in the background the sunset is hand-painted a mesmerizing red, orange and yellow. The picture is a snapshot taken by Bjaaland with his personal Kodak camera, as are many of the other images that survive from the final stages of the expedition. Amundsen's official camera broke down, and without Bjaaland's portable snapshots there would be no photographic record of the momentous journey.

The return from the South Pole had been gruelling but uneventful. The five exhausted men harnessed the remaining dogs to two sleds. The dogs had a rough time on the thirty-nine-day retreat, and five more succumbed to the bitter cold, a disheartening and somewhat melancholy series of deaths, since the men had to kill them as the animals became too weak to go on. About one of his favourite dogs, Amundsen recorded that it "had been latterly showing marked signs of shortness of breath, and finally this became so painful to the animal that we decided to put an end to him. Thus brave Fridtjof ended his career." The expedition nevertheless covered an impressive average distance of 36 kilometres each day, for a total of about 3,000 kilometres since leaving Framheim. They returned to Framheim on January 25, one day earlier than Amundsen had estimated.

Amundsen, Hassel, Hanssen, Wisting and Bjaaland arrived at what would have been nighttime to find the camp at Framheim silent. Despite their exhaustion, they scrambled out of their equipment and banged open the door, awakening Lindstrøm, Johansen, Stubberud and Prestrud. "Good morning my dear Lindstrøm, have you any coffee for us?" Amundsen asked. Lindstrøm's "hotcakes and heavenly coffee" were followed by tumblers of celebratory schnapps, poured all round in liberal quantities. Amundsen then announced, "Yes, we've been there, the whole thing went like a dream." Hanssen later wrote that "that gathering around the breakfast table at Framheim after the end of the trip belongs to the moments in one's life one never forgets."

Prestrud then related the story of his expedition with Johansen and Stubberud to King Edward VII Land—how they had narrowly beaten a Japanese expedition to explore this part of Antarctica. He also said that they had seen the *Fram* offshore the day before, but the ship had been driven away by pack ice. The famous ship came in again the next day, hooting its horn in celebration when its crew spied the unfurled Norwegian flags at Framheim announcing the return of the Polar Party. The meeting on the *Fram* was "a great, jubilant reunion." Amundsen learned what the men on the *Fram* had been doing for the past year while he and the Polar Party were marooned in Antarctica: they had completed the first oceanographic survey of the South Atlantic from Africa to South America. By the end of the voyage, the *Fram* had sailed over 54,000 nautical miles, a distance equal to more than two and a half times around the world. They were broke when they returned to Argentina the previous year, in need of supplies and repairs, and Peter Christophersen had taken responsibility for the ship and crew there. His support in refitting the ship and providing money and supplies enabled them not only to undertake the oceanographic voyage, which lent the expedition an air of scientific legitimacy, but also to return to Antarctica and pick up the Polar Party.

Once reunited, the crew did not waste time at Framheim. They were in a great hurry to rush back to civilization with the news, and transferred only the remaining thirty-nine dogs and a small portion of the most expensive equipment to the *Fram*. After two days of hauling goods out to where the ship was anchored, they were ready to leave Antarctica. Lindstrøm cleaned Framheim as best he could, so that "it was shining like a new pin," Amundsen noted. "We won't be accused of untidiness or dirt if anyone should happen to go there and look." As they cast off on January 30, the men watched from the deck as Framheim receded in the freezing fog. It was their last view of the bleak shores where they had lived for over a year, and where so much drama and hardship had changed their lives. None of them ever returned to the Great Southern Continent.

The month-long voyage from Antarctica to Hobart was a slow-going churn through high seas and storms. All of the crew just wanted the voyage to be done. During the miserable trip, Amundsen spent hours each day in his cabin, writing his story for the papers and preparing his correspondence, telegrams, articles and speeches for the media storm he knew lay ahead. He had gone so long without speaking English that the work proved more difficult than he had imagined. He enlisted Captain Nilsen, a fluent English speaker, to help with the writing and polishing of his speeches.

The *Fram* remained in Hobart for two weeks while routine work was done on its propeller and engine. Amundsen was busy with publicity. Interest in the "Great International Polar Race" had been building for several months in anticipation of either Amundsen's or Scott's triumphant return. Because they had obtained exclusive regional rights to the story from both Scott and Amundsen, the *London Times*, *Daily Chronicle* and *New York Times* each devoted plenty of ink to publicizing the race and the racers before any news arrived, and enlisted famous people such as Robert Peary and Ernest Shackleton to give them quotes. Nansen himself, in the February 1912 issue of *Scribner's Magazine*, compared and contrasted the parties and their chances of success. "If we compare their chances of reaching the South Pole I think that both expeditions have their special advantages. . . . The success of an expedition depends now, as it did before, chiefly on the man." While rumours flew around

London that Scott had reached the South Pole first, Shackleton felt that Amundsen and his party would emerge victorious because "Norwegians can live on the smell of a bone."

The March 8 *New York Times* special report on Amundsen's victory certainly took advantage of the newspaper's exclusive rights. In a bold proclamation at the head of the article, the newspaper announced its intention to prosecute anyone who violated its copyright. A large spread, the article featured maps and images to enliven a text, written by Shackleton, that offered nothing new but a promise that the details would appear in the paper "probably tomorrow." The newspaper also ran an article on how "Tasmanians fail[ed] to induce him to discuss exploit before his story reach[ed] the world." Apparently "Amundsen was attacked by reporters" in Hobart but maintained his "impenetrable reserve." It was big news, and the newspaper had paid a lot of money for the story, so it squeezed as much as it could from the event.

Meanwhile, Leon was working on his brother's behalf in Norway, answering correspondence, arranging deals and handling a flood of incoming donations. He met politicians and newspaper reporters and spoke for Amundsen on the world stage. In particular he was beginning negotiations with lecture agents to promote his brother's inevitably lucrative tour of Britain, Europe and America. Without the help of Leon and Nansen, two tireless supporters, there was no way Amundsen could have managed the financial and diplomatic logistics of the *Fram* expedition. Even Shackleton, who had an intense rivalry with and dislike of Scott, was working to help Amundsen, being instrumental in arranging Amundsen's publishing deals in London. Publishers in Britain and the United States, the largest markets, were vying for the rights to his as yet untitled, unwritten and untranslated book. The *New York Times* reported on March 17, just days before Amundsen left Tasmania, "Large offers have been cabled to him at Hobart, Tasmania, since the thrilling narrative in the *New York Times* and *London Chronicle*."

Amundsen parted ways with his ship and shipmates on March 20. He briefly toured Australia, giving a series of lectures while he had the world's undivided attention; he was broke and desperately needed some cash. Meanwhile, the *Fram* weighed anchor and cruised east from Hobart en route to Argentina. After nearly a month and a half of sailing, the ship rounded Cape Horn and headed north along the east coast of South America and up the Rio de la Plata, arriving in Buenos Aires on May 21. Amundsen, travelling to the city on a commercial steamer, soon met the *Fram* and his crew. One member was conspicuously absent. Amundsen had sent Johansen home on a separate cargo boat after he began drinking heavily and quarrelling with his shipmates in Hobart. His behaviour was an embarrassment and could result in bad publicity. Amundsen had never forgiven Johansen for his challenge the previous fall, and his "disgraceful" conduct in Hobart solidified Amundsen's determination to exclude him from any public celebrations in Norway. A bitter and disillusioned man, Johansen committed suicide not long after, in January 1913. Some observers blamed Amundsen for the tragedy, claiming the humiliation of not being included in the Polar Party drove Johansen to his death. But he had been in decline for the many years between returning from his adventures with Nansen and his South Pole expedition with Amundsen. Before leaving for the South Pole, he had failed in the army, abandoned his wife and child and fallen into a rootless and alcohol-fuelled life. The world he returned to in Norway in 1912 was similar to the one he had left, and none of the other men who were excluded from the Polar Party experienced similar problems.

In Buenos Aires, their elderly patron, Christophersen, who had been such indispensable help in outfitting the *Fram*, was excited and pleased to welcome the famous ship and its now equally famous captain and crew in their moment of triumph. "This is just like a fairy tale," he said. With the support of the Norwegian community in Buenos Aires, Christophersen organized a celebratory banquet for the crew with congratulatory speeches and many toasts. Amundsen was also honoured in an audience with the Argentine president and senior government officials. Until now, he had felt that everyone had abandoned him and his project after Peary's discovery of the North Pole, and that only King Haakon, Nansen and Christophersen were resolute in their support. He had been frustrated and hurt by what he felt was tepid support from his own government, and now learned that the Norwegian parliament had wanted to order the *Fram* home before he reached Antarctica but were unable to do so only because the *Fram* was not carrying wireless communication technology. He must have smiled when he heard the news. Yet here was Christophersen, a private citizen living in a foreign land, taking on the role that Amundsen felt should have belonged to his country, showering him with praise and giving him financial support as well. Amundsen truly was grateful and remembered to thank Christophersen profusely decades later, when he wrote his autobiography, claiming that "his timely aid with funds, sound advice, and personal good offices more than once saved the expedition from failure."

Christophersen again ordered the *Fram* repaired and refitted at his expense, to make the ship seaworthy enough to continue with its original expedition, the north polar drift. In the letter he had written announcing his change of destination from North Pole to South Pole, Amundsen had promised Nansen and the Norwegian public that the race to the South Pole was merely a detour and that he would resume his original expedition once the southern race was over. Several of his men, including Hanssen, Lindsrøm and Wisting, agreed to accompany him north. But they would all have to wait while the *Fram* was reprovisioned. Amundsen retreated to one of Chistophersen's estates to finish writing his book while most of his

crew sailed home to Norway on commercial ships. He was now dutifully, but slowly, working toward the original goal.

In the meantime, Amundsen's publishers and lecture agents were
persuading him to strike while the iron was hot rather than once
again disappear into the Arctic wastes for an unknown number of
years. Now was the time to capitalize on his years of work and investment, while the European and American publics were eager to
see and hear from the man who had won the great international
polar race. So Amundsen announced a change of plan: after finishing his book he would then embark on a multi-continent lecture
tour before resuming the north polar drift the following year, in the
summer of 1913.

On April 1, 1912, while the *Fram* was en route to Buenos Aires,
Scott's ship the *Terra Nova* arrived in New Zealand from Antarctica.
It brought the news that Amundsen had definitely beaten Scott to
the South Pole but that Scott remained in Antarctica. It was believed that he would be exploring the southern continent for another
season and would return the next year, when the ice would again
allow the *Terra Nova* to sail into McMurdo Sound. In fact Scott was
already dead by this time, but it would be another year before that
news electrified the world. Editorials in the British newspapers still
held hope that Amundsen had been beaten by Scott, some claiming
in a huff that even if Amundsen had been the first to the South Pole,
Scott "planned much scientific exploration while Amundsen was to
make only the dash for the Pole" and similar sentiments. Amundsen
suspected that something terrible had happened for Scott to have
failed to return from the interior of Antarctica in time to catch the
Terra Nova before it sailed; there were ominous rumours of scurvy
and poor ice conditions, which did not bode well. But he knew he
had to get on the lecture circuit while he still had the field to himself and was still heralded as a hero for his accomplishment. If in-

deed tragedy had struck the Scott expedition, Amundsen knew he had only until the next sailing season in Antarctica before that sensational news would overshadow his accomplishment.*

In a small country like Norway, the curse, or the joy, of fame such as Amundsen achieved was that everyone looked to him as either the cause of or the solution to a great many of their problems—sometimes both. Amundsen was uncomfortable with the role. He wasn't good at protocol and had to be constantly advised by Leon on what his public response should be to certain events and occurrences, such as the death or dishonour of old comrades, or business offers. Over the years, Leon managed his brother's public response to many diplomatic scenarios, understanding that personal opinions and feelings were not what people wanted from a famous explorer; they expected him to be larger than life, to give diplomatic public commentary on a great many issues, providing quotable comments that were suitably lofty and respectable. The problem was that Amundsen's opinions were often emotional and personal. He had to learn how to dissemble and provide morally elevated half-truths that gave the appearance of sincerity. His expeditions were merely one part of a large, ongoing business enterprise, and his public persona had to be managed with this in mind. It was a job for which Amundsen, unlike his compatriot Nansen, was not naturally suited, and this caused a certain frustration among his friends and family when he made missteps.

Amundsen remained in the blessed peace of Argentina until his book was largely written, as if by avoiding Norway he could avoid the annoying problems that awaited him there. His brother Gustav was again demanding money and defaulting on numerous loans,

---

*The sensational news that did soon dominate the newspapers was the April 15, 1912, sinking of the RMS *Titanic*.

blaming it all on Roald, who apparently didn't show him enough respect or give him enough money when he had returned from the Northwest Passage; Roald and Leon already supported Gustav's wife and had to bail out his creditors as well. At one point in mid-1913, Gustav threatened to kill himself if Roald didn't buy him a house. Perhaps Roald also feared confronting Sigrid Castberg, who had refused to obtain a divorce and marry him before he had left Norway two years earlier. His ardour for her had cooled during the years of hardship and strain in Antarctica. Maybe Johansen was on his mind—the erratic man descending into alcoholism might start writing embarrassing articles or giving interviews, undermining the deals he and Leon had arranged for exclusive rights.

But Amundsen could not hide in Buenos Aires forever. It had been nearly five months since he had announced his victory in Hobart. Reluctantly, he boarded a steamship and departed Argentina and the enthusiastic support of Christophersen, arriving anonymously in Christiania on July 31, just after his fortieth birthday. He had hardly spent any time at home before he was on the road again; he was a famous man, much in demand, even more so than he was after returning from his navigation of the Northwest Passage. The remaining months of 1912 were a whirlwind of public celebrations and events in Norway and around Europe. Amundsen had left anonymity behind long ago; the Norwegian parliament, having a change of heart now that he had succeeded, wanted to establish a professorship for him and vote him more money to undertake another Arctic expedition. He received notification from France that President Armand Fallieres would present him with the decoration of being made a Grand Officer of the Legion of Honour in October, when he would be in Paris speaking to the Geographical Society there. Prince Roland Bonaparte heartily congratulated him: "Your expedition has been among the greatest ever conceived and carried out by one man." The king of Sweden bestowed an award, the Norwegian parliament voted him a life annuity, and other citations followed. The lecture tour began in Gothenburg, then proceeded to Copenhagen, Berlin, Paris, Rouen, Rome and many other cities.

The excitement and novelty of talking about his accomplishments quickly wore off for Amundsen. As he had discovered after navigating the Northwest Passage, a lecture tour was work, not pleasure, and a type of work that he didn't enjoy. He was not in control of his routine, he could not get exercise easily, he could not eat what he wanted: he was not a free man. But in those days the lecture tour was the only way, other than newspaper stories, to make money from a sensational feat. As one of his lecture agents put it, it was "the man" that people came to see, even when they already knew the story.

So Amundsen persevered, being shuttled about, met at train stations by committees, delivering the same talk night after night in a series of well-attended lectures. In mid-November he finally arrived in London for something he had been both dreaming of and dreading for months, perhaps years: his address before the famed Royal Geographic Society.

11

A New Battlefield

The secret to my success has been due to self-control and willpower. Control yourselves, be your own masters, and at the same time develop determination. If you undertake anything, determine to accomplish your purpose and let no obstacle no matter what turn you back.

AMUNDSEN'S RECEPTION in Britain after his conquest of the Northwest Passage had been muted. His lecture tour of the country in 1907 had not been especially well attended, which was a disappointment, since he had been hoping for recognition of his historic feat there. So it's not surprising that in the anxious months before his second British lecture tour in the fall of 1912, Amundsen worried that his reception might again be tepid. Public sentiment was turning against him because he had beaten Scott. Lord George Nathaniel Curzon, the president of the Royal Geographical Society, made a public statement that Amundsen's decision to give no advance warning to Scott about his plans to race to the South Pole was unethical, and now newspaper editorials were claiming that there never was a "race" to the South Pole, that Scott was only there on leave from his officer's position in the Royal Navy

< 187 >

to carry out a scientific mission. Amundsen, worried that he was becoming reviled simply for being a foreigner, sought Nansen's advice as to whether he should cancel his trip to Britain altogether.

Amundsen's English lecture agent, Gerald Christy of The Lecture Agency, was horrified. In a series of letters to Leon, Christy repeatedly stressed that any sense of ill-feeling toward Amundsen was unfounded. "I think you will do well to put the notion of cancelling your brother's visit altogether out of your mind. Of course I attach a great deal of importance to Dr. Nansen's opinion, as he knows England well and I have known Dr. Nansen for so many years; but I venture to suggest, as I have stated above, that too much importance can be attached to one or two of the remarks that Lord Curzon made. The British people want to hear Captain Amundsen's story, and you must bear in mind that they will feel a little aggrieved if he goes to every other country in the world before coming here."

By July, while Amundsen was still in Argentina, the matter had still not been resolved. Christy wrote again: "I have lectures booked that represent pretty well 2,000 guineas. Halls have been definitely booked, and these cannot be given up without a severe monetary loss. As a matter of fact, I cannot lay too much stress upon the disagreeable situation that will arise if your brother does not now come to this country. . . . About this I am certain: your brother will have no reason to complain of the treatment he will get from Englishmen, Scotsmen, Welshmen and Irishmen. I have booked him in lectures in the four countries, so you can see that the interest in his exploit is general. . . . I cannot think of anything that they would resent more keenly than this notion that they could be guilty of what they would call un-sportsmanlike conduct." Even the king and queen of Norway urged Amundsen to go forward with his lecture tour of Britain: not to do so would cause international embarrassment and scandal.

Amundsen's lecture before the Royal Geographical Society took place on November 15 in Queen's Hall, London. His fears proved false, as the event was well attended and well received. The celebrities and notables in attendance included Shackleton, Lord Robert Baden-Powell and Sir Francis Younghusband. "Captain Amundsen delivered his lecture in the great voice of a man accustomed to shout against the winds and swiftly carried his audience of savants into the very atmosphere of the explorer's exploits," was one reporter's summary. In Amundsen's mind, however, the lecture was tainted by the opening and closing addresses given by Lord Curzon, who hinted at Amundsen's incredible luck and good weather, and then proposed a tribute to "those wonderful good-tempered, fascinating dogs, the true friends of man, without whom Captain Amundsen would never have got to the Pole." Later in life, when writing his autobiography, Amundsen remembered the event slightly differently. He recalled Lord Curzon proposing "'three cheers for the dogs!' [and] clearly indicating the next moment the satirical and derogatory intention of the phrase by turning to me with an unnecessary calming gesture and, though I had made no move, urging me with great earnestness not to make a rejoinder to the thinly veiled insult." The truth, no doubt, lies somewhere in between; it was subsequent events that coloured Amundsen's later recollection. But on this tour of Britain, during the remainder of November and most of December, his modest and self-deprecatingly humorous talks were made to full houses and met with an enthusiastic response.

His book *The South Pole: An Account of the Norwegian Antarctic Expedition in the Fram, 1910–1912*, was published in Britain in the fall of 1912, around the same time that he began his lecture tour. *The South Pole* presents a considerably different version of the adventure from the one revealed in Amundsen's private journals. The book makes everything seem easy, as if the entire venture had occurred without a flaw, hitch or complication. Part of the reason that some could later claim Amundsen's success was due merely to good luck was that he downplayed, and even removed, some references to hazardous weather and conditions—the extreme fog, blizzards and erratic snow conditions, crevasses and dangerous episodes such as the dash to Framheim that caused the rift with Johansen. He presented the journey as an amusing ski outing in which any challenges were easily overcome by the merry band. Amundsen wanted the adventurers to look perfect, as though they hadn't struggled at all to achieve their goal. All interpersonal quarrelling and rivalry is excluded from the book, as are any decisions that might have made him or his party look bad. In this account, Amundsen lavished great attention upon the dogs and their antics, and didn't shy away from the unpleasant aspects of their behaviour: the eating of their comrades, their fighting, their exasperating independence, their sneaky efforts to gain more food. He wrote about the dogs in a way that he couldn't write about his crew. With respect to them, all is presented as a unified front: all the quarrels and his inner worries are absent from the final manuscript.

It makes for a great story, but not an entirely honest account of the great adventure. The bonhomie of the jolly group going about their tasks without a care in the world is a pleasant fiction. As a result, the account lacks the vital ingredients of a thriller. Some have suggested that Amundsen was a poor writer, but the English translations of his books are infused with a lively jauntiness and lack of pretension that is refreshing for its simplicity. Amundsen didn't write a book about a harrowing adventure in the howling wastes of the most inhospitable place on earth; rather, he wrote about a grand sporting event, and he has been criticized for portraying what he wanted it to be rather than what it was. If he had exaggerated the danger and conflict and downplayed his extensive planning, he would have been praised for penning a gritty real-life thriller. The book was a good one, but it told only part of the story; nevertheless the reviews upon its release were generally positive. The *Times Literary Supplement* claimed that while Amundsen and his Polar Party "advanced in blizzards which less hardy men would scarcely have ventured to face," the book "conveys the impression that the whole affair was a sort of pleasure trip."

When he was finished lecturing in Britain, Amundsen boarded a steamship and crossed the Atlantic. On January 5, 1913, the *New York Times* published a review of the U.S. edition of his book: "An ancient Norseman's saga sung in the language of the twentieth century; 'Burnt Njal' divested of its blood-feuds, but with all its humor and quaint gossip of primitive men, their friendships and love of adventure." The paper also praised Amundsen for being "big-hearted" and the book for being "devoid of heroics; the exploit chronicled is apparently so easily within the grasp of the ordinary man." The review was a good start to Amundsen's American lecture tour, in which he was billed as the "Discoverer of the South Pole and Winner of the International Race for the Southern Extremity of the Earth." Despite giving many dozens of presentations of the same lecture and slide show, Amundsen was upbeat about this tour. His American lecture agent, Lee Keedick, had advised him to cut out much of the science in his lectures, to dwell on humorous and light-hearted incidents and to keep practising his English.

Amundsen liked the United States and its people. Newspaper accounts of his U.S. tour are different from those in Europe, peppered with quotes of him bantering with the press. In America, Amundsen seemed to have a more fluid and freewheeling relationship with the press. They seemed to respect him for his enthusiasm and stubborn self-motivation, and he was indulgent with questions that were only peripherally related to his adventures, whether they were about the merits of eating dogs, his friendship with Dr. Cook, his opinions on the future of exploration or his next expedition—the polar drift in the *Fram* that he had now delayed until the spring of 1914. "Although I have had offers of wireless installation for the *Fram*," he said in one rambling interview, "that also I declined. I don't care for it. It is very much better to be without news when you cannot be where the news comes from. We are always more contented if we get no news. A good book we like, we explorers. That is our best amusement and our best time killer."

Amundsen's openness with the American press earned him many favourable columns of print. The articles devoted as much time to the dress, décor, meals and distinguished guests in attendance at his lectures as they did to the speeches and accomplishments of the explorers. Like the society or gossip pages that concern themselves with celebrities today, the reporters following Amundsen wrote approvingly of the suit he wore and his stately bearing, commenting that he "was a younger looking man than when he was here in 1906." Amundsen was feted wherever he went, and treated to laudatory dinners after his lectures in dozens of cities and towns. His agents sold hastily printed souvenir books at his talks; his name and images from the expedition appeared in advertisements for floral design, bread, "Gentleman's Toupees," funeral homes, drug stores, shoes and countless other local businesses. In publicity pamphlets he was depicted as stern, rugged and handsome but always well groomed and well attired, and he was referred to as "the world's greatest living explorer, in fact one of the five greatest in the world's history."

One highlight of his U.S. tour was sharing the stage with Robert Peary in a full-capacity Carnegie Hall. Later, Amundsen and Peary were invited to lunch with President Theodore Roosevelt. The National Geographic Society hosted several of Amundsen's talks and announced in Washington that it was granting him $20,000 toward his next expedition. Amundsen also shared a stage with Peary there, and the National Geographic Society had Peary present him with the explorers' gold medal. In Philadelphia, he shared the stage with Peary and Shackleton; a photograph from the event shows the three men in formal tuxedos standing behind a small table displaying a giant globe tilted to show Antarctica. The photo bore the caption "The Three Polar Stars."

Amundsen also found the time to share his philosophy in less illustrious venues. At an address to students in the Great Hall of the

City College of New York, Amundsen, who "appeared to be amused" at the cheering of the three thousand youths in attendance, spoke of the traits that would lead to success in life: "There is one thing that I want to say to you boys, and that is that the secret to my success has been due to self control and will power. Control yourselves, be your own masters, and at the same time develop determination. If you undertake anything, determine to accomplish your purpose and let no obstacle no matter what turn you back. If you do this, my boys, no matter what your life work may be, I will promise to each one of you the fullest measure of success."

In San Francisco, it was reported that Amundsen had done something unusual: he had contracted for the purchase of two newfangled machines, "hydro-aeroplanes," that he would take north with him, and that before departing San Francisco he, Nilsen and Hanssen would "study flying scientifically for three months." While he was lecturing in Vancouver, he received word that the U.S. government would "offer him the honor of allowing the *Fram* . . . to be the first vessel, other than a warship, to pass through the Panama Canal" en route to San Francisco when he departed for his next polar expedition. "I am glad of it," Amundsen replied simply.

On February 10, 1913, the *Terra Nova* returned from Antarctica with the news of Scott's death. Several months earlier a relief party from the ship had discovered Scott and two other men frozen to death near one of their depots. Scott and his team, after reaching the South Pole a few weeks after Amundsen, had fought a horrifying struggle through vicious blizzards and punishing cold on their return journey. Naturally, the press sought out Amundsen for his opinion. He must have been anticipating some news around this time, as the Antarctic ice usually opened up for navigation in January. "I would gladly forgo any honour or money if thereby I could have saved Scott his terrible death," he said. In the days that followed, other newspaper reporters observed him in distracted agitation, unable to entirely control his emotions. "While those brave men were dying out there in the waste of ice," he mentioned quietly to a reporter in Chicago, "I was lecturing in warmth and comfort in Australia."

Amundsen, of course, had no direct responsibility for the disaster. He had never even met Scott, and although he felt that Scott's planning and logistics had been amateurish and foolish, and his hierarchical command structure and disdain for dogs and Inuit clothing a serious impediment, Amundsen naturally felt melancholy and perhaps even remorseful that these men had suffered and died in their brave quest. Though Scott and his men were ill-prepared, Amundsen thought that perhaps they wouldn't have extended themselves so dangerously to attain the pole if they hadn't known that Amundsen was also working toward the same goal at the same time. Perhaps his presence had prompted Scott to take additional risks. Amundsen also mused that the surplus oil he had considered leaving at the Pole might have saved Scott's life. "The day was bright and not very cold," he observed. "There was a general inspection of the outfit before we started back, and for some time I debated with myself whether or not to leave behind two five-gallon cans of oil I did not expect to need. In the end I did not leave the oil." When leading an expedition, Amundsen was ruthless and calculating; in victory, he was magnanimous and regretful. It must have been hard to continue to lecture about his own triumph when everyone now knew that the vanquished British explorers had perished miserably. Leon instructed Amundsen to express nothing publicly except heartfelt sympathy—make no comments about Scott's poor decisions or inept leadership.

While Amundsen continued to enjoy good press and sold-out halls in the United States, and the magnitude of his accomplishment was elevated when compared with the alternative; in Britain his triumph was quickly overshadowed by Scott's tragedy. It was even suggested that Scott and his men had died because they were heartbroken at seeing the Norwegian flag at the South Pole. No one wanted to hear that Scott's equipment was not up the task, that his ponies were all but useless with their hooves sinking deep into the snow, that his men were worn down by hauling the sledges themselves instead of using dogs, or that their inadequate diet led to scurvy. There were claims that Scott's failure was caused by bad luck, and the corollary, that only good luck had preserved Amundsen, that he wasn't deserving of respect since his accomplishment and survival were mere outcomes of chance. Scott's diary, purporting to be a truthful account of the expedition but in reality heavily edited to remove information that might show Scott in anything other than a generous and heroic light, was published in Britain as *Scott's Last Expedition.* Unsurprisingly, it became an immediate bestseller. Scott himself became a mythical figure, the embodiment of heroic but doomed struggle, a romantic figurehead and "the man who snatched victory from the jaws of death": in death, Scott had won.

Scott was a product of the British Empire in the gilded age before World War I, and he dragged with him to the pole all the baggage of the imperial behemoth of which he was an agent—including the inflexibility to adopt another culture's ways of doing things or to admit when purely British technology and the British naval hierarchy were insufficient to the task. Although his expedition was technically a private enterprise—Scott was on leave from his job as an officer in the Royal Navy—it was run very much like a national expedition. Just as Amundsen was always working under the stress of creditors who hounded him, and his life and accomplishments must be seen with the chronic lack of financing as a backdrop, so must Scott be seen as an appendage of the British Empire. But a positive assessment of Amundsen and his skills does not necessarily mean the opposite for Scott.

Without prejudicing opinions about Scott, it is fair to say that Amundsen was better prepared and had experience of polar travel and survival skills that were lacking not only in the British leader but in the British expedition in general. Amundsen had some good fortune, and perhaps slightly better weather. But in the end, his superior planning and leadership, attention to history and adoption of the knowledge of "primitive" peoples won the day. Is it any wonder that in a David and Goliath contest—as the expeditions can be considered in terms of financing and the might of their respective nations, where the gladiator of the establishment was defeated by the upstart—that the establishment rallied around their man, his legacy and his character? Scott was their anointed hero and to challenge him, let alone defeat him, was considered unseemly, somewhat like entering a restaurant and sitting down at someone else's reserved table.

Scott's demise, and his bravery in confronting it, is an oft-told story and an interesting study in how the control of information makes history: how the story of the "race" to the South Pole was manufactured with Scott as the hero and Amundsen as the villain, the man who may have technically won but didn't deserve the victory. Much has been written about the competition between Amundsen and Scott, with authors taking sides about whether Scott was more concerned with science, or somehow wronged, or whether Amundsen was devious, or the cause of Scott's death, and so on. But it's time for a decoupling of these two lives. The so-called race is a literary and historical conceit, contrived at the start by Amundsen and his brother Leon to generate publicity, and perpetuated by authors for nearly a century now, in which Scott's and Amundsen's stories are always told in tandem, with emphasis on their duel, their struggle, their ambition and their tragedy. But the fact remains that the two men never met and had no direct knowledge of each other's actions in Antarctica or before. The "race"—which only appeared in newspapers after both parties were incommunicado, en route to Antarctica—was always about selling newspapers and books and filling lecture halls, and it took on a life of its own, one uncontrolled by either of the two "racers."

It should also be remembered that Amundsen never considered the conquest of the South Pole to be his greatest achievement, although it brought him his longest-lasting fame and earned him a great deal of money. He lived for more than two decades afterward, never bothering to return; he pushed on with other interests and continued his rich and unusual life of adventure and challenge, undertaking creative and daring stunts that enthralled millions. The apparent antipathy for him that developed in Britain in the wake of Scott's death was something that Amundsen never forgot or forgave. In his memoirs he devoted considerable effort to detailing the ill-treatment he felt he had encountered in Britain, "[j]ust as in times of war it may be observed that the soldiers on the opposing sides retain a high respect for their foes in arms, while the non-combatants at home seem to feel obligated to engage in hymns of hate against their enemies." His dislike of the British establishment began with his reception after the *Gjøa* voyage and remained strong, perhaps unjustifiably so, and was based upon only a few mean-spirited remarks by a few individuals. But the British establishment, evidently, had a dislike of Amundsen as well, one that would see its full expression in the wake of Scott's death.*

Amundsen met with a more favourable reception in Europe and particularly in America. In America there was no need for the elaborate drapery of scientific camouflage: the contest, the struggle and the record were reasons enough to embark on geographical conquest. It was one of the reasons Amundsen was drawn to the country—he didn't have to pretend to be in the service of the greater deity of science but could simply do what he was good at and enjoyed doing. Admired by Americans for his energy and boldness, he

---

*Leon Amundsen did once express the opinion in a letter that it was fortunate that Amundsen had prevailed; otherwise, the British would have continued to send out one doomed expedition after another, condemning dozens to horrible fates, similar to what had occurred in the wake of Sir John Franklin's demise in the mid-nineteenth century.

was regarded as a successful entrepreneur in the field of exploration entertainment—a privately financed citizen, an underdog, challenging and defeating the state-sponsored champion of the world's greatest empire, and doing it with a showman's style and flourish.

Thus it came about that in the spring of 1913, about halfway through his six-month American lecture tour, Amundsen mused about selling his house in Norway and becoming a U.S. citizen.

As had happened many times before, Amundsen became a victim of his own success. With the North and South Poles already claimed, even with the additional financing by various geographical societies in the United States and Europe, he found it difficult to inspire public excitement for another polar drift. And he was not eager to embark on the voyage in any case—it lacked originality and promised much tedium, with little remuneration or fame. The voyage had already been pushed until 1914, and the *Fram* still languished in Buenos Aires. Nevertheless, at Nansen's urging, Amundsen dutifully signed up for courses in oceanography. His romantic life was likewise unsettled. Sigrid Castberg had moved on during his two-year absence. Amundsen soon began another romance, however, in an unlikely place: England. Kristine Elizabeth Bennett was the Norwegian wife of a much older, successful English businessman. Amundsen had met her through mutual acquaintances at a dinner in London during his lecture tour in late 1912. Vivacious, outgoing and flirtatious, Bennett saw in Amundsen a respite from the tedium of her otherwise dull life of wealth in the country.

Amundsen quietly met her on many secret trips to England and in Norway. It was the start of a lingering, complicated and ultimately unsatisfying affair, about which little is known. Amundsen was intensely secretive about his relationships with women as well as with his closest family and friends. He was a romantic at heart, and approached his love interests from that perspective; in geographical conquest, he was hard and uncompromising and above all practical, but in romance, he was the opposite. He had committed himself to seemingly unobtainable goals throughout his life, and this applied to women as well. None of this information ever made it into the press, and Amundsen wrote very little about it; in fact, only recently have the scantest references to his private relationships come to light in his correspondence. "Discreet" hardly describes his approach to affairs of the heart, and this new romance was probably one more reason he was less than enthusiastic about his impending multi-year polar drift, which now seemed like a form of penance imposed by Nansen for Amundsen's sin of secrecy in heading for the South Pole. Nansen wrote the foreword to the book *The South Pole*, and his description of Amundsen's proposed new voyage reads less like a colleague's celebration of the next victory than a judge's imposition of a sentence: "Next year [Amundsen] heads toward the Bering Strait," Nansen wrote definitively, "into the ice and cold and dark of the north, to drift across the North Pole Sea for at least five years." Amundsen must surely have been dreading such a prospect. What man newly in love would look forward to spending five years floating on a ship locked in the Arctic ice?

There seemed little way for Amundsen to back out of the north polar drift, particularly in light of Scott's death and his original public promise to Nansen that the jaunt to the South Pole was merely a stepping stone to the scientifically more important goal awaiting him in the Arctic Ocean. Nansen was relentless in urging him to push on with it, citing honour and duty as the key reasons. Amundsen was no doubt more interested in continuing his affair with Bennett, but on the professional side he would have preferred to return to the region of the Northwest Passage and devote some time to ethnographic studies of the Inuit. He had done what he had set out to do, he had wanted recognition for accomplishing it, and some money, but not the job of being a famous or respected person. He wanted to be known for his feat but then to be left alone until it suited him to go public again, with all the fuss and ceremony and the shackles on his freedom that this entailed. He was the "Chief" or the "Governor" while on his expeditions—there was no other way, he felt, to ensure success—but he resented having to play the role afterward. He had no interest in fulfilling the expectations of society, in being trapped by obligations. It was a paradox of his character that he craved public recognition for daring stunts and yet dreaded the tedium of repetitive lecturing in mediocre venues.

He returned to Norway and his home at Uranienborg for some months in late 1913, working unenthusiastically on preparations for the fourth voyage of the *Fram*. A skeleton crew, including many of his old comrades, were lined up. With Captain Christian Doxrud in command, the *Fram* had sailed from Buenos Aires north to the Panama Canal and was waiting for permission to sail through to the Pacific side. Unfortunately, work on the canal was behind schedule. The *Fram* was delayed for two months and could get no guarantee of when the waterway would be open, although the crew toured the whole length of the canal by train. By December 16, Amundsen had reluctantly made plans for the *Fram* to sail around South America and up to San Francisco, where he would join the ship along with some of the other expedition members. He also undertook another short lecture tour of Europe in November and December to raise a last bit of money, followed by another trip to Britain around Christmas to visit Bennett.

Trying to arrange all the details of his impending expedition by telegram from hotels while he travelled, Amundsen was too busy to do everything that needed doing because he refused to give up his personal life and wholeheartedly devote himself to the expedition. He was constantly delegating from abroad, even instructing Leon in basic personal obligations such as sending flowers for a funeral and arranging renovations of his house. He had delayed his 1914 crossing to America from February to April as he once again visited London for personal reasons, to steal a last few weeks of pleasure with Bennett before heading off to exile in "the ice and cold and dark," as Nansen had put it.

Meanwhile, other problems arose. The *Fram* had become infested with rats, cockroaches and worms while working its way down the South American coast. The delay at the Panama Canal and the slow progress south made it impossible for the ship to round Cape Horn and sail north in time to make it through the Bering Strait before summer ended and ice set in. This would postpone Amundsen's departure from San Francisco by another year, until the ice in the strait opened up again. Rejecting this delay, Amundsen abandoned his plan of entering the Arctic Ocean via Alaska and ordered the *Fram* to return to Norway. He would try the Northeast Passage, north of Siberia, instead. But the earliest the *Fram* could sail would now be in the spring of 1915.

The expense of sailing the ship up and down the Central and South American coast and then crossing to Norway was enormous: the provisions would be wasted, the ship worn out and the crew's wages paid, all to achieve nothing. Amundsen hadn't been on board the ship since March 1912, when the ever-generous Christophersen had again covered many of its expenses. But clearly Amundsen's heart wasn't in the expedition: the enthusiasm and tight control over the planning so evident during his earlier journeys had given way to a slackness and disinterest. He wasn't personally overseeing the expedition any longer, and being misled about the possibility of using the Panama Canal had wasted vast amounts of time and money. As a consequence he appeared to be observing the expedition as it progressed, making only vague and reluctant plans to join it when the time came to give up his real life. In this way the months of 1914 passed.

Although his South Pole escapades had made an enormous amount of money, the expenses had also been enormous, and the profits from his book went into the general revenue of the expedition rather than to Amundsen personally. He had also acquired another expensive pastime: flying, the thrilling path of the future, as he perceived it. He realized that he had accomplished all he could with dogs and sleds and skis; this approach was no longer novel or captivating, and there was nothing more he could do with it. It now bored him. But in San Francisco the previous year, during his American lecture tour, he had flown in a primitive biplane for the first time. The roaring contraption, piloted by a Norwegian-American aviator named Silas Christophersen, had bounced along a large field and lifted into the air for a few turns before returning to earth. Amundsen was stunned. This was exciting in a way he had never before experienced, and he became a devoted convert to the new technology and its possible benefits: speed over rough terrain and a good overview of a large area. He envisioned flight as a logistical aid to help orchestrate the movements of an over-ice expedition. And, not to be discounted, flight had the additional benefit of being novel and exciting. He had noticed the public acclaim awarded to the French aviator Louis Bleriot after he crossed the English Channel in a primitive plane of his own design in 1909, and no doubt Amundsen could imagine himself waving down to admiring crowds as he roared overhead.

He ordered two seaplanes to be ready for the *Fram* expedition in early 1914, and he enlisted the Swedish aviator Baron Carl Cederstrom. The aircraft, made of wood-ribbed frames and wire covered in tight canvas and propelled by a primitive 50-horsepower air-cooled engine, were waiting for him in San Francisco, where he planned to study flying for several months before heading north. But when the voyage was delayed again until 1915 and Amundsen had ruled out the Bering Strait as his entrance to the Arctic Ocean, he sent instructions for the biplanes to be sold. He set off for Germany and France to scout for new machines that he could more easily transport to Norway. He now planned to spend the better part of a year there—more time than he had spent in his native country in over a decade.

After finding a suitable aircraft, a Farman biplane, he ordered it to be sent from France to Christiania, to take on the *Fram*. This would be the first, and highly experimental, use of a motorized flying machine for polar exploration. In early 1914, Amundsen settled down for a few months to learn to fly, getting the first civilian flying licence in Norway on June 11—crashing only once during his practical exam. Excited by the prospect of the upcoming voyage and its novel plan to use airplanes, the Norwegian parliament voted a huge subscription toward the upcoming expedition. But other events, of international significance, began to intervene. Throughout the summer of 1914, Europe moved inexorably toward war. Amundsen's plans changed again: the explorer turned down the funding of the Norwegian parliament and donated his plane to the Norwegian military for the duration of the war, which everyone expected to be over quickly.

The north polar drift, so long a nagging, unfulfilled and unwanted obligation, an albatross around Amundsen's neck, was now officially called off for the duration of the war. The time for peaceful scientific expeditions had ended. Amundsen had temporarily escaped his exile.

12

The Frozen Reaches of Tartary

A glorious moon made the whole landscape glisten with a vivid whiteness. In several places we could see polar bears moving about on the ice. Added to the moonlight was a brilliant display of the aurora.

"NO ONE," AMUNDSEN wrote in his autobiography, "but a penniless explorer can realize the frightful handicap from which nearly all explorers suffer in having to waste time and nervous energy in their efforts to raise money to equip their expeditions. The heartbreaking discouragements, the endless delays, the blows to pride, if not to self-respect, involved in this search for funds, are a tragedy of the explorer's life. I now thought I saw an opportunity for once to avoid these sorrows." Although the war had delayed the *Fram*'s departure for the North Pole, giving Amundsen a respite from what he must have felt was his voyage of punishment for deceiving the world and rushing to the South Pole, it also left him essentially unemployed. But the war, at least in its early years, presented other opportunities.

Because considerable wealth remained from his South Pole exploit and, as he admitted, "I had nothing else to do," Amundsen decided to invest the bulk of his funds in shipping stock, all organized by his brother Leon. "Such an opportunity was obvious in all the neutral countries, and nowhere more obvious than in Norway. Ships were vital to the success of the Allies, and Norway's excellent merchant fleet commanded prodigious prices for its services." While he was silently on his way to doubling his fortune in under two years, Amundsen had plenty of spare time to pursue his relationship with Kristine Bennett, alternately in London and Norway, where she frequently returned to visit her family and Amundsen. For the first time, he eased into the life of a well-off gentleman with both time and money on his hands.

But keeping secret his affair with a married woman was not easy, and at the end of 1915 and in early 1916, he spent several months in Britain attempting to persuade Bennett to get a divorce and flee to Norway with him, something she refused to do. It is easy to conclude that when Amundsen declared that this was the time to continue with his plans for polar exploration, being spurned by his paramour was the reason. The relationship did not end, though, and perhaps he imagined that Bennett would be ready for him after his next adventure, after all, her children were nearly grown and her husband was much older. In either case, "not being in business for any love of business," Amundsen cashed in most of his investments and began planning his next expedition. Around the same time, he purchased an apartment in the same Christiania neighbourhood as Bennett's sister. On March 24, 1916, his plans were announced and reported upon in the *London Morning Post* and the *New York Times*. His expedition would leave from Point Barrow, Alaska, in the summer of 1917.

When Amundsen went to inspect the *Fram* in Christiania, he was shocked by the old ship's condition. Its long exposure to the warm southern waters had rotted its hull and rendered it unseaworthy. The cost to get the vessel in shape would have been so high that Amundsen decided he would be better off buying a new ship, one designed to his particular specifications. Doing so had the added advantage of making him the owner of the ship (the *Fram* was still owned by the government of Norway); also, the expedition wouldn't be hampered by historic ties to Nansen. Amundsen took his design to shipbuilder Christian Jensen, who worked the sketch and ideas into a proper design and began building the unusual vessel. It would be about 40 metres long and 13 metres wide, and have an unprecedented shape: "half of an egg cut through its length." The hull would be nearly a metre thick and be made from specially imported timber from Holland that involved "extraordinary expense." According to Harald Sverdrup—the adventurer who voyaged on the new ship for many years, became famous as a scientist and anthropologist in later years and wrote Amundsen's biography—"her shape made her behave excellently under heavy pressure from ice, but in the open sea she rolled like a wash basin." To help pay for the construction, Amundsen, or more likely his brother Leon, arranged for the issuing of a special Norwegian stamp series to augment the ship's building fund. The brothers also arranged to sell postcards that would be carried on the voyage and "cancelled" with a "Royal Norwegian Post Office that has been installed onboard" at the ship's farthest-north destination. The advertisement showed polar bears staring across an icy sea at a distant sailing ship.

Meanwhile, Amundsen was back to his peripatetic ways. Once the ship's construction was set in motion, he made a summer trip to Britain and then in November crossed the Atlantic to the United States, which, like Norway, was a neutral country in the war at this time. He spent several months arranging for the provisioning of the expedition with his companion Herman Gade, spending Christmas with Gade's family in Chicago, just as he had on several previous occasions. As usual, Amundsen was received with great interest in America. He appeared in the *New York Times* the day after disembarking from the steamship that had brought him across the ocean. "Captain Amundsen's hair is white and his face is weather beaten from many years of exposure to wind, sun and sea, but his blue eyes seemed as steady and bright as they were years before, and he walked down the pier at Hoboken with the springing, rolling gait of a mariner."

The reporters were much taken with Amundsen's claims to be bringing an airplane on the ship, "to fly to the North Pole from the nearest point that we pass on the ship." His stated plan, dutifully reported in the press, was to sail through the now-opened Panama Canal and then north to Alaska, hugging the North American coast. From Alaska he would enter the Bering Strait, cross over to Siberia, and proceed north until the ship became stuck in the ice. As it drifted about the polar basin, Amundsen would await his chance to launch his airplane and cruise to the North Pole. He would be gone for three to five years, he said.

In addition to arranging to receive bacon from Armour's and other general provisions from Sprague, Warner & Company in Chicago, Amundsen as usual attended several dinners and awards ceremonies and delivered a few speeches. (He mentioned these companies specifically in his autobiography, so he must have felt they had given him a good deal, did an especially good job or were otherwise deserving of being singled out.) He always liked his public role in the United States, and immediately slipped into his customary good-natured banter there. Perhaps he had less to fear in the way of public scandal in America; but the U.S. press also felt a natural affinity for him and his accomplishments. There was a feeling that he was welcome, that he deserved his fame and had not merely crashed someone else's party. This may be why Amundsen still planned to sail from Alaska, despite his new ship's being built in Norway. His only disappointment was that airplanes were in short supply even in a neutral country—they were valuable war machinery that might be needed for defence, so he had to abandon his plans of incorporating flying into his explorations. It was a bitter blow; Amundsen was excited about the prospect of flying to the North Pole, and he instinctively knew such a feat would be novel enough to generate great interest in the expedition.

He sailed from New York to London in early February 1917, for obvious personal reasons, and then returned to Norway a month later. The war at sea was complicating his plans, and the cost of his expedition's supplies was rising. At the end of April, Germany launched an unrestricted U-boat war against all neutral and Allied shipping, and the United States entered the war. Although Amundsen had ordered his supplies while the United States was neutral, once the nation joined the Allies, wartime restrictions applied. Now, he had to obtain a special licence that would allow the goods to leave the country, and those goods would cross the Atlantic at great expense in order to avoid the U-boats. The provisioning for the expedition was proceeding slowly, and the war at sea was escalating rapidly. Meanwhile, Amundsen's new ship was launched to great public fanfare in Oslo in June. There had been much speculation about the name Amundsen would choose, and in the end he named it *Maud*, "in honour of our beloved queen."

But the delays in getting his supplies across the Atlantic meant that even though the ship was ready, he could no longer sail in 1917. Another year would have to pass before he set sail. He would now have to cut out the publicity-friendly voyage to Alaska and instead proceed to the Arctic by sailing north along the Norwegian coast. He also gave up on acquiring an airplane for the expedition. Once Germany began its attacks on neutral, specifically Norwegian, shipping, the possibility of invasion became much more real, and Norway could not let something so valuable as an airplane be used to fly to the North Pole. The time for such civilian heroics had passed.

Amundsen brooded about Germany's "ruthless methods of carrying on submarine warfare" throughout the summer and early fall of 1917. He was not unsympathetic to the German cause; he had admired Germany and German ingenuity ever since his early student days, and this, coupled with his quiet dislike of the British, kept his opinion balanced on the fence for the early years of the war. "I did not then, nor do I yet, see any reason to criticize the Germans for using their submarines to destroy enemy shipping, or even neutral shipping where there was reasonable evidence that it was engaged in carrying contraband of war," he wrote. But when "the Germans threw humanity overboard and proceeded to indiscriminate sinkings without warning, I shared the hot indignation of all civilized people." In October, one particular incident galvanized his opinion. A German U-boat torpedoed a Norwegian merchant ship in the North Sea, "destroying all those on board, and even firing on such lifeboats as could be launched in the confusion." After deliberating on a course of action for twenty-four hours, Amundsen collected in an envelope all his German decorations and medals, several of which had been personally pinned to his chest by Kaiser Wilhelm II, and proceeded to the German legation in Oslo. He marched into the office of the German minister, a man with whom he had been acquainted socially. When the man smiled and reached out his hand, Amundsen met the gestures with tight-lipped determination. He refused the handshake and instead read from a handwritten note that expressed his "indignation and resentment" and brought forth his precious envelope, "to be returned to the Emperor."

Evidently, returning his awards wasn't meant to be an entirely private gesture, since it became international news. "Amundsen Rebukes Berlin" reported the *New York Times*, quoting his comment that his actions were a "personal protest against the German murder of peaceful Norwegian sailors on October 17 in the North Sea." Amundsen then decided on a greater wartime role for himself and began exploring the possibility of joining the British Royal Navy. Although he was now middle-aged, Amundsen, like many others, was galvanized to take a stand in response to actions he considered dishonourable. His international fame precluded him from being sent to the trenches or into battle; he was much more valuable as a figurehead.

The U.S. government invited him on a tour of the front lines in early 1918, and he reported from Paris on February 5 that "the qualities that impressed me the most in the American troops at the front are their cheerfulness, confidence, and certainty of being able to do their part in beating the Germans." Again showing his mastery of the press, he claimed, "I felt in those shell-swept trenches—for they are shelled every day—that there the mighty preparations of America were beginning to be realized, and that the end would be the overthrow of autocracy in Europe and safety for the world. . . . It was a tonic to a friend of America."

Naturally these sentiments were well received, and he soon crossed the Atlantic again for another quick tour of some of the northern U.S. states, to see to his provisions and to give speeches to Scandinavian Americans, urging them to support the war, to "put all their strength into their work so that more ships might be built and the submarine menace swept away." He made an impassioned plea to his audiences: "I say to you that no man can be a slacker and at the same time be a patriot. Every idle man who takes a day a week off just to suit his own whim may be the cause of death to many more men, some of whom may be dear and close to you." Amundsen widely praised the American troops in the trenches of Europe, claiming in another interview that "there is no fear that the Germans will break through that part of the line." He had certainly become a skilled speech writer and public speaker.

American newspapers praised Amundsen as "a born leader of men," noting that "the driving power of the man is tremendous" and that "he has a magnetic personal charm that attracts heroic spirits to him." He was on his way to becoming an American hero. Before the *Maud* headed to sea, President Woodrow Wilson sent him a cable message extending his best wishes for the expedition. Hardly surprisingly, Amundsen's request to export American provisions to

Norway for his adventure was soon granted, and, by April 1918, he
was back in Europe completing the preparations for the *Maud*'s
maiden voyage. The crew consisted of several old hands from the
South Pole expedition: Helmer Hanssen as captain, Oscar Wisting as first officer, Martin Rønne as sailmaker and Knut Sundbeck
as engineer. The new recruits included Harald Sverdrup and four
other men, for a total crew of nine. Amundsen was now forty-seven
years old.

A few months later, on June 24, 1918, the *Maud* sailed north.
Amundsen chose the date based on information sent to him by the
U.S. Navy; its intelligence reports suggested that U-boats had returned to their bases and would no longer be in the northern waters. By mid-July the *Maud* had left behind its final port, Tromsø,
reached the northern coast of Norway and turned east, entering the
fabled Northeast Passage. The men did not relax until the end of
the month—they "knew that until they had passed the White Sea,
we could not be sure that some stray submarine might not be cruising in the waters there." The tension was so high that on one occasion, when Amundsen spied the turbulent waters of an approaching
storm and called out "all hands on deck. Quick!" some of the men
scrambled up from below clad "in the scantiest of night apparel,
some with pieces of other men's clothing pulled on awry, and one in
a complete suit of civilian street clothes, bowler hat and all, with his
suitcase in his hand."

The *Maud* continued east through the famous passage, which
centuries earlier had been hailed as a possible sea route from England to the Orient but was soon abandoned because of its extreme
cold, dangerous seas and crushing ice floes. Amundsen noted, typically, that "it offers no great difficulties to experienced navigators."
He hoped to reach the Bering Strait in one season. Soon, however,
one of the passage's challenges began to present themselves—increas-

ingly icy waters—and the *Maud* was stopped completely on September 17. The expedition was frozen in for the winter near Cape Chelyuskin, on the Siberian coast. (Although Russia was in the throes of the Bolshevik Revolution, Siberia was not closed to foreigners until several years later.) Amundsen called the little winter shelter "Maudhavn." The men went ashore on the stony beach to build depots, observatories and kennels for their twenty dogs. Then they spent weeks shovelling snow into great mountains around the sides of the ice-locked *Maud*, to shelter it against the "searching Arctic winds [that] are the greatest handicap to comfort in winter quarters." Discomfort, however, would not be Amundsen's chief worry during the winter of 1918–1919. His luck—something he famously claimed was merely good planning, yet ironically also mentioned as one of the necessary qualities of an explorer—could not always prevent accidents.

Every day, Amundsen went for a morning walk. He was in the habit of carrying one of the pregnant dogs down the gangplank to the ice from the *Maud*'s deck so that the animal could stroll about. One morning another dog rushed up as he was coming down and bumped into him while he had his arms full. He stumbled and "plunged headlong down the steep slope at the side of the runway," landing heavily on his right shoulder. The pain was excruciating, and he staggered back to the ship. Wisting, who knew a little first aid, helped to set the badly broken bone. Amundsen was so debilitated that he remained in his bunk for eight days before emerging to perform light duties with his arm and shoulder in a tight sling.

A few weeks later, when one of the dogs was playfully bounding about on the ice, Amundsen carefully picked his way down the slippery gangplank and followed it into the fog out of curiosity. He stopped when he heard strange and eerie sounds coming from the obscuring mist, and soon the dog came running toward him followed by a furious polar bear. "This situation had its humorous side," Amundsen commented, "but I did not pause to enjoy that."

He stared at the bear and it stared at him. He wondered what he should do. He was alone on the ice, with a bound arm and shoulder, so he turned and sprinted toward the ship. But the bear was faster. It came up behind him, and Amundsen heard its loud rasping breath before being smacked to the ice by a mighty paw. The fall reinjured his arm, and the bear began to maul him, tearing at his clothing. Only when one of the dogs returned to torment the beast did it leave Amundsen alone and take off after the dog. Amundsen staggered up the gangplank and into the ship, bleeding from gashes in his back. Only his heavy leather clothing had protected him from worse injury. Amundsen later wrote in his autobiography that in the moment when he felt that death would surely come to him "laying at the feet of the bear," his mind did not dwell on "the chief incidents" of his life, the ones that were reputed to pass before a person "in vivid and instant review" at the moment of death. Instead, eccentric as always, he focused on an all-consuming question that "although vivid enough, was certainly frivolous": the number of hairpins that "were swept up on Regent Street in London on a Monday morning."

The winter days were now at their darkest and coldest, and Amundsen began a slow recovery from his injuries. Although the gashes made by the bear, once stitched and bandaged, healed on their own, Amundsen's arm was another matter. It was so damaged that at first he couldn't even lift a pen to write. "Several times a day, therefore, I would sit in a chair, brace my body, grasp my right fist in my left hand, and with the strength of my left arm force my right arm slowly upward a short distance, repeating the painful operation time after time." Even by the end of December he could barely lift his arm as high as his face, and it took many more months to fully heal. Years later Amundsen had the arm and shoulder X-rayed in Seattle. The physician expressed shock at the damage and at the fact that he could move it at all. "Thus," Amundsen wrote, "among such distinctions as I possess must be counted also the one that I am an impossible but successful surgical phenomenon."

This formal portrait of Amundsen, circa 1918, shows the classic profile of "the White Eagle of Norway."

Amundsen's custom built ship, the *Maud*, in Christiania fjord soon after it was launched, 1918.

Reading in the cabin of the *Maud* along the Northeast Passage

Amundsen feeding his pet polar bear Marie along the Northeast Passage in the winter of 1920.

21

Amundsen, looking relaxed at the helm of the *Maud*, Nome, Alaska, 1920.

22

Amundsen, Kakonita and Camilla in Seattle. It must have been a culture shock for the two girls who had never been away from their tiny Arctic communities before, and who were about to visit New York and cross the Atlantic by steamship to Norway.

The fuselage of N25 being unloaded from the transport ship Hobby onto the ice at Kings Bay, May 1925.

The flying boats being assembled on the frozen rim of Kings Bay. Note the open cockpits, the lack of landing gear, and the mighty engine on the wings above.

Amundsen looking
cool, leaning against
the side of his plane
before the flight.

Amundsen, Ellsworth being drawn through the crowd-lined streets of Oslo in
celebration, July 5, 1925.

Umberto Nobile, displaying his customary smug expression, and his pet dog Titina, the first dog to reach the North Pole.

The *Norge* leaving Leningrad for Norway, note the men outside tending the engines. The Italian members of the crew had never seen snow before.

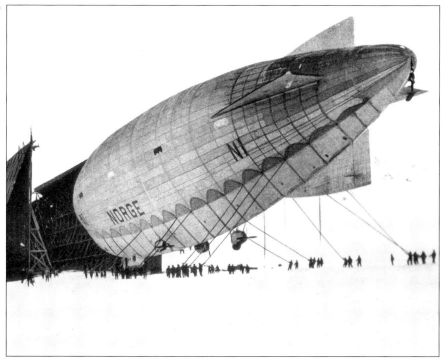

29

The *Norge* is hauled from its green canvas hangar in Kings Bay on May, 11, 1926, in preparation for its historic flight. The mighty open-roofed shed was constructed at great expense with imported materials in the month before the flight.

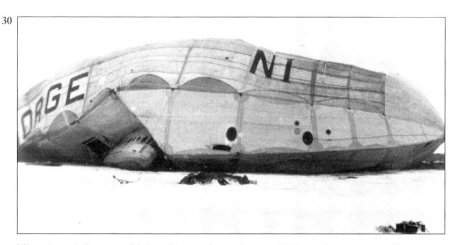

The *Norge* deflating in Teller, Alaska. Amundsen and Ellsworth went on to Nome while Nobile remained to pack up the damaged airship, May 1926.

Amundsen and Ellsworth posing in celebration after the pioneering flight that disproved the existence of land surrounding the North Pole.

The leaders of the *Norge* expedition, Amundsen, Ellsworth, Nobile (seated) and Riiser-Larsen (far left), posing for a photo as they cruised south to Seattle, June 1926. The relaxed atmosphere conveyed in the photo belied the undercurrents of disgruntlement, frustration and distrust that soon erupted into a bitter public feud.

Amundsen restricted himself to sedentary activities while his wounds healed at Maudhavn. Just before New Year's Eve, he trudged from the *Maud* to an observatory on shore to spend several hours recording the weather and magnetic forces. The grandly named "observatory" was little more than a single-roomed hut with no window. The lighting was provided by a Swedish kerosene lamp, which also heated the tiny room. Absorbed in his work, Amundsen began to feel drowsy and disoriented, and then noticed that his heart was beating unusually fast. By the time he fully realized the danger, he could barely stand. He struggled to the door, on the verge of unconsciousness, and stumbled out into the snow. Toxic fumes from the malfunctioning lamp had "thoroughly impregnated" his body. For days his heart continued to beat erratically and quickly, and for months afterward even the slightest exercise sent his heart into a wild flutter. It was years before the effects of the fumes fully wore off. In early February 1919, two months later, he nearly collapsed with exhaustion after struggling up a small 15-metre hill to observe the return of the sun. A few years later, doctors advised him to give up exploration, and indeed any strenuous exercise, if he wanted to survive. It was a recommendation he jocularly dismissed. He boasted that "at fifty-five years of age, I would cheerfully wager that I could outrun most young men of twenty-five."

The rest of the winter was a monotonous string of days, spent waiting for the ice to break. Amundsen was unable to leave the ship for any real travel, so he devoted himself to being the expedition's cook, apparently to good effect. Some of the men went on expeditions in April and May, but they were short, desultory affairs. There is an old saying that bad luck always comes in threes. By this reckoning, Amundsen should have been done; but fate decreed otherwise. As the ice lingered throughout the summer of 1919, one of the young men on the expedition, Peter Tessem, complained of headaches and melancholy and wanted to go home. Another young man, Paul Knutsen, volunteered to accompany him on a 650-kilometre overland trek south to a Russian outpost on Dickson Island, at the mouth of the Yenisei River. Both men were experienced overland travellers and hunters who had been to Siberia before. With six dogs, a year's worth of provisions and the expedition's scientific records and mail, the two men departed the *Maud* and were never heard from again. Years later, Tessem's body was discovered near the meteorological station at Dickson; Amundsen sadly called it "the one real tragedy in all my Polar work."

Through the summer the ice continued to imprison the ship. Open water was in sight but unobtainable. Drawing on his many years of experience, Amundsen remembered Frederick Cook's solution on the *Belgica* more than two decades earlier. He had his men drill holes in the ice in a channel leading toward the open water, fill the holes with sticks of dynamite and detonate them simultaneously. When high tide came on September 12, the ice cracked up and the *Maud* sailed free on a beautiful night when "a glorious moon made the whole landscape glisten with a vivid whiteness. In several places we could see polar bears moving about on the ice. Added to the moonlight was a brilliant display of the aurora."

The *Maud* continued along the Siberian coast, in the region historically known as Tartary, but met with an unusual quantity of ice. After a few weeks of sailing, before September had even ended, it was stuck again in the ice, this time at the mouth of the Kolyma River, near Anyon Island. They were still 800 kilometres from the Bering Strait, where the polar drift was supposed to start. It was a demoralizing setback, to have hardly progressed at all and to be stuck again in surroundings that were already familiar. With Amundsen still weak and lacking the will to fully take charge of the expedition, personality clashes dominated the winter as the men became slightly deranged from boredom and frustration. But here, at least, they would not be entirely isolated from human contact. A band of native Chukchi had made their winter base at the mouth of the Kolyma. The Chukchi were a remote and little-known people who had al-

most no contact with or influence from their nominal Russian over-
lords. They spoke their own language and lived a nomadic lifestyle,
following the migrating herds of reindeer. Amundsen was still too
weak to be involved in any physical activity, but he retained his fascination with polar peoples and urged Harald Sverdrup to leave the
ship for an adventure, to travel with the Chukchi. Sverdrup spent
over seven months with them as they pursued the reindeer across the
tundra of Siberia, learning the rudiments of their language and culture and later writing a book detailing the experience.

That same winter, Amundsen also sent Wisting, Hanssen and
another man on a quest by dogsled to locate a Russian wireless station and report on their situation. Their original destination was
Nome, Alaska, but it proved impossible for the trio to get a boat to
sail from Russia across the Bering Strait in February. While Wisting remained in East Cape to recuperate, Hanssen continued on
alone, skiing south with his dogsled until he reached the Russian
outpost at Anadyr, on the Bering Sea, near the end of March. Despite the recent revolution, Russia's borders had not yet closed, and
Amundsen's emissaries had no trouble in getting their news relayed
across to Alaska. It didn't hurt to be the representatives of the famous Amundsen, then ice-locked along Russia's own northern
coast. Hanssen returned north with his news and picked up Wisting.
They proceeded back to the *Maud*, arriving in mid-June 1920, after
a six-month journey of nearly 1,000 kilometres.

After Hanssen had made contact with the outside world,
Amundsen's actions became fodder for the press. In the previous
two years there had been much speculation about where he might be
wintering, about ice conditions, and whether the expedition was in
danger, but now that he was known to be near America again, adventuring not far off the coast of Alaska, the media circus began. By
this time in Amundsen's established career, his ongoing exploits
were pure entertainment. There were weekly reports of Amundsen's
plans, his setbacks and his progress. Amundsen was now a celebrity.

In addition to being famous for his novel adventures, he was famous for being famous. When there was nothing new to report, the papers were filled with columns of opinion and older information to help people catch up on anything they might have missed. "Amundsen in Siberia" proclaimed one report; "Doubt Amundsen Reached North Pole" went another. There were many reports in the *New York Times*: "Doubts Amundsen Failed," "Amundsen to Try Again for Pole" and "Amundsen Caught in Ice." Sometimes the dispatches were completely inaccurate, as was the one claiming that Sverdrup was leaving the *Maud* to lead an expedition to rescue the two men who left the ship during the first winter. Another fabricated and false story was headlined by the intriguing claim "Amundsen's Ship Wrecked in Siberian Ice Pack—Alaskan Missionary Brings Details of Explorer's Plight to Seattle."

A few weeks after Wisting and Hanssen's return, the *Maud* was freed from the ice and pushed east again, but not north toward the North Pole. Amundsen was headed toward Nome, to resupply and again communicate with the world. The crew arrived on July 27, becoming only the second expedition to navigate the entire Northeast Passage. Amundsen was met with a collection of mail from prominent American scientists and explorers such as Vilhjalmur Stefansson, president of the Explorers' Club, and Henry Fairfield Osborn, president of the American Museum of Natural History, welcoming him to Alaska and congratulating him on navigating the Northeast Passage. This accomplishment, combined with his Northwest Passage voyage, made Amundsen the first person to complete a circumnavigation of the Arctic Ocean. But during the two-year voyage he had made no progress at all toward the North Pole, and he considered the expedition a failure. Although he soon learned that Kristine Bennett and her husband had moved into a new estate near London, he waited in vain for a declaration of love.

At Nome, three members of the crew decided to leave the expedition, including Amundsen's old companion Hanssen. Amundsen was displeased with Hanssen's performance as the captain of the ship and had considered sending him and another man home in any event. But the loss rankled for a long time; although magnanimous in victory and loyal to a fault, Amundsen reacted with anger when he felt someone had let him down. It is, however, hardly surprising that the men wanted to leave after three years of tedium and quietly stressful danger; in the face of several more years of the same, and without the glory of conspicuous achievement to counterbalance it, who wouldn't be homesick? Amundsen didn't easily forgive the men, whom he considered to be deserters, and he offered to help them on their way home only as far as his legal obligations required.

No doubt his illness and lack of enthusiasm for the expedition also played a part in the low morale on the ship. By the time he was in Nome, however, Amundsen had apparently regained his vigour and energy. A local physician pronounced his injuries to be healed, and those who remembered him from the last time he had been in town, fourteen years earlier, when the *Gjøa* had completed the Northwest Passage, noticed that he seemed as energetic now as then. He had apparently shaken off the lethargy that had beset both him and the crew during the disheartening Northeast Passage voyage, and he was eager to leave again, in order to pass through the Bering Strait before it was plugged with ice for the year. Evidently, he felt that he couldn't yet cancel the expedition because it hadn't accomplished anything noteworthy. What did he have to show for his enormous expenditure of money and time? He had endured two years of pointless Arctic drifting, and was about to give it a purpose.

After spending only ten days in Nome, the *Maud* was ready to head out again. Only Sverdrup, Wisting, Amundsen and a Russian man, Gennadij Olonkin, elected to remain on board, along with an Inuit cook whom they called Mary. Newspapers reported that Amundsen didn't want to hire any local men because the wages demanded by sailors in Nome were too high and he couldn't afford them. Perhaps this was true: Amundsen had been shovelling money into the *Maud*'s maintenance and supplies for over three years and had not earned enough to compensate for those expenses. His fortune was quickly depleting as the *Maud* sat stranded in the ice in various locations along the Northeast Passage. This latest attempt to float north also proved fruitless—the ship was again imprisoned in the ice along the Siberian coast. Wisting and Sverdrup went on another 1,200-kilometre ski and dogsled expedition, leaving Amundsen the only Norwegian on board the *Maud* for a while. But that winter turned exciting in other ways.

The *Maud* was again wintering near a band of Chukchi, and Amundsen "became well acquainted with them." One of the men brought his sick four-year-old daughter, Kakonita, "a charming bright eyed little creature," on board. The girl's mother had died, and the father felt he was incapable of taking care of Kakonita; in fact, she was nearly starving and clearly suffering from neglect, and likely would have died without Amundsen's intervention. The man left her aboard the *Maud*. Once Kakonita had been nursed back to health, Amundsen devoted himself to her. Since her father had essentially abandoned her and claimed to be unable to take her back, Amundsen began teaching her how to speak English and Norwegian and introduced her to European customs.

This idyll soon ended. When the *Maud*'s propeller was damaged by ice, Amundsen was pushed beyond the limit of his patience. Restless and annoyed, and with Kakonita in tow, he left only three men to sail the three-masted *Maud*, set off with a dogsled south along the Russian coast and searched for a boat to take him across to Alaska. He and Kakonita caught a supply ship to Nome and another ship south to Seattle, arriving in July. (The *Maud* eventually sailed to Seattle as well, once the ice cleared, arriving on August 21 with help provided by some Chukchi boys and a coastguard vessel.) En route to Seattle, Amundsen brought along another girl, Camilla, the nine-year-old daughter of Clarendon Carpendale, an Australian fur trader and agent of the Hudson's Bay Company, and his Chukchi wife, as a companion for Kakonita. Carpendale was eager for his daughter to receive a more formal education and be exposed to life away from the remote Siberian coast. Amundsen took on the role of devoted "grandfather" and eventually brought the two girls to Norway to be schooled.

In Seattle, Amundsen was quickly welcomed, particularly by the city's large Scandinavian community. He was given accommodations and an office, and again was a featured guest at many public events—he was still popular. Soon after settling in, he received a telegram from Leon informing him that despite the voyage's setbacks the Norwegian government had voted a large sum of money to overhaul the *Maud* and keep the expedition going. Relieved of his financial burdens, Amundsen bought himself a car and toured Seattle and the surrounding region throughout the fall of 1921, always accompanied by his foster daughters, who became known in the press as "Amundsen's Esquimaux" and who "attracted the greatest attention." Amundsen also met Haakon H. Hammer, a Danish American shipbroker and businessman who quickly became Amundsen's confidant and agent in America.

While no doubt flattered by his increasing fame, Amundsen had other more prosaic matters to address. During all those years along the Northeast Passage, the expedition members had hunted and collected many specimens of interest to museums of natural history. To engender good will, he planned the disposition of some of the expedition's more exotic booty, including mammoth teeth and various arctic birds, many of which he prepared to be shipped back to Norway as a gift to the state. There was also a large collection of prime furs he wanted to give to Kristine Bennett. Evidently he was still thinking about her, even though they had been apart for many years. He dedicated his hastily written book *Nordostpassagen* (which was not published in English) to her, albeit obliquely. Also, he had consigned his house to her in his will, though she was already quite rich. "[Amundsen] Says He Will Try Again," claimed the *New York Times* in a dispatch from Nome—a claim that might be applied to his pursuit of Bennett as well as to his quest for the North Pole.

The expedition had dragged on far longer than planned and, even with the melodramatic reporting of the previous year, it lacked the competition and drama of his earlier exploits. As a result it was not earning him a great deal in endorsements or donations. Ever the optimist, Amundsen forged on, though his sense of his finances, never a strong suit, was inaccurate. He grossly overestimated the value of the furs and bird specimens that he hadn't given away, and he had wildly optimistic projections of his book sales. Thus his prospects for additional funding did not look promising before Leon's news of the Norwegian government's latest donation to repair and refit the *Maud*.

Amundsen's lofty dreams, however, were never tethered to his earthly finances. He was bored with ships and dogsleds, and now that the war was over and the economy was rebounding he returned to his love of airplanes. This time his goal would be to fly to the North Pole, without any scientific pretension at all. While his two remaining crew, Wisting and Olonkin, worked to repair the *Maud* in Seattle, and Sverdrup began an association with the University of Washington, Amundsen took a train across the United States. He planned to sail to Norway to secure more government support. In January 1922, the *New York Times* reported: "Amundsen Coming East."

PART FOUR
NORTH

Bering Strait

Nome

Herschel Island   Wainwright   Anyon Island

Gjoa Haven   Victoria Island

Hudson Bay

Flight of the Norge

Baffin Island   Ellsmere Island

✦ NORTH POLE

Greenland

Kings Bay

Spitsbergen

Iceland

Tromsø

Oslo

London

13

Grounded Dreams

I had never had any opportunity to acquaint myself
with business methods. I had always had to rely upon
others for the management of any business details.
Thus far my trust in others in these matters had never
caused me any trouble.

IN 1903, WHEN the thirty-one-year-old Amundsen had set out
for the Northwest Passage in the *Gjøa*, another milestone in the
history of technology was achieved thousands of kilometres to the
south and east. Orville and Wilbur Wright made their first tentative
hops in a motorized heavier-than-air machine in a field in North Car-
olina. During the following two decades, the progress in flight was
remarkable, yet the technology was still in its infancy. The Atlantic
Ocean had been crossed, but only in the "easy" direction, from America to Europe. More aviators had crashed into the ocean than had succeeded in crossing it. A British dirigible floated west to America in
1919, and a German airship did so in 1924. These airships, while
slow, stayed in the air for long periods and didn't crash every time
they had engine trouble or headwinds. They did, however, have their
own set of problems, such as manoeuverability, their large size and
the danger from the combustible gases they used for lift.

Engineers and pilots were designing and experimenting with new machines throughout Europe and the United States, trying to work out the practical aspects of long-distance flying. In the period of freedom from regulation during the 1920s and the 1930s, aptly named the "Golden Age of Flight," private air flight was not yet common or regulated, so engineers could take risks with materials and designs, and pilots could challenge distances without interference. Flying in the Arctic was just another challenge—enduring remote locations, freezing temperatures, unknown and unpredictable winds—although many thought the exercise foolhardy and reckless.

Amundsen's early success as an explorer was based primarily upon his mastery and adaptation of two historical traditions from different cultures—the Inuit use of dogs and light sleds, and the Scandinavian use of boots bound to wooden planks to travel over snow. But he was not nostalgic when he knew their time was over. He quickly perceived the advantages of air travel in exploring the frozen zones. In 1913, when he first observed primitive airplanes in France and Germany, he saw the future: "I stood with fresh memories of the long sledge journeys in Antarctica, and watched the machine in the air cover distances in one hour that would have taken days and cost fearful effort in the Polar regions." He learned to fly and was only delayed in bringing airplanes to the Arctic by the war. "The future of Polar exploration lies in the air and I am cheeky enough to claim that honour for myself as I was the first serious polar researcher who realized this and who practically demonstrated this method's potential," Amundsen wrote in his autobiography. While this may have been an accurate boast, his early efforts to use airplanes in the Arctic were not always successful.

After his six-month sojourn in Seattle, organizing the repairs for the *Maud* and touring the countryside, Amundsen set out east across the United States with his two Siberian foster-daughters, Kakonita and Camilla. The girls eventually proceeded ahead of him to Christiania under the care of Oscar Wisting's wife, Elise, who had travelled from Norway to meet the expedition in Seattle. In New York, Amundsen met with the directors of the Carnegie Institute to discuss polar scientific issues, conferred with airplane manufacturers about the possibility of a spring delivery of aircraft, and then crossed the Atlantic by ocean liner to Europe. He hadn't been "home" for over three years, and he would be gone again in less than two months. He spent a few weeks in London first, ostensibly to consult a prominent physician about his heart, but he had a personal motive as well, with Kristine Bennett living so near. He left London at the end of February 1922 and arrived in Christiania secretly. He went directly to Uranienborg and settled his foster daughters in his brother's home, registering them in school and other activities. He and Leon began planning the next expedition while holed up in Uranienborg, the snowy hills behind them and the icy fjord visible through the front window.

Around this time, Amundsen began referring to himself as the Norwegian counterpart to the Flying Dutchman, "doomed to life-long travels in the Arctic Ocean." In fact, after so long away from his homeland he didn't really have a home or a stable base of family and friends. His personal life took place on his ship and in various hotel rooms. His house still stood where it always had, the view from its windows was the same, but there was no real spirit to the place. Amundsen was an aging bachelor who didn't want to face his situation; constant travelling, meeting and planning allowed him to avoid confronting the deficiencies in his life. So long had he been away from urban life, from any semblance of a stable routine, that he had become unmoored from the rhythms of a settled life, unable to fit in or to find satisfaction when at Uranienborg. To whom could he relate as a peer? He stayed only long enough to meet with some government officials, sign papers and enjoy a few family dinners. He was anxious to get going. He was already dreaming of the fulfilment of his long-held dream of polar flight.

Only when Amundsen left Norway on March 17 was a press release circulated revealing that he had been in the country. A great crowd turned out to see the famous hero as he embarked on the ship that would take him across the Atlantic again, and he dutifully waved from the bridge while the crowd sang the national anthem. In the United States, Amundsen embraced his public role, or at least he was comfortable with it; in Norway, he seemed to shun it and travelled in disguise, doing the bare minimum to generate positive press for his latest venture.

Leon had ordered two airplanes to be picked up in New York. On board the ship with Amundsen was a young pilot, Oscar Omdal, a lieutenant on leave from the Norwegian navy, whom Leon had selected to be the expedition's chief pilot. The airplanes would be "more important to the expedition's economic profits than anything else," Amundsen speculated. He understood publicity, even if he did not understand business—airplanes were expensive whether they were exciting or not.

Newspapers in the United States were quick to report the details of Amundsen's latest expedition. His plan, as he informed reporters, was to "drift from Alaska over the roof of the world to Norway" in his quest to "seek the sources of storms." But, as exciting as he tried to make it sound, that is only what the new crew members of the *Maud* would be doing. Amundsen had decided on something altogether more daring for himself. In January, when he was in Norway, he had heard of the new record-breaking flight of a Junkers aircraft that had remained in the air for twenty-seven hours without stopping. This gave him a bold—some would say crazy—idea: to "fly from continent to continent across the Polar Sea," from Point Barrow in northern Alaska to Spitsbergen—something that (naturally) had never been done before. Amundsen put aside the goal of reaching the North Pole itself, claiming that "the crossing of the

Arctic Ocean was still a virgin opportunity." It was, after all, as he stated in an interview in the *New York Times*, the "largest of the earth's surfaces (land or water) that yet lay unexplored."

As always, Amundsen was in need of new attention-generating schemes to finance his lifestyle. He no doubt enjoyed the respect his fame brought him, even though he was fed up with the monotony of the lecture circuit, unless it was a prestigious engagement; but he felt humiliated to have to fall back on talking-up past exploits. Leon was a master at dreaming up new schemes to capitalize on his brother's fame. He had done a fine job of putting Roald in the spotlight after his triumph at the South Pole, and now he extended it even further. One of the fundraising initiatives they again employed for this latest adventure involved postage stamps. The brothers decided that since Roald would be flying over the top of the world, he could easily deliver air mail over the North Pole. They created a postcard, *North Star Air Post, Amundsen North Polar Expedition*, and arranged for it to be sold through various newspapers, with the papers doing their own advertising and keeping a commission for their efforts. Some of the postcards had the word "air" replaced with "ari," perhaps to create the aura of a rare and extra valuable collector's issue.

Amundsen calculated that his flight would be about 3,200 kilometres through a frozen, fog-ridden area that had never been thoroughly explored. Robert Peary claimed to have reached the North Pole, but the larger Arctic region was essentially *terra incognita.* An advance expedition led by Godfred Hansen, who had sailed with Amundsen on the *Gjøa* two decades earlier, had already sailed to leave a supply depot for Amundsen on Spitsbergen. Leon had already sold exclusive newspaper rights to the event, which was portrayed as merely a reconnaissance of the region, which would later be thoroughly and scientifically explored by the crew of the *Maud.* Amundsen was only interested in the sporting side of the expedition, but he had to justify the Norwegian government's financial backing. He publicly claimed that his new scheme would have scientific merit too, as the mysterious poles were "climate makers." He speculated confidently that "the air currents that wheel about the ends of the earth have more effect on the temperature day by day in New York or Paris than any other influence except the sun alone.

"My interest, therefore, in this North transoceanic flight was not in mere adventure," he hastened to add. "It is geographical and scientific." Certainly this was true—geographic exploration is scientific in itself—but with Amundsen the emphasis was always on adventure, on something stirring and unusual to generate publicity and to help with fundraising. "Captain Amundsen prefers to talk more of the adventure that is to come than the perils of the last expedition," reported the *New York Times*. "He looks to this as the supreme effort of his life, because the discoveries may be of immense value in the charting of the weather of all the continents." Whether Amundsen believed his own press or not, he, in consultation with his brother, certainly knew how to put a lofty spin on his plans: he wouldn't merely be searching for a way to gain public attention in order to finance his dream of cruising in airplanes in the Arctic—he would be working to unravel the mysteries of the global weather machine. This was an altruistic act of incalculable benefit: scientists would be able to "prophesy" the weather "for a long time in advance."

Before Amundsen had even crossed the Atlantic, the newspapers from Seattle to New York began reporting these latest plans. The *New York Times* announced, "Explorer May Fly to Seattle to Test His Arctic Machine." As usual, regular updates followed, telling the story of the man who "has the imagination of all great explorers and an invincible optimism."

As soon as he arrived in New York, Amundsen set about visiting the offices of two airplane manufacturers. He purchased a large German-designed Junkers, which had a passenger capacity of nine and a great cruising radius, and a smaller American-made Curtiss Oriole—a gift from the manufacturer, which was gambling on the publicity it would generate. The Oriole would be used for shorter reconnaissance flights. Amundsen named the Junkers *Elizabeth* and the Curtiss *Kristine*, the two names of his married paramour. No explorer before had so utilized his position to promote products in this way. Roald and Leon Amundsen had stumbled on a business model that would drive professional sports for generations: create a public spectacle that draws media attention—in Amundsen's day, newspapers and magazines, public speeches and ceremonies, slide lectures and, by the mid-1920s, some live radio broadcasts—and then, with the presumption that the public eye will be turned on them for their exploits, sell the attention as advertising. Amundsen sometimes endorsed products directly, but usually products and individuals received their publicity by public association with Amundsen and his exploits.

Amundsen decided that rather than transport both of his new flying toys across the country by rail, he would fly across the country to Seattle to test the Junkers and ship only the smaller Oriole, landing in key cities to generate news coverage. After all, "a railroad train is too slow for Roald Amundsen," noted one newspaper. Four people would accompany him on this series of test flights: a pilot from the aircraft company, an engineer, Oscar Omdal, and Amundsen's long-time friend and benefactor Fredrik Gade. The route would take them through Cleveland, Chicago, Omaha, Cheyenne, Salt Lake City, Reno, Sacramento and then north to Seattle, where the *Maud* lay waiting. On April 10, 1922, the Junkers took to the air from a field on Long Island. After cruising for about 550 kilometres, the plane's engine began to overheat and stall, and the pilot glided down from an altitude of 2,000 metres for an emergency landing in a rough field in northwestern Pennsylvania.

The plane clipped the top of some trees and then bounced on its huge rubber tires a few times before hitting a tree root and flipping over, which bent the wings and tossed the five men around. As they crawled out from the wreckage, they determined that none of them were seriously injured. Amundsen and Gade were "stiff front and back. It might be our age," Amundsen admitted. After a day of waiting, he boarded a train to Seattle while some of the men tried to repair the plane in order to ship it west. The damage to the plane proved to be extensive, however, so a new, even larger, Junkers was packed up and shipped west from New York to Seattle. Not surprisingly, the exciting near-disaster made the international news—probably not the sort of publicity the Junkers company was banking on.

In Seattle, Oscar Wisting was overseeing the provisioning and victualling of the *Maud*. He welcomed the new crew in May. Including Wisting and Sverdrup, who took a leave from the university to continue his polar research on the *Maud*, the expedition now had eight crew, including three pilots, one of them a young Canadian officer from the British Royal Air Force, Elmer G. Fullerton. After a last infusion of money arrived from Peter Christophersen in Argentina in early June, all was ready and the *Maud* lurched out to sea with the two airplanes stowed in several crates on the deck. Amundsen, who suffered from seasickness, decided to take a passenger ship to Nome and meet the *Maud* there, avoiding the corkscrewing and heaving of the unwieldy and overloaded vessel. On the SS *Victoria*, he met an attractive Alaskan woman, Winnipeg-born Bess Magids, who was to occupy an increasingly important role in his life in the coming years.

In Nome, Amundsen gave a final press conference; the mayor had declared a holiday in honour of the explorer's visit, and for days dogsleds had been bringing people to town to see the famous man off. With his voice "deep with feeling," Amundsen gave a speech that concluded: "I want to thank the citizens of Nome for many kindnesses and courtesies and the generous hospitality they have always extended to me. Four times I have sailed to the north from Nome." Asked about their chances of success, the Canadian pilot, Fullerton, then smiled and answered: "It's either success or death for us." Even this local ceremony on the northern fringe of the "civilized world" made news headlines.

A few weeks later, on July 16, near the village of Deering on the north Alaskan coast, Amundsen celebrated his fiftieth birthday. The *Maud* had also proceeded there. Not coincidentally, Deering was where Magids lived with her husband, Sam, the proprietor of a series of remote trading stations. Amundsen wanted a greater spectacle, perhaps to impress the young and beautiful Bess, so he and his crew spent a week flattening a landing field for a test flight of their little Curtiss airplane. (The flights were filmed by Reidar Lund and titled "With Roald Amundsen's North Pole Expedition to the First Wintering Place.") Apparently Fullerton then had a dispute with Magids, whom Amundsen was flirting with, and with other members of the expedition. When Amundsen told him that his services as a pilot were no longer required, since there was only one plane to fly, Fullerton declined to do the polar drift on the *Maud* and Amundsen sent him home. In Vancouver, Fullerton reported to the press that, to his "regret and disappointment," Amundsen's plans had changed and there was no more need for him, as his only goal was to fly to Spitsbergen. After a few weeks in Deering, Amundsen and Omdal took passage on the supply ship *Holmes* north to Wainwright, Alaska, along with the new Junkers, while the *Maud*, carrying the small Curtiss, which they planned to use to scout ice conditions, continued into the ice near Wrangel Island and was frozen in for the drift, with Wisting in command. The *Maud* would now be on an expedition of her own, frozen in the ice and out of communication with Amundsen for several years, until October 1925, when it would sail south to Seattle for a shocking welcome.

For Amundsen and Omdal, the winter of 1922–1923 was one of great physical exertion and, unexpectedly, social outings. When they arrived in Wainwright, it was too late in the season; high winds and storms prevented them from attempting their audacious polar flight. Since Point Barrow, which had only a few hundred inhabitants, seemed too small a place for them to spend the winter, Amundsen and Omdal settled in Wainwright for the long dark season—Amundsen as cook, Omdal as carpenter. The two men built a small two-bedroom house with a dining room and a kitchen, as well as a primitive airplane hanger for storing the valuable Junkers. In November 1922, Amundsen left Omdal to work on assembling the Junkers while he set off on an overland adventure south to Nome.

The previous fall, a London physician had minced no words: "No more expeditions! If you expect to live more than a few years longer you must avoid all strenuous exercise." Amundsen proudly paid no attention to this advice and wrote, "I started on foot from Point Barrow through the snow with a native mail carrier and made the run of 500 miles to Kotzebue in ten days, at an average speed of 50 miles a day. The next two days I ran 90 miles from Kotzebue to Deering to Nome; and in the following four days, I ran 200 miles from Deering to Nome. In other words, after having been 'counted out' by a heart specialist in February, I did the hardest travelling of my life in November, covering practically 800 miles through the snow at an average speed of nearly 50 miles a day, stopping only a few hours every night to sleep." He wrote this not to "boast," he claimed, but to demonstrate the result of "a conscientious regimen of life from youth onward to preserve it in the prime condition in which nature intended it to function." This account was written five years later, when Amundsen was in his mid-fifties and showing a preoccupation with his continued strength—the concern of an athletic man in later middle age worried about the inevitability of physical decline. In 1921, many of Amundsen's teeth had been pulled and replaced with gold teeth, so "my mouth looks like a true Klondike man's unfortunately" (probably the reason why Amundsen is seldom seen fully smiling in any photographs from this time).

Amundsen briefly visited Magids on his way through Deering, but he spent most of the winter in Nome, taking advantage of the free accommodation on account of his celebrity and enjoying festivities that included dancing, drinking and dogsled races. In Nome, he also had to face the realization that once again his finances were in trouble. He had burned through his modest fortune and most of the new government funds, and his expedition was again in debt, particularly in the United States. Haakon Hammer, Amundsen's new American business agent, wrote a letter to Leon in Norway and asked for funds to cover the U.S. debt, but he was rebuffed; Leon did not trust the man, even though Hammer claimed to be paying various ongoing costs from his personal funds. Even if Hammer was not entirely trustworthy, Amundsen was notorious for racking up expenses without a care for how they would be repaid; it was a strategy that had worked so far in his life. The problem was that he was now trying to finance two expeditions—a scientific voyage with the *Maud* and a daring polar flight—but with financing in place for only one. As usual, he was sanguine, believing that his flying stunt would vanquish any problems that presented themselves. He sold a small property in Norway and used the proceeds to satisfy the immediate claims of various U.S. creditors who had contacted him through a bank in Nome.

While Amundsen was essentially incommunicado in Alaska during the winter of 1922–1923, a scandal was developing in the southern United States. A rival explorer, Edwin Fairfax Naulty, a man of lofty ambitions who had never been to the Arctic, claimed that Amundsen had stolen his plans for the polar flight. Naulty pronounced that Amundsen was a foreign agent bent on deceiving the United States by using its territory to launch an expedition to claim new land for Norway. He also complained that Amundsen was stealing an "American" plan—that is, his own—in the same manner, he falsely claimed, that Amundsen had stolen Scott's plan and route to the South Pole. Although Naulty's was a strange and illogical argument, he was getting coverage in newspapers, probably for this very reason, and because Amundsen was a celebrity.

Amundsen had no idea that he was being slandered, but Hammer responded to the challenge for him in a special to the *New York Times.* Hammer wrote about the absurdity of someone claiming priority in the idea or concept of a polar flight, something Amundsen had been considering for nearly a decade, and something that Peary had also mused about for many years. In his final paragraph, Hammer wrote,

> I know the real American admires a true sportsman, regardless of nationality; admires the man of daring, the man of action, the man who really does things and thereby proves that he is a two-fisted, red-blooded human; that is Amundsen, the man who is now about to attempt one of the most daring feats in exploration annals, and I am quite sure that in spite of Mr. Naulty's talk a large majority of Americans are proud to regard Captain Amundsen not as a citizen of any specific country, but as a citizen of the world. . . . His discoveries, geographic or scientific, are the property of the world and not the property of a specific country.

Certainly Amundsen spent far more time in the United States than he did in Norway. Legality aside, Amundsen was more American than Norwegian at this point in his life.

Naulty's claims were also quickly discredited by Henry Woodhouse, president of the Aerial League of America, who pointed out that he was with Amundsen, Peary and the explorer Robert Bartlett in 1916 when the three of them had discussed the logistics of a polar flight. Amundsen never bothered to personally reply to Naulty's claims, and the issue faded from interest after a few months. But it was also around this time that Leon sent his brother a telegram detailing Hammer's shady business dealings in Denmark. However eloquent the Danish American businessman appeared to be, his history was enough for Amundsen to hastily rescind Hammer's power of attorney over his expedition and return it fully to Leon, at least temporarily.

In the spring of 1923, excitement was building for the polar flight, and Amundsen was making the final preparations. Many people wrote letters to newspapers offering their opinion on how he should proceed or organize his expedition, while others complained that he had wronged them or made other spurious claims. One writer advised him to use walrus-skin pontoons, another predicted his failure, and yet another advised him on how much fuel to take. One writer of a letter to the *New York Times* wondered "just what [Amundsen] expects to accomplish, outside of a long-distance airplane flight under ideal weather conditions." A New York woman claimed to be Amundsen's long-lost daughter (this was proven false). A report, following an X-ray he had in Nome, announced that "Arm Troubles Amundsen." One day the papers reported that he was about to leave on his flight, and a few days later the report was that the flight had been delayed. One day the Norwegian government was supposedly planning a "relief expedition" and a few days later, the relief expedition had supposedly been called off. Amundsen was in the media circus, part of a never-abating commentary on his life and actions. Fortunately for him, he was insulated from most of the hoopla by the remote regions of his endeavour and the lack of efficient communications technology.

Amundsen set off from Nome to Wainwright by dogsled in April 1923, travelling over the snow of early spring with a handful of stories for his planned book and the foreboding knowledge of his foundering finances. He arrived on May 9, and after consulting with Omdal fixed the date for the great trans-polar flight, announcing that it would take place on June 20. During the winter, Omdal had assembled the Junkers from the parts that had been shipped in three giant crates and had replaced the landing wheels with skis. On May 11, he fired up the engine while the plane rested on a flat patch of ice out on the bay. The propeller roared to life, and the machine taxied along the icy expanse before lifting into the air. Omdal cruised in circles over the village of Wainwright for a while and then steered the plane back to the cleared runway. As soon as it touched the ice, the left ski "crumpled like a piece of cardboard" and the Junkers spun in a circle over the ragged frozen surface of the water, scraping a wing. Omdal was uninjured, but an investigation of the inner structure of the airplane revealed that it was severely damaged. Worse, the structure of the airplane was so ill-suited to the impact of landing on skis that Amundsen and Omdal feared it would never work as planned. The company that designed the airplane in Germany knew of Amundsen's plans and should have warned him of the risk, but Amundsen should have done a better job of inspecting it before testing it. He was no longer adhering to the philosophy guiding his earlier expeditions. So much planning and testing had gone into his Northwest Passage and South Pole ventures, but so little into this polar flight scheme, and the results confirmed that. In his defence it must be said that aviation technology was primitive, although rapidly evolving, and Amundsen was attempting something never accomplished before.

In frustration, Amundsen initially blamed Omdal for the crash, even though as the leader he was more to blame for attempting a polar flight without first checking his equipment. Omdal and Amundsen attempted to repair and reinforce the landing structure with the limited supplies on hand, but when they tested the airplane again on June 10 it again crumpled. The entire scheme had to be called off. All the air mail that had been pre-sold would now remain undelivered. Added to this was the disappointment of all the other sponsors, the numerous creditors and the Norwegian government, which had sent a ship to Spitsbergen to await the historic arrival of Amundsen's airplane from across the top of the world. Amundsen had finally failed. The next year would bring what he later described as "a series of events that led to the most distressing, the most humiliating, and altogether the most tragic episode of my life."

Although he might have been feeling dejected and humiliated, the public fascination with Amundsen did not abate. People were as interested in his failures as his successes. Newspaper articles continued to detail his plans, to print defences of him and attacks against him. One article mocked him, saying he orchestrated the crash because he was afraid, that it was all just for publicity; another accused him of abandoning his ship for the attention-seeking stunt of a polar flight. What is true about celebrity culture now was true about the activity surrounding Amundsen in the 1920s: interest in celebrities is greater when they are experiencing personal setbacks or in the midst of a scandal. Seeing a great man fall, and recording his ordeal and his actions, are all part of the story. The newspapers, and therefore presumably their readers, were caught up in the ongoing Amundsen saga. What would he do next? How could he possibly recover from this humiliating failure? When Amundsen retreated ignominiously to Seattle in September 1923, newspaper reporters had their proverbial knives out, and were looking for a story to carve.

The events that Amundsen described as the worst in his life began with his association with Hammer in Seattle, and he attributed them to his "lack of business experience." Of course, he could not admit defeat. He had not lost faith in his scheme; he knew it could be done with the proper equipment. He planned another polar flight and just needed money to purchase the proper planes. Hammer had written him en route to Spitsbergen, where he had travelled to await Amundsen, about the possibility of getting several new Junkers aircraft from Germany, but Amundsen now knew that they were unsuitable for Arctic flying. He needed money for new machines that suited his plans: he wanted "flying boats," airplanes equipped with pontoons rather than skis or wheels. Amundsen met Hammer in Seattle, and Hammer promised he would raise the money; in desperation Amundsen believed him. "I had never had any opportunity

to acquaint myself with business methods," he wrote in his own defence a few years later. "I had always had to rely upon others for the
management of any business details. Thus far my trust in others in
these matters had never caused me any trouble. I did what I was told
and everything came out all right."

While Hammer went to work searching for financing, Amundsen rode the train from Seattle to New York, and then sailed to
London before making his way back to Norway in November. He
again handed over his business affairs to Hammer, along with power
of attorney. This time, his reception in Norway was frosty. Once
the man who could do no wrong, he was now attacked for misman-
aging the *Maud* expedition and for failing in his ridiculous stunt of
a polar flight. Under Hammer's management, Amundsen, with the
bad press, seemed amateurish, and the financial support provided
by the Norwegian government and people appeared to have been a
bad investment. As usual, Amundsen kept a low profile at home,
researching airplanes and visiting with his foster daughters—whom,
he was pleased to note, were doing excellently at school. Despite the
general antipathy toward him in Norway, he was able to persuade
the government to issue a special stamp to commemorate the new
polar flight, from which he would gain additional financing: most of
the stamps would never be used, but would be kept as collector's
items. Back in the United States, Hammer printed about seventeen
thousand postcards advertising "The Trans-Polar Flight Expedition," with an image of a chart projection of the North Pole and an
airplane zooming toward it. The caption read "In commemoration
of Amundsen's trans-Polar flight, 1924." Hammer sold about ten
thousand of them for a dollar each. He also went ahead with signing newspaper and magazine deals, and even film rights.

After a few weeks, Amundsen departed for Copenhagen to meet
with aircraft manufacturer Claud Dornier at his factory to discuss the
possibility of using his planes in the Arctic. At first, Amundsen liked
the Dornier Delphin, but he soon calculated that its range was too

limited. He settled on the larger, newly designed and more expensive Dornier-Wal flying boat. Equipped with two 360-horsepower Rolls-Royce Eagle engines, mounted in tandem (one pulling and the other pushing), it had twice the range of the Delphin, enough for him to fly to the pole from Spitsbergen. The design element that interested Amundsen was that the Dornier-Wal had no landing gear; the aircraft was like a giant metal tube that had wings and engines bolted to its exterior. By his calculations, he would need three flying boats, one of which would carry extra fuel that would be pumped into the other two planes before being abandoned on the ice so that the remaining two flying boats could continue on to Alaska. On January 7, 1924, Amundsen signed a contract for the delivery of three planes, to be built in Pisa, Italy, to his specific requirements, at a price of $40,000 each. They would be ready for pick-up in June. Hammer negotiated a minimal down payment, using Amundsen's celebrity and good name as assurance. He then convinced Amundsen that the funds would be in place by spring. Ever the optimist, Amundsen went to work on planning the expedition and hiring the crew, apparently unaware of the old maxim, "If something looks too good to be true, it probably is." Another truism comes to mind: "What we wish to be true, we readily believe." Amundsen was merely the latest in a great parade of the optimistically deluded, a gathering that would include a great many famous explorers as well as military commanders, gamblers, lovers and investors.

His partnership with his brother Leon was an ideal match. Roald's daring and preoccupation with the details of an expedition's field were was balanced by Leon's tact, diplomacy, gravitas and responsibility: piratical gambling and a mastery of hardship, balanced against caution, respectability and social standing. But with the portly Hammer, who had pretensions to call himself a polar explorer and who was mocked for it in the press, the partnership was a disaster. To make money from an expedition as a business enterprise, more was needed than just the execution of the deed—someone had to be the face and the voice of the expedition when the explorer was incommunicado. The "Amundsen" enterprise was indeed a business, and if the explorer himself wanted to participate in only half of it, he needed someone else to manage the other aspects of the expeditions, such as paying wages and dealing with creditors, quietly and confidently reassuring officials, and pursuing new fundraising and advertising opportunities. Amundsen provided the daring spectacle, but he needed someone else to ensure that money was being made while everyone was paying attention.

An awkward situation arose relating to the possible discovery of new land during the flight. A great swath of the Arctic was essentially unknown. It was still a realistic possibility that a yet-to-be discovered landmass existed somewhere in the Arctic. If so, it would be the last great undiscovered and uncharted land on the planet. Who would own it? Which flag would be planted when the airplanes landed on the ice? Amundsen let it be known in Norway that he would of course plant the Norwegian flag; after all, he still depended upon some government financing, and the expedition planned to fly from Spitsbergen. Yet in the American papers he intimated that he would not claim any new land for Norway, and he let this vague, noncommittal statement stand. Hammer, meanwhile, was promising potential American backers that of course the new lands would belong to the United States. The American and Norwegian foreign officers began talking about the theoretical new land. Amundsen, however, had not lost his touch for diplomacy. He had arranged special permission to enlist Lieutenant Ralph Davison of the Naval Air Service, selected from over thirty American applicants, to be one of his pilots, a move that not surprisingly generated positive press in the United States.

In April 1924, Amundsen rode the train to Pisa to inspect the new aircraft during their construction. Although Dornier-Wal was a German company, under the terms of the Treaty of Versailles that ended the First World War, Germany was prohibited from constructing large airplanes at home and had to contract out the work.

Everyone at the factory seemed optimistic and excited about the new airplanes, but Amundsen heard some rumours about Hammer that began to disturb him. Apparently Hammer was bragging to the Italians about his flying prowess, claiming to be an Arctic explorer and boasting that he would be included in the flight party to the North Pole. "Nothing could have been more absurd than the idea of taking such an utterly inexperienced person as he upon an expedition which at best was fraught with the greatest hazards." At first Amundsen found the claims hard to credit, but then they were confirmed by some of his Norwegian compatriots, at which point Amundsen began to suspect (or finally admitted that he suspected) that all was not well as far as Hammer was concerned. Because the stories were "so numerous and explicit," Amundsen fired Hammer and publicly announced that their business relationship had ceased. Hammer quickly fled to Japan, and Amundsen was left to unravel the tangle of strange and complicated business dealings that he left behind. Hammer had "made commitments far beyond any resources I could possibly muster," Amundsen related, and had set the entire expedition upon a fraudulent foundation, leaving Amundsen, in his own words, "humiliated beyond my powers to express it."

The commitments that Hammer had made in Amundsen's name were numerous and outrageous. No amount of profit from the expedition could ever hope to pay for them. There remained in the expedition's funds nothing to pay for the three Dornier-Wal flying boats. Amundsen was forced to issue a public statement that must have galled him: "As it has been impossible to secure sufficient financial backing the expedition will have to be postponed until further notice." Without the airplanes, he had no expedition; without an expedition, he had no way of earning money; and with no money, he couldn't hope to repay his debts.

The discovery of even greater debts from other sources, about which Amundsen had no idea but for which he was legally responsible because of Hammer's power of attorney, were so high that Leon became fearful that he would never be able to claim his own repayment from his brother—of a debt that ran to a considerable sum. Leon had been paying the wages of the *Maud*'s crew when Roald's finances no longer permitted it, with an unwritten assurance that the money would eventually come once the expedition was a success or the ship was sold. In the past a solution had always presented itself, yet now it all seemed doomed. Amundsen was still responsible for financing the continuation of the *Maud* expedition, which was stuck in the ice somewhere, yet he knew there would be little profit to be made from publicity on that front—there was nothing dramatic about that endeavour, and he wasn't even on board the ship.

An unseemly and bitter feud erupted between the brothers over their collapsing financial affairs. Amundsen aired his one-sided version of events publicly in his autobiography in 1927. But as usual with feuds, whether within families, between former business partners or during a divorce, reality becomes distorted as each side retreats to an unreasonable defence of its actions and its version of the truth. Such was the case with Roald and Leon. Although some records of their correspondence exist, they reveal only part of the story. Anyone who has ever written a diary knows that its entries are unreliable as proof of one's attitude or opinion, since they reflect a brief moment in time, a conversation with oneself. Letters to others, on the other hand, reflect how one wants to be perceived by the recipient or how one feels at the moment of writing, even if that opinion later mellows. Harsh words were evidently spoken between the brothers, but the precise nature of their quarrel remains a secret. But it was no doubt related to the fact that Roald wanted to sell his properties to free up money, and Leon blocked the sale, fearing the loss of his own unsecured debts. And Roald blamed Leon for some accounting deficiencies. When times are good, these types of minor disputes between siblings or business partners are easily overlooked, but when both the present and future look bleak, years of grievances and feelings of inadequate support come to the surface.

Amundsen still had considerable assets in the *Maud* and in his house, and he could have pulled through financially if he had sold them—although it was impossible to sell the *Maud* while the ship was stuck in the ice. He was also too proud to beg for more assistance from the government and so, once he had settled upon the idea of bankruptcy, in September 1924, he seems to have refused to give it up. It seemed the easiest thing to do, especially since Amundsen was estranged from both of his business managers and didn't have a good understanding of either his debt obligations or the surrounding legal issues. Nor did he want to begin learning about these things now that he was in his fifties; he was still dreaming of airplanes and undiscovered Arctic lands. He claimed that he was declaring bankruptcy in order to gain access to the books and do a full accounting of all his financial obligations. Out of pride or spite, he did not want his property to be owned by his brother. As a result, the legal wrangling with Leon continued for months, even after Amundsen had left Norway.*

Following his announcement of insolvency, the press turned against Amundsen. "Now that I was helpless and embarrassed," he wrote in his memoirs, "the same lips that described my career as a glory of the nation did not scruple to repeat lies of the most transparent fabrication, in a cruel effort to besmirch my private character and tarnish my name." He saw his whole life and legacy implode before his eyes, a slow-motion train wreck over which he had no control, even if he had precipitated it. There were spurious claims that the bankruptcy and public quarrel with Leon were part of a conspiracy to defraud creditors. There were suggestions that his two foster daughters were his own biological children—an impossibility, easily countered by comparing the dates of their birth with Amundsen's whereabouts around the time. And there were other

---

*The *Maud*, which had been drifting in the ice north of Siberia, eventually cruised into Nome in August 1925 and was promptly impounded for debts. Temporarily freed, the ship continued south to Seattle and was again impounded, eventually being sold to the Hudson's Bay Company.

hurtful and false accusations about his morality and his skills as an explorer. At least in the United States, Amundsen received some understanding: a lengthy article in the *New York Times* in the fall of 1924 offered sympathy "for the gallant Amundsen in this perhaps cruellest stroke of destiny."

The besieged explorer remained holed up at Uranienborg for the summer and fall of 1924, brooding and hiding from the press. He became a lonely and bitter man, wounded by the attacks of his countrymen and not on speaking terms with his brother, sister-in-law and nieces and nephews, who lived nearby. It was a miserable time. His companion Sverdrup later claimed that "he had to pay a high price for his success. His faith in human nature."

Amundsen's behaviour, particularly his fight with Leon over the expedition's finances and his readiness to declare bankruptcy, seemed so erratic that some of his few remaining friends questioned his sanity. He later devoted many pages of his short autobiography to a detailed litany of abuses he suffered. "Undoubtedly, I was guilty of a grave mistake in trusting my business concerns so implicitly to others," he wrote, referring specifically to Hammer, "though I do not see how I could have done otherwise than to trust somebody. For that mistake I deserved the punishment of bankruptcy, but certainly I did not deserve the contumely and ingratitude of my countrymen." All of this is true, but he appears not to have been willing to take responsibility for choosing Hammer to represent him or for so willingly shuffling all the responsibility of the business over to him.

Ever the indomitable spirit, however, Amundsen refused to entirely give in to despair. In the fall of 1924 he set off for the United States, where he knew he would get a positive reception. He would undertake a lengthy lecture tour to raise funds for a new project and to help pay the wages of the men still stuck on the *Maud*. He was down but not out.

14

The Arctic Phoenix

I haven't done so much. All else has been training for
this, the big thing. . . . If we leave the planes we shall
build a snow house every night. . . . Yes, we might be
gone a year or two. Who knows? Time is nothing.

AMUNDSEN WAS dreaming of Alaska. When he left Norway
in 1924, he thought he might never return to Europe but instead head north to the little cabin he and Oscar Omdal had built in
Wainwright, Alaska, so he brought many crates of his belongings
with him in his planned exile. He intended to write Kristine Bennett
to let her know that he would await her in Wainwright, though
surely he must have known the unlikelihood of that ever happen-
ing. He was unanchored from his previous life, having broken with
Leon and several of his companions from previous adventures; what
could he offer Bennett now that his finances were in disarray and
his reputation at an all-time low? Nor was his American lecture tour
going particularly well. He had only old stories to tell and his syn-
dicated newspaper articles were not bringing him funds sufficient to
undertake another expedition. It was "not encouraging," he recalled.
"I worked out that if nothing unforeseen occurred, I could be ready
to start when I was 110 years old."

In early October that year, Amundsen was brooding in his hotel room in New York. The Waldorf-Astoria was not a cheap establishment so he could not have been entirely destitute, but his peace was frequently disturbed by the rustling of summonses being slipped under the door and the ringing of creditors calling to discuss the debts Hammer had racked up. "It seemed to me," Amundsen recalled, "as if the future had closed solidly against me, and that my career as an explorer had come to an inglorious end." Now fifty-three years old, he found himself in the same financial situation he had been in thirty years earlier, when he had stolen into the night on his first adventure, sailing the Northwest Passage. "I was nearer to dark despair than ever before." When the phone in his hotel room rang on October 8, he suspected another unpleasant talk with a creditor. A voice he didn't recognize asked if the caller could come up and visit him in his hotel room. "I met you several years ago in France, during the war." Amundsen was suspicious and remained brusque and noncommittal until the man said, "I am an amateur interested in exploration, and I might be able to supply some money for another expedition." Amundsen was stunned, and immediately bade the caller to come up. The man was Lincoln Ellsworth, a forty-four-year-old engineer, pilot and leader of two small expeditions in South America. More importantly, he was the only son of a millionaire.

Ellsworth had long regarded Amundsen as one of his heroes and had applied to join the *Maud* expedition in 1918, but had been turned down. To Ellsworth, Amundsen was a "virtuoso of exploration. . . . [W]hen I heard his voice, I was excited as a young hunter who has an elk in his sights for the first time." The two men met several times throughout October and concluded the terms of their partnership. Ellsworth gave Amundsen not only access to funds for a new adventure, something to rejuvenate his flagging reputation, but also the adulation and respect of a younger man who had been an admirer for many years. He validated Amundsen's sense that his career and life had indeed been, and now would again be, heroic and noteworthy. Amundsen gave Ellsworth the reflected glow of this fame, which the young American would use to further his own ambitions as an explorer, as a way to carve a niche for himself independent of his domineering father.

Amundsen and Ellsworth agreed to become partners, with Ellsworth putting up the money and Amundsen acting as the leader of an expedition that would fly under the Norwegian flag. They would obtain airplanes and fly toward the North Pole from Spitsbergen the following May. "The gloom of the past year rolled away," Amundsen recalled, "and even the horrors of my business experience faded into forgetfulness in the activities of preparation." Ellsworth wrote, "Thus I came to Amundsen as a godsend, bringing not only new blood and enthusiasm to bolster his spirits, but a chance as well to secure financing for some magnificent adventure."

Amundsen threw himself entirely into the preparations for the expedition. They would now be able to use the Dornier-Wal flying boats he had been unable to pay for in June, taking possession of them the following year. The only complication was that Ellsworth, although not a spring chicken, had only a portion of the money in his possession; the rest would have to come from his father as part of his enormous inheritance. A flight over the North Pole was obviously extremely dangerous, and perhaps foolhardy, considering the primitive state of aircraft design and the deadly region they would be flying over. Ellsworth knew that his father, James W. Ellsworth— who owned coal mines in Pennsylvania and had estates and chateaux around the world—would never agree to finance such a trip without the cachet of international fame that a man as celebrated and competent as Amundsen brought to it. When the aging patriarch reluctantly agreed to meet the polar explorer, Amundsen took a train to the enormous Ellsworth estate in Ohio and sat down with the tycoon, a tall, distinguished-looking man with a large moustache and a stern expression. The younger Ellsworth described them eyeing each other suspiciously, taking measure: "the grim, old, white-faced financier facing the gray, bald but vigorous, weather-beaten old Viking!"

Amundsen made a good impression, detailing in clear but accented English his past expeditions and his reasoning for why this extraordinary feat of aerial daring should succeed. He knew how to spin a lurid tale and a self-deprecating yarn, but he also knew when not to—when, instead, to confidently outline a plan in concise, plain language, acknowledging danger yet explaining how it would be overcome. This he did, and soon the required $85,000 was promised, plus an additional $10,000 that Ellsworth told his father's lawyer was for parachutes. A few days later the men met again in the library of the Ellsworth mansion in New York to sign the documents. The elder Ellsworth had added a stipulation. He had always disliked his son's habit of smoking a pipe, and demanded that he quit smoking altogether if he wanted the money. Ellsworth the son grimaced but agreed and signed the contract, although he later reneged, claiming he had signed under duress.

The newspapers enthusiastically reported the new plan, interviewing Amundsen and Ellsworth and announcing that the duo had invited "seven prominent New York men to serve as an Advisory Committee." Amundsen knew the value of bringing powerful people onside and making them feel like his success was their success. He was also astute when responding to questions, such as what would any new lands they might discover be the used for: "air stations and bases," he replied, displaying an appreciation for the future. "The short route from England to Japan or California is over the top of the earth. The short route from many other parts of Europe to Asia is over the top of the earth. With the development of dirigibles and airplanes, the north route will be used, and if there is land there it will be of the greatest importance. In case of future wars air bases in the Arctic will undoubtedly be of the greatest value."

He responded to every question about possible trouble with "I have prepared for that." He was once again a darling of the press, with one writer from the *New York Times* stating in a feature piece on his life and achievements that Amundsen was a "giant in stature and strength, physically fit and as competent in endurance and vitality as any athlete. We walked for miles at a brisk pace through the streets of New York. He wore no overcoat, though others were bundled and scarfed and panting in the frosty air. He carried a stick in a gloveless hand, now and then transferring it to the other while he stuck a blue-cold fist into his coat pocket." Always looking to the future, Amundsen even claimed that his past exploits were nothing compared with this latest adventure: "I haven't done so much. All else has been training for this, the big thing." And if they crashed? the reporter asked him: "If we leave the planes we shall build a snow house every night . . . Yes we might be gone a year or two. Who knows? Time is nothing."

Throughout the winter, Amundsen and Ellsworth worked out the details of their plan. They would need two planes, each with three crew members—a pilot, a navigator and a mechanic—and to arrange for provisions, calculations of fuel, details on how to get the planes from Italy north to Spitsbergen, the construction of a base on Spitsbergen and many other details, not the least of which was arranging newspaper and magazine rights to the story. Amundsen sent Oscar Omdal and Hjalmar Riiser-Larsen—Norwegian airmen he had tapped for his previous, aborted polar flight—to the Dornier-Wal factory in Pisa to learn all they could about the new planes. He selected two other crew members, the Norwegian pilot Leif Dietrichson and Karl Feucht, a German mechanic.

In America, Ellsworth was having a feud with his father, whose health was rapidly deteriorating. The senior Ellsworth had changed his mind about allowing his son to go on the adventure and threatened to cut off his inheritance. He even tried to call in a favour at the White House in order to have his son's passport cancelled, after becoming convinced that his only son would surely die on the expedition. "Father was no more yielding than a granite crag," Lincoln wrote in his autobiography. But he claimed that he would rather risk his soul than bow out, and it was only the intervention of his sister and a promise to his father—to alter the trip plans slightly—that ensured that the funds were finally forthcoming. Ellsworth had to promise his father that he would not attempt to fly over the pole to Alaska but only from Spitsbergen to the North Pole and back, which James believed to be safer. The younger Ellsworth, despite what he had agreed to in any contracts, later admitted that he and Amundsen planned on doing whatever they wanted when the time came to make the decision—the unexplored land that lay between the pole and Alaska was the true prize. When Lincoln left for Europe in March 1925, his father stubbornly refused to see him off; he died without ever seeing his son again.

In January 1925, Amundsen had gone on another cross-country lecture tour of the United States to promote his latest adventure and to raise funds. The three-week tour was a grand success, characterized by filled halls. But it was tempered with an unsettling lack of letters from Kristine Bennett in London, to whom he regularly wrote and professed his love. In early February he boarded a ship for London, to see her before going on to Italy and Norway. As ever, he was only partly satisfied with the meeting. Bennett had indeed been growing distant; the lingering and tortured affair was now in its thirteenth year. She claimed illness for most of Amundsen's visit and couldn't see him often, keeping him always in a state of uncertainty that could only have been unsatisfying and demoralizing. From London, he took a boat and train to Pisa, where he met with Riiser-Larsen, the genial, six-foot-four, pipe-smoking pilot who was to be second-in-command but who in reality was doing most of the detailed work for the expedition, including the day-to-day organizing.

Amundsen as usual was the charismatic front of the expedition, generating the overarching idea and drumming up publicity through tours and interviews. A new company had been formed to deal with the expedition in order to keep Amundsen's disastrous personal finances separate from it. This had been one of the conditions stipulated by the Norwegian government before financing the navy rescue required after Amundsen's failed polar flight expedition of the previous year. The new corporation's board of directors included Rolf Tommesen, the chairman of the Norwegian Aeronautical Association, and several other prominent individuals including Johann Sverre, the Norwegian delegate to the International Olympic Committee—a fitting choice, since Amundsen's exploits were now international sporting and entertainment extravaganzas.

Back in Norway in March, Amundsen disembarked from the train one stop before Oslo* to avoid the crowds waiting for him there. As usual, he avoided publicity in Norway, particularly before departing on an expedition; he loved celebrating with crowds for a while after he returned. He asked for and received a small donation from the Norwegian state and settled in for a few weeks at Uranienborg. When Ellsworth arrived, he stayed at Uranienborg, enjoying numerous feasts and celebrations with "these hearty people, surrounding the festive [smorgas]board, eating and drinking, laughing and telling stories." One day, he drank so much fiery aquavit that he forgot to pack his collar for a formal dinner engagement. "At the end of the second day of such feeding," he noted, "I threw up my hands in surrender. 'After what you told me in Oslo,' I reproached Amundsen, 'I expected only black bread and soup; but, my heavens, you live better than we do in America.' And I added: 'Norwegians are certainly big eaters.' A twinkle came into the squinting grey eyes. 'You ought to see the Swedes eat,' said Amundsen."

Amundsen's home was again filled with visiting family and friends, but it was missing his brother Leon and his foster daughters. The girls had been sent back to Alaska during his bankruptcy proceedings the previous year. Of course, they had never been his daughters in a traditional sense; Amundsen was hardly ever in Norway, and they had been shuffled among various relatives and friends for years. He wanted

---

*In 1925—twenty years after Norway gained its independence from Sweden—the Norwegian capital, Christiania, was given its original medieval Norwegian name, Oslo.

them to return to their homeland in the north. He had taken them in, if his own later writings can be believed, as a sort of experiment to prove to the world that they were just as capable of learning and becoming "civilized" as any European. The experiment done—and proved, in his mind—now he wanted them to return to their families and communities, especially since he could no longer afford their upkeep. His older brother Gustav had arranged for both girls to return to the Carpendale family along the Siberian coast.

His actions now seem rather callous, but they should be considered in light of the times. It was widely believed that "primitive" peoples were incapable of "civilized" behaviour; that they were in fact not as intelligent or developed as Europeans. Amundsen, who had lived with, emulated and admired many aboriginal peoples during his life, knew this not to be true, and his foster daughters were part of his effort to disprove the claims of racial hierarchy then prevalent—soon to be elevated to a horrific level by the rise of Nazi Germany and, in a slightly different form, by the eugenics movement in North America. He never intended to be the girls' actual father—he had very little in the way of a domestic streak—and had brought them to Europe to prove a wider point: that they were capable and intelligent, regardless of their ancestry.

Nevertheless, Amundsen was so busy with his projects, travels and financial stress (the *Maud* had still not returned from the ice when he was about to fly north with Ellsworth) that when he delegated responsibility for something, of necessity he quickly dismissed it from his mind. It's hard to avoid the conclusion that Amundsen wasn't always honest with himself about his moral, if not legal, responsibilities.*

---

*Much later, Amundsen received a letter from Clarendon (then known as "Charles") Carpendale informing him that the family had kept both girls instead of sending Kakonita to her negligent father, and that eventually they had all fled the arrival of the Bolsheviks and escaped from eastern Siberia to Nome. By November 1927, the Carpendale family had moved to Surrey, Vancouver, British Columbia, where Kakonita married and had three children.

When Ellsworth arrived in Oslo at the end of March, he was just in time to attend a grand dinner hosted by the Norwegian Aeronautical Association at the Grand Hotel. There was a fancy cake decorated with airplanes circling a rendition of the North Pole, and many speeches and toasts were dedicated to the daring adventurers. The next day, Amundsen and Ellsworth boarded a train north to Bergen and then a steamship to Tromsø. The aircraft were also transported by train and steamship to Tromsø, and from there they all travelled overseas again, to the tiny coal-mining settlement of Kings Bay on Spitsbergen, which consisted of little more than a few wooden houses on a stony beach. Their boat was caught in tremendous swells, and Ellsworth and Amundsen were horribly seasick. By early May the six men had made themselves at home; they had unpacked and begun assembling the flying boats near the beach, not an inconsiderable task—the temperature was about −10°C (14°F), although they had endless daylight.

During their first "council of war," as Amundsen put it, he outlined a plan to which he hoped the others would agree. Two airplanes would set off for the North Pole together and land as near the pole as possible to take observations and solidify their claims to actually having been there. Then, Amundsen explained eagerly, looking around at the other men to gauge their reactions, he and Riiser-Larsen and a mechanic would board one plane and continue on to Alaska while the other plane returned to Spitsbergen. Fortunately, more realistic heads prevailed: the planes had never been tested in the Arctic, the others observed; nor did they have any realistic idea of how fierce the winds would be at the North Pole, nor the rate of fuel consumption, nor the ice or water conditions. If the two aircraft stayed together, then if one plane developed problems, the other could come to the rescue or at least fly out for help. The men all voted down Amundsen's plan. Then Riiser-Larsen mentioned that while he was in Italy he had heard of a dirigible that was for sale, second-hand, for about $100,000. It was of a newer design by the Italian engineer Colonel Umberto Nobile. Ellsworth was intrigued; he and Amundsen had discussed airships and concluded that whatever their merits, they were far too expensive for their purposes. But at this price, Ellsworth vowed to purchase it. The next summer they could leisurely traverse the entire region while this year contenting themselves with a jaunt to the North Pole and back. Two years earlier, when he had been in Italy, Amundsen had actually flown in the very airship that was now for sale, and he now began making of list of alterations that would better outfit this dirigible for use in the Arctic.

Kings Bay was still covered with a sheet of ice. This made it difficult to get the airplanes to shore, but it would be a boon for takeoff, because the fuselage could glide over ice with far less drag than in open water, allowing the travellers to stow an additional tonne of fuel—fuel that probably saved their lives. Perhaps it would even compensate for the fact that they wouldn't be carrying radios with them; the radios hadn't arrived by mid-May, and the brief window of opportunity for flying in the Arctic would close if they didn't leave soon. Most of the technical work was completed by Riiser-Larsen and Dietrichson, including bringing Amundsen and Ellsworth up to speed on the techniques of navigation. All that was left for Amundsen was to teach Ellsworth how to ski; despite claiming a great desire for polar exploration, Ellsworth had never skied. The crew waited patiently for weeks until the weather calmed, and on May 21 they prepared to fly. Amundsen was unfortunately preoccupied with the welfare of Kristine Bennett, who had undergone a minor operation in London. One can't help but feel sorry for the great explorer, to be so obsessed with a woman whom he rarely saw and who surely by now would have left her husband for him if that was her intention.

The settlement's coal miners were given the day off from work to watch the historic takeoff. Many, if not all, believed the adventurers to be lunatics, a view shared by the small European and American flying community. From Kings Bay to the North Pole and back would be about 2,400 kilometres through airspace that had never before been flown. In the early morning, the six heavily bundled men crunched across the ice to the two flying boats with purpose, donned their bulky parachutes and climbed onto the wings to enter the aircraft. One photo of Amundsen, a trim and muscular man, shows him looking like a puffy sausage in his layers of flying clothing, including woollen underwear and sweaters, a leather jacket, two pairs of woollen pants, a sealskin greatcoat, a leather flying helmet, gloves, scarves and heavy boots. He would, after all, be flying in an unheated, open-cockpit airplane across the Arctic Ocean, at high speeds and in freezing air.

The engines roared to life, and the first heavily loaded airplane, N25—Amundsen's plane, naturally—surged forward across Kings Bay and toward the mountains. N25 was slow to rise, and Amundsen glanced over at Riiser-Larsen to gauge his expression. "Had he been seated at the breakfast table he could scarcely have looked less concerned."* Soon the lumbering aircraft gained enough altitude and cleared the mountains. It circled around waiting for N24, and then upon the two aircraft sighting each other in the golden glow of the rising sun, they headed for the North Pole. Amundsen, the visionary and the dreamer, was again going where no one had gone before. N24 and N25 cruised over a vast sea of ice covered in wispy fog. The takeoff, particularly for N24, had been rough, and some of its rivets had burst under the pressure, causing a small gasoline leak,

---

*Archival film footage of the event, restored by the Norwegian Film Institute, shows N25 skidding down an incline and wobbling on the uneven ice while a crowd of enthusiastic onlookers waves and cheers: "Roald Amundsen-Lincoln Ellworths Flyveekspedisjon 1925.mp4," www.youtube.com/watch?v=xEHmD-FDUEU.

although no one knew this at the time. For several hours the two airplanes cruised without incident over monotonous terrain, until the fog cleared and the vast majesty of ice presented itself, a frozen plain stretching to the horizon, empty and featureless in all directions. Amundsen glanced out the window as his plane roared north at 120 kilometres per hour, covering in mere hours a distance that would have taken him more than a week to travel by skis and dogsled. Using binoculars, the men's radius of vision was extended to nearly 100 kilometres, or about 15,000 kilometres each hour, of terrain never before seen. It contained no surprises: "At least I thought we might see a bear," Amundsen commented.

After eight hours they had travelled about 1,000 kilometres, and Amundsen thought they must be near the North Pole. He began looking for a spot to land, but when N25 descended, he saw rough blocks of ice thrust up in pressure ridges, cut by serpentine gashes of open water and plugged with icebergs and frozen detritus. As the two aircraft cruised above the treacherous terrain, one of N25's engines began to sputter. Riiser-Larsen reacted swiftly, steering the lurching aircraft into a narrow channel of slushy open water that was bounded by icy walls on either side. In a masterful display of dexterity and nerve, he eased the stricken flying boat between the ice outcroppings and zigzagged along the waterway until the slush brought it to a stop just in front of a giant iceberg.

Dietrichson, in the other airplane and without a radio, had no idea what had happened. He flew N24 for ten minutes further along, until he spied a wider, safer-looking lagoon, and dropped the craft into the slush. But the channel was too short. The airplane bounced across the surface and crashed into a mighty, 200-metre-diameter ice floe. It began to take on water. "Omdal! Omdal!" Dietrichson called. "The plane is leaking like hell!" Dietrichson, Omdal and Ellsworth quickly leaped out of N24 and into a metre of snow.

Suddenly there was silence. Looking around, Ellsworth saw a lone seal regarding them from the water's edge. One of the plane's engines was mangled, and water had filled parts of the damaged craft. Dietrichson grumbled that Amundsen had probably flown on without them to the North Pole, until Ellsworth pointed out that they would have heard the engines above them. The men quickly set up a tent. They began pumping water from the hull and heating water for soup and coffee. "We owed ourselves a drink," Ellsworth recalled. (It was the era of prohibition in the United States.)

The next day, they climbed a nearby ice hummock, from which through their binoculars they spied N25 across the expanse of ice. They couldn't communicate except by waving flags back and forth—a tedious process, since no one understood Morse code or semaphore. It seemed too dangerous to risk walking the 5 kilometres or so between the two downed planes, since the terrain was impassable with jagged ice, chaotic crevasses and shifting channels of thin ice and open water. For the next several days the two parties worked independently, unloading their planes, setting up their camps and working on repairs as best they could. The first challenge, however, was to somehow prevent the ice from freezing-in the airplanes when the temperature dropped.

On the second day, when they found they could do nothing to move their heavy flying boat back into a level position, Ellsworth and his two companions tried to reach Amundsen's group. They set off on skis, and were making progress through the heavy snow, ridges and crevasses before they were faced with a channel of open water. The ice continued to drift, and fortunately it brought them closer to their companions rather than farther away. They set off again, carrying 50-kilogram packs and carefully pushing across the thin ice that had formed over the previous day's open channel. It was dangerous, but they had no choice. Omdal took the lead, followed by Ellsworth and then Dietrichson. Without warning the ice sagged and split, and Omdal and Dietrichson plunged into the Arctic Ocean, soon to be followed by Ellsworth, who lost his balance and slid from view. Arms flailing, Ellsworth grabbed hold of an ice chunk and hauled himself up from the channel. He quickly unstrapped his skis and held one end out to Dietrichson, who managed to drag himself from the ocean. Omdal, still strapped to his massive pack, clung to the ice edge, but the current was dragging him under. "I'm gone," he called, "I'm gone!" But Ellsworth crawled closer, using his skis as a brace, and reached out to cut Omdal's pack loose; it quickly swirled under the ice. His hands numb from the cold, Ellsworth clutched Omdal's coat and dragged the barely conscious mechanic onto the ice. Omdal's hands were cut and bloody, and five of his teeth had been smashed, but he could still move. The three men immediately began to crawl to the safety of more solid ice. Amundsen and Riiser-Larsen, who had picked their way across the ice from N25 to meet them, quickly helped their three freezing compatriots back to the camp around the N25. Shivering and exhausted, they had a shot of liquor, changed into dry clothes and warmed up with hot chocolate.

"Here we were, 600 miles from civilization, landed upon the ice with airplanes equipped for landing upon water, with the engine of one of the planes utterly out of commission, and with provisions adequate for full nourishment for only about three weeks." It was now that Amundsen displayed the leadership characteristics for which he had won so many honours. He calmly but quickly organized the men into groups, established work shifts and patterns to divide up the endless daylight: eating, working, resting, smoke breaks, sleeping. The men began hauling the miraculously undamaged N25 from the icy hill it was perched upon, and pulled on ropes while the engines roared, rocking the airplane back and forth. The six men were able to accomplish what had been impossible for three, and soon the plane was level on the ice's surface.

For the next few weeks the men worked at levelling a runway on the ice—clearing the snow and hacking away the ice ridges. They had only a single axe and improvised cutting tools, which they constructed by attaching knives to the end of ski poles. They spent days walking around the floe, flattening the piles of snow, aided by the freeze-thaw cycle. Amundsen organized the rations so that they would have food for twenty-five days, until June 15, at which time he suggested that they try to trek overland toward Greenland, even though they would be out of food by then. There was no more discussion of continuing on to the North Pole; merely getting back in the air and returning to Spitsbergen would be challenge enough. It was now life or death. They were trapped on a floating island of ice and snow. Soon, the brutal work made the men weary and sickly. Unable to wash, they became filthy. Amundsen's face became lined, and his beard came in white. He appeared to have aged ten years in a few weeks.

The constant sunlight wasn't the only reason sleep eluded the men: the ice beneath them was always shifting. At one point they left N25 in a small pool while focusing on the runway, only to have the ice start to close in, threatening to crush the airplane. "I expected at every moment to see the side stove in like a concertina," Amundsen wrote. Once alerted to the danger, the men hacked at the newly forming ice and rocked the floating plane back and forth to make sure that ice formed under it rather than around it. They all knew that if their craft became frozen-in or damaged, they would certainly die. The stress began to take its toll, and the men quarrelled about even minor things; certainly the possibility of death hovered over everyone. None of them wanted to end their lives here, spending their last moments with companions who sighed in their sleep, let their biscuits crumble into a mess or dropped precious strands of the diminishing tobacco supply into the snow.

After making a few aborted attempts to take off on shorter distances, Dietrichson now knew approximately the length of runway they would need.

Now on half rations, the men were becoming weaker and their work slower. For breakfast they had a small cup of hot chocolate and three medium-sized crackers; for lunch, a cup of soup, and for dinner, more hot chocolate and crackers. It was not much nutrition for men doing heavy work in cold temperatures, but it was all the airplanes were able to carry. "I should estimate," Amundsen wrote, "that we moved at least 500 tons of ice in the twenty-four days." They still found the time to take numerous measurements of ocean currents, depth and temperature; Amundsen wanted to have at least a little scientific data to show for the expedition's efforts—just enough to make it into the papers, and to prove that there was no land near their accidental camp.

After more than three weeks of work, the "day of decision" arrived. The runway was done; it was in fact about 100 metres longer than they had hoped for. "If someone offered me a million kroner for those extra hundred metres, I would not accept," Amundsen recalled, echoing the common sentiment: the distance was barely enough for the plane to take off, in Dietrichson and Riiser-Larsen's view, even assuming the airplane's fuselage was structurally sound enough to go skidding over a rough ice field before lift-off. On that day, June 15, fog shrouded the airplane and obscured the lumpy runway. But there was no delaying their departure: they had run out of food and it was not possible to extend the length of the runway any farther because of a thick ice ridge. The men unloaded everything unnecessary from the fuselage—extra clothes, camp equipment, skis, tents, guns, tools, movie camera, canoe—and flung it all unceremoniously onto the ice in a great pile. They had only this one chance, and if they failed to lift off in time, the plane would smash into the ice ridge. Six people weighing down one airplane would be a close thing, but if they didn't try this they would surely die. There was no talk of leaving anyone behind.

Four men crawled into the back of the flying boat while Amundsen sat next to Riiser-Larsen, the pilot. The Rolls-Royce engines "trembled and shook, shivered and piped" as the N25 bumped along on the rough ice on its fuselage and lower half-wings, nearly flipping on its side before righting itself. As its speed increased, the airplane began to make terrifying screeching sounds. The 7-metre high ice ridge at the end of the runway loomed ahead in the fog, and Riiser-Larsen gave full throttle ahead. The plane first skipped down into a small pool and then slowly began to rise as it approached the ice ridge. It seemed to take "terrible hours. . . . Thoughts and sensations crowd fast at such a moment," Amundsen recalled.

The Dornier-Wal lurched upward and cleared the ice ridge by mere centimetres, and the men released weeks of tension in a ragged cheer as the airplane continued rising and began heading back to Spitsbergen. Amundsen could now see the discarded equipment piled on the ice below, and a little distance away the carcass of the other flying boat. The flight home was accomplished in dense fog that the plane alternately flew under and over, sometimes nearly skimming the ice to get a better view ahead. Its only navigational tool, the compass, did not work properly because the plane was so near the North Magnetic Pole. The fuel gauge showed an alarming decline as the airplane hauled the six men southward across the ice for eight and a half hours, with no land in sight. Then, with only half an hour of fuel remaining, the men spied the distant, snowy peaks of Spitsbergen jutting from the frozen sea. In celebration they ripped open the final remaining package of chocolate bars that Amundsen had ordered kept closed in case of a further emergency, and wolfed them down; Ellsworth gobbled seven of them right away and was soon feeling sick.

In Amundsen's world, nothing was easy. It soon became apparent that part of the plane's steering mechanism, the lateral control, was malfunctioning. It was a minor problem during the flight, but Riiser-Larsen finally announced that he no longer had control and would have to drop the plane instantly. Yet landing on the ice would rip the fuselage to shreds and probably kill all the occupants in a crash. The only option was a small open lead of water. Spotting one, Riiser-Larsen masterfully brought the N25 down in Hinlopen Strait, where the airplane taxied to shore in a deserted ice-bound bay on the far side of the island from Kings Bay.

Before Amundsen could even calculate how long it would take to traverse several glaciers on the uninhabited region of the island in order to reach Kings Bay, the men noticed a sail on the horizon. They jumped up and down on the stony beach, yelling and waving their hands, but men on the boat—sealers preoccupied with pursuing their quarry on the ice floes—sailed on. The adventurers once more leaped into the airplane and Riiser-Larsen fired up the engines. The flying boat rushed across the choppy grey waters, pursuing the sealers' boat. Begrimed, sunburned, unshaven, weary and half-starved, Amundsen wasn't recognized by the sealers until he displayed his famous beaked profile.

"You're all supposed to be dead," they claimed.

15

The Dirigible and
the Fascist

*It was only a year ago that the German airship flew
over to this country. It is going to be the great means
of transportation in the north. There will be regular
routes over the North Pole. It may take a few years,
but it is bound to come.*

AMUNDSEN, ELLSWORTH and the others had indeed
been given up for lost. When their flying boats had failed to
return within a few days, newspapers began speculating on their
fate. Rescue expeditions, too, had been mobilized; ships began to
patrol the waters around Spitsbergen searching for evidence on the
ice floes. But after three weeks, everyone had given up hope that
the adventurers could possibly have survived—after all, they hadn't
taken with them any survival equipment, surplus food or even a
radio. Several rescue plans were being discussed in Europe and in
the United States; maps were brought out and scanned. Could they
have tried to ski to Greenland? What if they had discovered new islands or the continent that Robert Peary claimed to have seen on
his expedition?

All the speculation proved unnecessary when the six dishevelled adventurers turned up on June 18, thirty-two days after taking off from Kings Bay. Once the sealers had recovered from their surprise, the old sealing ship attached tow ropes to N25 and slowly hauled the flying boat along the Spitsbergen coast to Franklin Strait, where it was safely moored. Then they continued to Kings Bay, arriving in the harbour in time to see two rescue ships, *Hobby* and the larger warship *Heimdal*, preparing to depart for the search. As they neared shore, Amundsen and his five compatriots waved vigorously to onlookers and were soon met with jubilation and astonished shouts. A small crowd gathered on shore as they strode up to the small town. Fritz Zapffe, Amundsen's friend from Tromsø and the expedition's storekeeper, who had been nervously waiting for days, now smiled and rushed to get the box of celebratory cigars to hand them around. The exhausted, dirty explorers stood around and smoked, just as they had after the South Pole success, and photographers snapped their pictures. The gathering crowd of miners and the sailors from the rescue ships broke into song, the Norwegian national anthem. Amundsen recalled that "it was hard to remain dry eyed."

During the next several days, the explorers cleaned themselves up while the news of their dramatic struggle for survival was cabled around the world to newspapers that had paid for the exclusive rights to the story. Dozens of congratulatory telegrams flooded in from old acquaintances and former adventuring comrades, including one from Kristine Bennett in London. Several days later, after a small fireworks display and to the rhythms of a brass band, the explorers marched down to the bay and boarded a coal ship that would take them and the now-famous N25 south along the Norwegian coast to Horten, from where they would fly to Oslo for a grand celebration. The Norwegian public quickly forgot its general condemnation of Amundsen the previous year, in the aftermath of his public bankruptcy; he was again the hero of the nation, his position as the king of explorers restored by his latest heroic deed and miraculous survival. It was the first and last time that Amundsen completed one of his adventures in Norway.

In Oslo, the whole city was celebrating. Huge crowds lined the streets, and thousands of small boats cruised the harbour, which also hosted a British fleet of thirteen Royal Navy ships. As the hastily repaired Dornier-Wal circled overhead, the sound of its engines booming across the water, the great guns of the fort gave them a thirteen-gun salute. They were rowed ashore and, like Roman generals returning from an ancient victory, were paraded down the crowded streets in an open horse-drawn carriage to a ceremonial platform at the residence of the king and queen. Speeches were made and anthems sung. The reception was "royal," exceeding even the pomp following Amundsen's South Pole success. Ellsworth was given a gold medal for saving the lives of Dietrichson and Omdal, and Amundsen publicly praised him for saving the entire expedition and all its participants' lives. The acclaim was overwhelming and unexpected: after all, they hadn't even reached the North Pole— they had crashed on the ice and barely survived. But it was grand entertainment: the danger, the heroism, the dramatic struggle, the adventure. Amundsen provided Norwegians with a vicarious escape from the humdrum routine of daily life. Over the next few days the adventurers were treated to a series of public lunches and celebration dinners. If fame and public recognition were what Ellsworth was seeking from his association with Amundsen, then he got his money's worth.

The next adventure in Amundsen's career had been secured before the two flying boats had even launched from Spitsbergen in May. When Amundsen's crew returned in June to find that the world had given them up for dead, Ellsworth discovered that his father was the one who had died—on June 2, while the son was struggling to clear ice and snow to make a runway. The younger Ellsworth had come into a vast inheritance, enough to finance any number of ambitious expeditions. He soon returned to the United States to deal with his father's estate, but not before agreeing to put $100,000 toward the purchase of the Italian airship. As soon as they arrived in Oslo, Amundsen sent off a telegram to Italy, asking Colonel Nobile to meet him, Ellsworth and Riiser-Larsen in Oslo to discuss the purchase of his airship, in order to complete what Amundsen called "the big trip." The meeting took place at Uranienborg in mid-July. But what Amundsen, Ellsworth and Riiser-Larsen didn't fully appreciate at the time was that Nobile was more than just the designer of an airship; he was also, and perhaps foremost, a senior officer in the Military Air Service of Benito Mussolini.

Amundsen stayed at Uranienborg for a rare few months. He began working on his book and preparing the slides and talking points for his new lecture, with the help of Riiser-Larsen. In mid-August, he delivered the premiere of his latest lecture to a full audience and rave reviews at the National Theatre in Oslo. A week later, on August 22, the *Maud*, having completed her Arctic survey, docked in Nome and was seized by the bailiffs as part of Amundsen's ongoing bankruptcy proceedings, while its crew quietly made their way home. Amundsen and Riiser-Larsen then took the train to Rome to continue negotiations with Nobile and Mussolini for the purchase of the airship. The two Norwegians continued on the lecture circuit in a few European cities en route, where their reception was astounding—except in Germany, where public antipathy was high because of Amundsen's public denunciation of German actions during the war, and because he and Riiser-Larsen had selected an Italian airship instead of a German one. Amundsen let the younger members of the expedition take a greater role in the publicity than they had in the past, by giving speeches and lectures themselves. So, in the fall, while Amundsen toured the United States, Riiser-Larsen lectured in Europe and Dietrichson toured Great Britain, Sweden,

Denmark and Norway. Some primitive films of the expedition were also being shown in Europe.

Amundsen briefly returned to Norway before again setting off for London and America. His stay in London was short. After thirteen years, he and Kristine Bennett had finally ended their sporadic relationship, and Amundsen's emotional attachment to her dwindled. At first he tried to claim that a minor ailment would prevent him from lecturing in Britain, but his financial and moral obligations prevented this social retreat. It was a London correspondent for the *New York Times* who interviewed him and provided some insight into his plans for the next year. "I expect to start next May from Spitsbergen," Amundsen claimed, "where the airship will be taken from Italy in March. I shall fly from Spitsbergen right across Alaska." Always looking to the future, he took the opportunity to recast his past adventure in a way that would promote his upcoming venture. "That flight largely was made in order to gather information for the coming expedition," he claimed. "On our last trip we passed over more than 200,000 square miles of unexplored country, which must have tremendous potentialities." According to the new spin, the thrilling flight of a few months ago wasn't a stand-alone adventure, made possible only because of the timely intercession and financial support of Ellsworth. This random stitching-together of opportunities as they arose was actually part of a long-term strategy. Before Amundsen even boarded his ship for New York, the planning for his airship expedition was underway, organized primarily by Riiser-Larsen with the help of the Norwegian Aero Club. Nobile was working on the agreed-upon adjustments to the airship, while a location for a hangar in Kings Bay was being scouted and material to build it was being ordered.

Amundsen again had to raise some money and generate publicity in America—a task for which he was uniquely suited. He arrived in New York on October 9 and once again booked into his favourite hotel, the Waldorf-Astoria. He was immediately interviewed by newspaper reporters. It was all about the new expedition: its dangers, its goals, his likelihood of success. A great talker, Amundsen delivered what the reporters needed to fill their papers: opinions on undiscovered lands, risks to be taken, problems to be overcome. A favourite topic was the future of dirigibles. Dirigibles were much better suited to Arctic travel than airplanes were, Amundsen claimed, "experience having shown that when a plane once descends near the Pole it is a great hazard whether it will ever rise again." He also predicted a secure future for them as a means of transportation. "It was only a year ago that the German airship flew over to this country. It is going to be the great means of transportation in the north. There will be regular routes over the North Pole. It may take a few years, but it is bound to come."

The newspaper stories about his lectures and ideas were now complete with pictures of airships and portraits of the aging adventurer, looking like a weather-beaten old Viking from another age, although in person he was always dressed impeccably for any public display or talk, with a fondness for double-breasted suits and bowler hats. While in New York, Amundsen was also continuing his affair with Bess Magids. Although still married, she was seen dining with Amundsen at the Waldorf-Astoria. Her nephew William Hensley recalled that "she was a dynamo. She loved politics; loved to gamble, party, and drink. And she loved to spend money." Like Amundsen, Magids was apparently equally at home dining in a fine New York hotel and driving a dogsled around the Arctic. Amundsen's involvement with Magids was the relationship that probably allowed him to free himself from his unrewarding and hopeless romantic entanglement with Kristine Bennett. Although he remained friends with Bennett and her sons, he had moved on—as, indeed, she probably had, years ago—but there was no bitterness.

Amundsen rode the train from the U.S. east coast to the west, visiting most large cities in between. His lecture tour, however, was a mixed success. He received excellent press coverage for his polar flight and his planned airship expedition for the following year, but the crowds attending his lectures were less predictable. He had some full halls, but also others with some empty seats. Playing to his American audience, Amundsen astutely highlighted the role and heroic actions of Ellsworth whenever he spoke, emphasizing the American element in the next expedition even though it would be flying the Norwegian flag: "Explorer tells Carnegie Hall Audience that Ellsworth's Rescue of Two Saved Entire Party," read one headline. He had many opinions and an amusing, folksy way of expressing them. "The exploration of this great area can be accomplished in no other way except from the air," he pronounced. "You cannot reach it from a ship because of the ice. I tried that for three years." The failure of the expedition to reach the North Pole must have been on his mind. "I'd rather fly over the Arctic Circle in a dirigible than over Ohio," he declared. "Air conditions are better. The air isn't so bumpy." He conveyed a manner and personality that people wanted to see and hear: a sort of swaggering, devil-be-damned attitude, far removed from the prosaic and mundane aspirations of the average person. Certainly it was an act—Amundsen had a great flare for theatre—but it was also the truth.

Newspapers were fond of reporting on things that had nothing to do with his current adventure at all, just about his life and plans. In Los Angeles he suffered an attack of the flu, and of course the papers reported on it—in case readers wanted to know, Amundsen's physician told him to stay in bed for a day and he was recovering nicely. Reporters would also occasionally remind readers that Amundsen was "at 53, still blessed with the physical strength and enthusiasm of a man twenty years younger." When he was in Edmonton, Alberta, after taking in ski races in Canada's Jasper National Park, a reporter asked him: "What new thrill is there for you after you have conquered both Poles?" Amundsen replied, "Nothing probably, but marriage . . . although I have yet to find the girl." When one reporter from the *New York Times* asked him what his plans were for the coming years, Amundsen answered, "I have been at it a long time, you know. After next year, I might want to leave it to my partner, Mr. Ellsworth." It was the first public hint that he would ever consider retirement.

During this latest tour, Amundsen had some fun with Ellsworth when the two explorers met to do some planning for the next year's expedition. With Ellsworth, Amundsen could drop the frosty reserve that had enveloped him in recent years and reveal his light-hearted self: "Nobody was warmer hearted, no boy could frolic more joyously than Amundsen in his fifties," Ellsworth recalled fondly. Their book *Our Polar Flight: The Amundsen-Ellsworth Polar Flight* was published in the United States in late 1925, to positive reviews and strong sales. (The Norwegian edition had been a bestseller a few months earlier.) The *New York Times* called it "an epic of Arctic adventure," praised Amundsen's "indomitable spirit" and concluded: "Out of the vast 'whiteness,' out of its clutches, away from its sentence of death, the Norwegian Captain, the young American Ellsworth and their stout-hearted companions had flown back to amaze the world that had given them up for lost."

One event sounded a sour note near the end of his nearly five-month American tour: Amundsen went to visit his old companion Dr. Frederick Cook, the same Cook who had been publicly discredited and blacklisted over a decade earlier for his false claims to have reached the North Pole ahead of Robert Peary. Cook was now serving time in Leavenworth Prison in Texas for property fraud. Amundsen stopped in to visit his old friend—"I could not have done less without convincing myself of base ingratitude and contemptible cowardice"—and was beset by reporters looking for a story immediately afterward. Apparently people were still interested in the controversial feud even after a decade had passed. After he had been asked about his opinions on Cook and the North Pole, it was soon in the news—owing either to a misinterpretation of his remarks because of his Norwegian accent or, most likely, a deliberate "misinterpretation" by the reporter—that Amundsen had suggested that Cook's evidence of reaching the North Pole was as solid as Peary's (both claims are now generally considered to be false).

Amundsen heard the news of what he had said about Cook when he was in Montreal, en route to New York. He immediately declared that he had been misquoted, that he had in fact never made any comments of that nature, that the reporter of the "purely mythical interview" in a Fort Worth newspaper had written "pure fabrications." Nevertheless, the damage was done, and his scheduled address to the National Geographic Society in Washington, D.C., was abruptly cancelled, as was his hefty speaker's fee. "There is something wrong somewhere," Amundsen said, as he tried to fend off numerous additional questions about why this had happened, what he really believed and if he was offended or angry. "I don't want to get into any controversy," he replied to one reporter for the *New York Times* on March 3. "I am told I am very indignant, but I am not. I am rather amused than otherwise at the childishness of things. Maybe they will grow up some day."

He left New York for Europe a few days later, on March 6, but not without giving a final interview in the hours before his ship sailed. What more could possibly be said after five months and hundreds of interviews—more than a dozen in the *New York Times* alone—during this lecture tour? He disliked overcoats. Amundsen apparently tugged and itched at the collar of his overcoat "as often as Huck Finn tugged at his uncomfortable new Sunday suit," the reporter noted, before quoting Amundsen: "So many people stare at me when I go without an overcoat in winter that I felt I had to go out and buy this one. I don't like to wear them. It isn't pleasant to feel the long tails of the coat flapping against you when you walk. And I never had a cold when I went without one." He was certainly a charming eccentric in America, and this only served to boost his popularity and gain him more publicity. But now he had to return to Europe quickly; he was supposed to be departing from Spitsbergen in two months, and he hadn't done anything to prepare for the technical side of the next expedition. The giant airship was about to leave Italy, and Amundsen needed to be at the ceremony.

~

Umberto Nobile was born in 1885, in a town in southern Italy near Naples. His father was a middle-ranking government official, and both parents encouraged his education. He graduated from the University of Naples in engineering and soon turned his considerable talents to the new field of aeronautical engineering, particularly airship design. A slight man, compared with Amundsen, he was not an athlete or a sportsman. Handsome and cultured, he fit the image of a university professor and a scientist. At the University of Naples, he founded the Institute of Aerodynamics and was a lecturer in the School of Engineering. He was far more interested in the problems of airship design than in being a pilot, and had limited experience flying the machines that he had devoted his professional career to developing.

After the First World War, Nobile settled in Rome, where he became the director of the military airship facility. When Benito Mussolini and his Fascist Party seized power in October 1922, Nobile and his fellow aeronautical engineers were inducted into the Italian armed forces. By 1925, Nobile was a colonel and worked for the undersecretary for air, one of the four most important officials in the Fascist leadership, where he designed the N-class semi-rigid airships. But Nobile was neither a man of action nor a natural leader, and he probably wouldn't have minded a more behind-the-scenes, technical or consultative role in the Amundsen-Ellsworth expedition. But Mussolini and the Fascist leadership had a different plan.

~

Lighter-than-air airships, dirigibles, or aerostats, are buoyant aircraft that remain in the air without propulsion. They use a series of propellers and small rudders to manoeuvre what is essentially a large floating bag of gas. Airships are unlike airplanes, which use the force of air propelled under a wing to provide their lift; if the motor fails, the airship doesn't come crashing to the ground, a virtue that Amundsen and Riiser-Larsen speculated would ideally suit airships for exploring the Arctic, with its unpredictable climate and terrain, and avoid the problems they had so recently encountered with their flying boats. Jean-Pierre Blanchard first crossed the English Channel in 1785 in a balloon propelled by an odd-looking, self-powered, flapping-wing contraption that had a rudder for steering. There were improvements to this design throughout the nineteenth century, including attempts to use steam power for propulsion. Other power source options included having eight people pedal to turn propeller cranks like rowers in a galley and, by the end of the nineteenth century, electric motors and early internal-combustion engines. The "golden age" of airship design began in the early twentieth century, with countless designs being tested for buoyancy, propulsion and steering.

The original airships were the fully rigid German zeppelins— large cigar-shaped machines with metal frames covered by a stiff outer layer of rubber-coated fabric and filled with hydrogen. The first airship of this design was built in 1900. A non-rigid airship, or blimp, in contrast, is distinguished by having no frame at all. Blimps are essentially balloons that have a compartment or gondola strapped beneath, and they rely on air currents for horizontal movement. The Germans, Italians and French used airships for reconnaissance and bombing raids during the First World War, but with little success, since airplanes proved more useful for military applications—the airships were cumbersome to manoeuvre and highly flammable. In 1919, a British airship made the first double crossing of the Atlantic Ocean. Dirigibles were fashionable in the 1920s, creating thrilling aerial spectacles that captured the public imagination as much as or more than airplanes did. But airships were not without their problems.

There were several high-profile accidents with airships when they were caught in storms and buffeted to the ground.*

Nobile's airship designs were semi-rigid, a hybrid of the two other airship designs, combining much of the strength and manoeuvrability of the zeppelins but without their enormous weight and corresponding size. Amundsen felt they would be the perfect blend of functionality for use in the Arctic, which is what led him into dealings with Nobile and the Fascist government of Italy—a government for which he had little respect or political sympathy. He convinced himself that everything would turn out for the better, and perhaps he would retire thereafter.

In the mid-1920s, disasters had not yet dampened public enthusiasm for airships, and they were widely believed to be the future of long-distance or oceanic travel. The media spectacle of a dirigible cruising over the North Pole was the key reason Amundsen's latest venture was financially possible on such short notice. Despite the infusion of Ellsworth's money, it would be quite a task to get the airship to Spitsbergen. Bases for the airship would have to be constructed near Oslo, at Vadsø on the north Norwegian coast and near Kings Bay on Spitsbergen, requiring the construction of mooring masts, giant hangars and stockpiles of gas and engine fuel, in addition to the other equipment needed for the expedition. Much of this work was under way while Amundsen was on his publicity tour of the United States; it was organized by the Norwegian Aero Club. There were cross-currents of expectations between the principal leaders long before most of them had even beheld the dirigible *Norge* at Kings Bay.

Ellsworth wanted to be named co-leader of the expedition because of his financial contribution, in spite of his lack of experi-

---

*The most famous airship disaster occurred much later, in 1937, when the German airship *Hindenburg* burst into flames in New Jersey after successfully crossing the Atlantic Ocean from Europe. Over a third of its ninety-seven passengers and crew died in the accident. The disaster was caught on film, thereby ending commercial passenger airship service.

ence or skills. Amundsen, as always, wanted to be the overall leader of the expedition, a task for which he was admirably suited, and to be the official discoverer of any new lands they might find in the Arctic; he would be the public face of the expedition. But Nobile considered himself to be far more than a mere hired pilot. As an officer in the Italian military, his task was to highlight the superiority of Italian engineering to the world. Dr. Rolf Thommessen, president of the Norwegian Aero Club, was a great admirer of Mussolini and more than willing to give credit to the Italian contingent of the expedition, even above Amundsen, and above Riiser-Larsen, who had taken airship training in England and would be second in command.

Amundsen should have been more attuned to these competing interests. He had previously observed and noted that problems arose in expeditions when there was a lack of complete authority in one person; different factions could develop and threaten the cohesiveness of an expedition. In Amundsen's very first meeting with Nobile, at Uranienborg, Nobile had made an astonishing offer: that he and the Italian government would give the airship to the expedition for free if it would fly under the Italian flag. Mussolini's interest in the expedition had increased when he realized its enormous potential for publicity. It was an offer that Amundsen had outright refused. It should have been apparent to him then that he was not dealing with a private individual or business: Nobile was an agent of Mussolini, and his airship was actually the property of the Italian state. "I did not realize it at the time," Amundsen recalled, "but it is now clear that it was a deliberate effort on the part of the government to gain for the present Italian political regime in particular, and for the Italian people in general, a world wide advertisement. My idea of a transpolar flight was thus subtly to be appropriated as their own by the Italians, and my skill in Arctic exploration was to be utilized as the means of a dramatic achievement for which the Italians would take the credit."

Before Amundsen had even returned to Europe, complications arose around the original agreement: Nobile felt his contribution was large enough to warrant his being the coauthor of the official book. Amundsen, who counted on lectures and book sales for his income, refused to agree to this. Then Nobile wanted the expedition's name changed to the Amundsen-Ellsworth-Nobile Transpolar Flight, which Amundsen and Ellsworth were forced to concede, although newspapers in the United States still referred to it by its original name. The *New York Times* on March 14, for example, ran an article headlined "The Coming Polar Flight—By Amundsen," wherein it was revealed that Amundsen and Ellsworth, whose portraits featured prominently, were "ready for hardships." But the three co-leaders also argued over who would have final decision-making authority over where and when the airship would fly. It was finally agreed that Amundsen and Ellsworth would be the "expedition leaders" while Nobile would hold the title of "airship commander." They would vote on any disagreements. Nobile wanted most of the crew to be Italian, while Amundsen and the Norwegian Aero Club, naturally, wanted them to be Norwegian. Eventually it was agreed that only six of the sixteen-person crew, including Nobile, would be Italian. But Ellsworth was concerned the American participation was being minimized, and he demanded that American newspapers be offered first rights to the story. Ellsworth and Amundsen had also made the usual promotional deals involving stamps and postcards, as well as various additional serial rights to their story and images, that would be penned either by themselves or by others.

Amundsen and Ellsworth were essentially aligned to exclude Nobile; after all, they were already "companions in danger and in achievement." Amundsen had no problem in sharing the fame with his American friend, but he did not want to share it with the Italians, though the Italian contribution, and particularly Nobile's, was arguably just as important. Amundsen probably wouldn't have been so opposed to sharing credit with Nobile if the colonel hadn't been an officer in the Fascist government, and if he had felt that Nobile was, like Amundsen and Ellsworth, working toward the same personal goal, rather than being more concerned with creating propaganda. Not only were there potential rivalries in the leadership; Amundsen and Nobile had each chosen key loyal men as part of their contingent, creating two factions that were divided on linguistic and cultural lines as well as personal loyalty. The Norwegian crew were ready to quit over Nobile's leadership before the airship even left Rome, and Ellsworth was apparently jealous of Riiser-Larsen's role and didn't want the tall Norwegian to have any role in writing the official account of the adventure. There was plenty of intrigue and jockeying for prestige, resulting in squabbling that only grew with the scope of the undertaking.

Amundsen included Riiser-Larsen, Oscar Omdal and his old companion Oscar Wisting, who had only recently returned from being stuck in the ice with the *Maud*. He reasoned that since Wisting been with him at the South Pole, he was entitled to be at the North Pole too if he wished. In fact, Amundsen offered a right of first refusal to the entire crew of the *Maud*, loyalty to his crew being extremely important to him, more so than loyalty to his family: he left behind his nephew Gustav S. Amundsen. At the last minute, however, he displaced the Russian radio operator Gennadij Olonkin, who had served on the *Maud* for many years, with a Norwegian man, to ensure that Norwegians on the voyage were not outnumbered by Italians. Amundsen was apparently and belatedly realizing the overriding politics of the voyage, in which nationality trumped loyalty. In hindsight, the personality problems, from the leaders to the air crew and the ground crew, were so hopelessly politicized and partisan, putting many qualities above competence and skills, that a positive response to any disaster could hardly have been expected.

Nobile's task of ensuring that the ship could cross thousands of kilometres from Spitsbergen over the North Pole to Alaska was perhaps not as simple as Amundsen thought it was. The known problems associated with airplanes were being exchanged for a new set of challenges associated with airships. Amundsen would be relying on the technical expertise of men he didn't know, dealing with problems he didn't fully understand. For example, hydrogen gas expands with increases in elevation and temperature, both of which vary throughout each day. When pressure in an airship became too high, it had to be "valved off" to prevent a rupture in its outer skin. To counter the loss of gas throughout the trip, ballast would have be jettisoned to keep the airship balanced and under control. The trip over the North Pole to Alaska was planned to take about fifty hours of flight time, with no place to land or refuel or re-ballast, so Nobile would have to monitor ballast and hydrogen carefully to ensure that the dirigible had enough of each to get to Alaska. Nobile, for his part, had no real experience with snow and ice, never having seen either, except on his winter trip to Oslo a few months earlier. Amundsen wrote that Nobile kept slipping in the snow when walking. He grew more nervous about the expedition's prospects.

Piloting an airship was anything but a routine exercise. The *Norge* was 106 metres long and 19.6 metres wide through the middle. It was propelled by three 245-horsepower Mayback internal-combustion engines and could easily cruise at about 80 kilometres per hour in the right conditions. When Nobile was calculating the weight of the men and equipment, he had little room for error, since he had already used up most of the excess weight that the airship could carry in strengthening and reinforcing the hull. Although Amundsen and Ellsworth were annoyed at Nobile's preoccupation with minutiae such as what clothing each man would be wearing, Nobile had reason to worry: he felt that the airship was at the threshold of its carrying capacity for such an unpredictable flight.

Amundsen later discovered that Nobile's clothing and luggage restrictions apparently applied more to Amundsen and the Norwegians than to Nobile and the Italians; unbeknownst to Amundsen or Ellsworth, Nobile and his men loaded additional cases of equipment, mostly clothes and uniforms. Nobile also brought along his tiny pet dog, Titina.

At a ceremony held on the grassy fields of the airport in Rome stood Mussolini, impeccably outfitted in trim suit and bowler hat rather than the Fascist black shirt. Amundsen and Ellsworth were likewise attired in their finest suits, while Nobile stood erect in his colonel's uniform. They all gazed solemnly at the looming bulk of the airship and watched as the Italian flag was taken down from the stern of the newly named *Norge* and the Norwegian flag was hoisted in its place. Then there were bombastic nationalistic speeches in Italian and the raising of the Fascist salute. Mussolini, his face inscrutable, folded the Italian flag, handed it to Nobile, and said loudly: "This is to be dropped on the ice at the Pole!" The crowd dutifully cheered, roused by the thought of an Italian airship reaching that famous spot. More speeches followed before the congregation broke up and the men went their separate ways. Amundsen noted with distaste that Thommessen had agreed to Mussolini's request to have the original name of the airship, N1, and some distinctive Italian colours remain on the vessel. It was far too late to back out now, but Amundsen was feeling an increasing unease about the choice of Nobile as airship commander.

A few weeks later the *Norge* was ready to fly again. It dropped its mooring cable and set off for Spitsbergen on a round-about journey that would take it to publicity stints in England and Oslo before pressing on to Leningrad and then north to Spitsbergen. The Norwegian and Italian crews were aboard for the brief European tour, continuing their training on airship operation under Nobile's direction. The tour was meant to generate publicity for the upcoming flight; many people had never before seen a dirigible, and its mere presence was a public spectacle. Amundsen and Ellsworth travelled by train instead, delivering a few speeches and ceremonial lectures before crossing the choppy, storm-bound waters to Kings Bay on April 12, 1926.

The ocean was clear of ice, but the mountains and town were still smothered in snow. At the tiny mining settlement, work continued on the mooring mast and the hangar. Both should have been completed, but severe winter storms had delayed their construction. The Norwegian Aero Club was responsible for the hangar, an enormous three-sided but roofless building near Kings Bay that would protect the *Norge* from the Arctic winds while the crew awaited perfect conditions for departure. All the materials for the enormous wooden frame and canvas sides had been hauled north to the remote spot by ship at great expense in the previous months. While Amundsen began overseeing the final details, the *Norge* waited in Leningrad for the hangar's completion before making the journey to Spitsbergen. On April 29, all eyes watched as an American ship steamed into Kings Bay. On board were visitors who were not entirely unexpected, nor were they entirely welcome.

16

A Massed Attack on
the Polar Regions

*Think of what it will mean, to fly in comparative
comfort and security above treacherous ice which has
threatened other explorers at every step. Never before
have I entered an expedition with so few misgivings.*

KINGS BAY IN 1926 consisted of twenty-two houses and a
company store clustered around a mine shaft. One American
newspaper writer rhapsodized, "[A]ll about, the high silent white
peaks shine down in the reflected sunlight dazzling to the eyes of
the 'tenderfoot.'" Giant snow banks filled the spaces between the
wooden houses, which "looked more like summer cottages at the
seashore than homes for the Arctic. All need a stove in every room."
The reporter commented on northern hospitality and the friendliness of the people, but added, with a dramatic flourish Amundsen
would have appreciated, "the Arctic smiles now, but behind the
silent hills is death."

In the summer of 1926, Amundsen was not alone in his attempt
to reach the North Pole. American and British teams were also planning polar flights. In April, the *New York Times* had announced:

"Massed Attack on the Polar Regions Begins Soon." Tiny Kings Bay was a hive of activity as news correspondents from around Europe and America arrived to report on the spectacle of competing national teams racing into the Arctic wastes to seek glory and fame in their new-fangled flying machines, and perhaps to announce the existence of the earth's final undiscovered islands. There was also a competing Norwegian-German airship expedition, which planned to cross over the North Pole the following year, using a much larger, fully rigid airship of German design, and Australian aviator George Hubert Wilkins was leading an American expedition to fly to the North Pole from Point Barrow, Alaska, in spite of Amundsen's failed attempt from there two years earlier. There were even reports of a Russian overland expedition.

Bernt Balchen, a young Norwegian pilot and air force lieutenant who was part of Amundsen's ground crew, recorded the arrival of a mysterious ship that was part of the "massed attack": "All morning long we have paused now and then in our work, and glanced at the smoking funnel on the horizon, and muttering uneasily to each other. We are not sure yet. It could be a supply ship for the mine, or a sealer headed for the ice pack. We look over the tar paper roofs of the mining camp, toward the superintendent's house on the hill where Captain Amundsen is living. Has he heard yet, does he know?" The ship neared Kings Bay before it radioed ashore. It was the American ship *Chantier*, carrying Lieutenant Commander Richard E. Byrd of the U.S. Navy, his pilot, Floyd Bennett, fifty men who formed the expedition party, and two Fokker Trimotor airplanes packed in crates, one named the *Josephine Ford*. The young and ambitious Byrd, who had made an exploratory flight in the vicinity of Greenland the previous year, was now planning to fly to the North Pole and return along the same route Amundsen and Ellsworth had attempted the previous year. Byrd later claimed that "[a]ll three of us—Amundsen, Wilkins and myself—are seeking to discover new land and also to conquer the

Arctic from the air. It is not exactly a race, but there is an element of competition in there."

Naturally, some of Amundsen's crew were suspicious and un-friendly. "All work at our base has halted," recalled Balchen, "and the men of the Amundsen expedition stand in silent groups along the bluff. We resent this foreign ship coming here to our country to snatch the prize, which we feel belongs to Captain Amundsen alone. We of his party are loyal to him to the point of worship, and any one of us would lay down our life without question for one of the greatest of all living explorers." Balchen's colourful description then focused on Amundsen, who had skied to inspect the newcomers. "We all look up to the lone figure on the hill behind us. People al-ways turn to look at Roald Amundsen, as their eyes would be drawn to the tallest mountain. . . . His face is expressionless and we cannot read it. Beneath the thick tufts of his eyebrows, white as hoarfrost, his eyes in the deep sockets are hidden in shadow. His cheeks are leathery and folded in hard creases, with a fine network of wrinkles spreading out from the corners of his eyes like a map of all the dog trails he has run. The most prominent feature of his face is the thin and arched nose, which gives him the look of an eagle. It is a face carved in a cliff, the face of a Viking."

Amundsen's crew stood watching their leader on the ridge, wait-ing for him to speak, "but he pivots on his skis without a word and strides back to the headquarters building." Amundsen never shied from a race—it was good for publicity—and he probably didn't care much whether Byrd flew over the North Pole first; the North Pole, everyone believed at the time, had already been visited first by Peary, and the object of Amundsen's expedition was grander in scope: the *Norge* would cross over the Pole and continue through the unex-plored regions of the Arctic Ocean to Alaska. But Amundsen knew that if Byrd failed, the *Norge* would be commandeered into the res-cue operation, probably ruining the chances for his ambitious Arc-tic crossing that year. Furthermore, the publicity stemming from any disaster that befell Byrd would detract from Amundsen's own objectives.

The July 1925 issue of *Popular Science Monthly* earnestly profiled the polar race and its personalities, dubbing it "the most sensational sporting event in human history." In its June issue, it had proclaimed, "None of us need be surprised if from the desolate North is flashed the news of some of the most far-reaching events of modern times—events that will affect the lives of all of us." *Boy's Life* headlined its lead story "The Attack on the Pole," filling it with much talk of brave men doing battle with the bitter Arctic. Various other publications displayed similar sensational headlines, some suggesting that the race was the greatest heroic undertaking since the war, if not "in human history." Amundsen himself provided a thoughtful comment: "Think of what it will mean, to fly in comparative comfort and security above treacherous ice which has threatened other explorers at every step. Never before have I entered an expedition with so few misgivings."

In addition to the usual raft of reporters for numerous newspapers, there were now also cinematographers with their primitive movie cameras filming the goings-on at Spitsbergen. The newspapers ran a near-daily update on the participants, their equipment and, of course, the weather. Unlike the media that had been available to cover the race to the South Pole a decade and a half earlier, advances in wireless communication meant that regular updates were possible and indeed became common. In the *New York Times*, the Amundsen-Ellsworth polar expedition was covered so extensively that some updates merely indicated that "snow and winds keep *Norge* in shed," continuing with a description of the snow and the winds and just how they were keeping the *Norge* in its shed. Other articles speculated on what Amundsen expected to discover, where he planned to land in Alaska and where he would seek refuge in the event of disaster. Nearly every literate person must have known about the event, given the quantity of print coverage.

Every few days, reporters stationed in Kings Bay also sent back reports about Byrd's preparations, including the details of how he unloaded his planes from the ship, how the construction of the runway was progressing and when a supply ship arrived. Of great interest was the ways in which the rival groups entertained each other in the isolated settlement. Amundsen and Ellsworth invited Byrd and Bennett and several others to "the big mess hall where four languages are spoken at every meal. There are no flowers in Spitsbergen yet, so the table decorations of sprouting onions in tin cups were the only green things on the island. It was difficult to know whether to eat or admire such blossoms," the reporter admitted.

The explorers were on their best behaviour with the press; however, the problem was that Byrd and Amundsen had each sold exclusive rights to the documentation of their adventures, but to competing syndicates. The result was that one group's reporters couldn't photograph, film or write about the activities of the rival group without violating exclusivity contracts. Amundsen would be in violation of his contract if he allowed the media following Byrd's enterprise to document his own expedition in any way, and vice versa. But Kings Bay was a small place, and the media really couldn't help but stumble over one another. A sort of media war broke out as each group of journalists tried secretly to get a scoop from the other, particularly after the *Norge* cruised into its hangar on May 7 after a difficult ocean crossing from Europe. The ground crew manoeuvred the spectacular cigar-shaped airship into its hangar with ropes and pulleys. The hangar dominated the scenery around Kings Bay and was impossible to ignore, being 30 metres high and 110 metres long.

There were "undercover operations and secret infiltrations," according to Balchen. "Scouts from the rival syndicates creep past each other, the Amundsen raiders disguised in American sailor hats, and the Byrd snipers wearing Norwegian ski caps." With no night, thus no darkness, to conceal furtive actions, the task was made more difficult, but even so a flash bulb might pop and motion-picture cameras whirr near the *Josephine Ford* and the *Norge* when least expected. "A skulking still photographer pops out of an empty crate to click a close up of the *Josephine Ford* or as we enter the dirigible hangar we see a pair of heels disappearing out the other end, the scurrying figure bowlegged under a heavy camera and tripod."

At first there was some unhelpful competition between the two expeditionary groups, born of the crews' excessive loyalty to their commanders. When Byrd wanted to unload the components of his airplane at the dock, the Norwegian captain of the coal boat stationed there refused to move his ship, so Byrd and his men were forced to haul the equipment ashore across the ice floes that clogged the bay. Although Amundsen had no authority over a local coal ship, Byrd felt that Amundsen was trying, however passively, to obstruct his efforts even while remaining outwardly friendly. Ellsworth felt that he and Amundsen had "every reason to be disgruntled" for what he believed was a trespass on their prior right to be in Kings Bay. Byrd's presence was feared to be damaging their chances of recouping their enormous expenses by flooding the market with more books, lectures and motion pictures. Saturation was an uncomfortable prospect.

Amundsen, however, could not retreat into defensive partisanship. He did not want a repeat of the competitive situation with Scott and the race to the South Pole a decade and half earlier. Amundsen's initial seemingly unhelpful attitude toward Byrd probably stemmed from a fear of violating the exclusive media contracts he had signed. After Byrd had failed in several attempts at a lift-off, Amundsen offered the aid that ensured Byrd's success. In particular, he got his men to help with the selection of a suitable location for Byrd's runway and with its construction. He also advised Byrd on the best time to attempt a lift-off, provided tips on when the ice was hardest and therefore offered the least resistance, and supplied Byrd and his pilot with emergency supplies and equipment—snowshoes, warm boots and a small sledge—none of which they had brought.

Perhaps most importantly, Balchen helped construct stronger skis for the *Josephine Ford* after two had cracked during a test flight, something he said he did at Amundsen's request but which Byrd at the time felt was done in spite of Amundsen (Balchen and Byrd later became friends). Byrd could hardly have gotten into the air without Amundsen's help: "We had much to learn," he admitted privately. When Byrd commented that Amundsen was being very generous to a competitor, Amundsen replied that he didn't feel they were competing but were engaged in different facets of the same goal; that Byrd was merely flying to the North Pole, while Amundsen and the *Norge* were crossing to Alaska—what else could he say? "Nothing stimulates like competition," Amundsen claimed, "nothing encourages exploration more. It seems absurd that all should stay away from a place that someone had announced his intentions to explore."

Nobile had wanted the *Norge* to depart before Byrd did, but perhaps to counter the lingering notion that he had been devious in rushing to the South Pole without informing Scott of his intentions, Amundsen flatly denied Nobile the chance to ready the *Norge* to leave before Byrd had completed his flight. It was the first public disagreement between the two proud men. Amundsen was determined to give Byrd his chance to fly to the North Pole, but Nobile was displeased at losing a chance for further glory for himself, his airship and Fascist Italy, probably in that order. Also on May 7, a cable arrived from Point Barrow, where Wilkins had finally brought his planes. Wilkins asked about the weather in Spitsbergen: was it good for a crossing from Alaska? But he would have no better luck at Point Barrow than Amundsen had had in 1923; his airplanes were damaged in the test flights, and he was forced into an ignominious retreat.

In Kings Bay, Amundsen, Ellsworth and their crew anxiously waited for good weather—clear skies and low winds—while Nobile worked on the *Norge*, repairing a damaged engine and adding glycerine to the cooling system to prevent the engine from freezing. Balchen was hastily giving skiing lessons to the five willing Italians, who had never seen snow—"the poor souls longed for their sunny Naples," he wrote. On May 8, Byrd and his men had finally readied the *Josephine Ford* for the flight, but the airplane still couldn't lift off, and Balchen suggested that Byrd try again at midnight, when the snow would be firmer and offer less resistance. Its engines roared to life once again, and this time the *Josephine Ford* shot down the icy runway and lifted into a clear sky. When silence returned to the base, the men tried to get on with their regular duties; but there was an edge of anxiety that disrupted everything. Occasionally they stopped to turn and listen while scanning the northern sky.

The next day they were sitting down to dinner in the mess hall, about fifteen and a half hours after takeoff, according to Balchen, when "one of the Italian soldiers comes bounding into the mess hall, out of breath. He chatters in broken English, 'she come—a motor!'" They dropped their forks and rushed to welcome the incoming airplane, photographers and reporters readying their equipment. Because Byrd was arriving several hours earlier than expected and his American media crew were still aboard their ship, it was Amundsen's motion picture crew who filmed the momentous event. As Byrd and Bennett climbed out of the machine onto the snow, Amundsen organized "nine good Norwegian cheers." A photograph shows Byrd and Bennett dressed in their flying furs, Amundsen and Ellsworth standing on either side, shaking their hands and congratulating them. Amundsen probably should have been a little curious about the timing of the flight—Byrd had returned ahead of schedule and with broken navigational equipment, and he claimed to have made the return flight by dead reckoning. Given the known speed of the Fokker airplane that Byrd and Bennett were flying, it has since been established that reaching the North Pole would have been impossible in that timeframe. On that day, though, Byrd was heralded as a hero for his aeronautical feat.

On May 11, Nobile pronounced the *Norge* ready to fly. Cables were attached to the enormous airship, and dozens of men were hauling it slowly from its hangar onto the snowy field when an unexpected wind blew up partway through the operation. There had been disagreements among the organizers. Nobile had slaved all night, getting the airship loaded and ready for the flight because he was planning to leave around one in the morning, when it was coldest and the airship would have the greatest lift. But as the Norwegian contingent failed to arrive, Nobile anxiously waited for hours, valving-off gas three times as the temperature rose, until Amundsen, Ellsworth and Riiser-Larsen slowly trudged over after having had their breakfast. Nobile, tired, hungry and irritable after his vigil, noticed that the wind had picked up again and wanted to cancel the flight for that day. Amundsen, however, dismissed Nobile's concerns as "nervous excitement," and Riiser-Larsen proceeded to organize hauling the *Norge* from its hangar while Nobile stood by, nervously "supervising"—a quick gust could spin the airship into the side of hangar and break a delicate fin or an engine. No one knows why the Norwegians arrived so late, or indeed why Nobile didn't just go and rouse them from their cabins, but the language barrier is the probable culprit: the Italians didn't speak Norwegian and the Norwegians didn't speak Italian, and Ellsworth spoke neither language. So English became the operational language of the expedition, even though many of the crew did not speak English except in the most rudimentary fashion.

Fortunately the *Norge* was not damaged by the gusts, and the flight crew quickly boarded. The ground crew let go of the ropes and the dirigible shot into the air, propelling its way toward the North Pole in a cloudless blue sky. As the icy peaks of Spitsbergen receded in the distance, the North Pole was 1,200 kilometres away and the cruising speed of the *Norge* was about 80 kilometres per hour. Byrd and Bennett, who had fired up the *Josephine Ford*, flew alongside the *Norge* for a while before returning when the airship reached the pack ice. The next day, newspapers around the world ran special editions to celebrate the launch. In Italy, in an incident that didn't augur well, it was proclaimed that the airship was sailing "under an Italian flag, in the spirit of fascism." Norwegian newspapers were equally possessive. The *Norge* flight had become politics, not mere entertainment, and certainly not science—there were no scientists on board.

As the *Norge* buzzed ever northward across the frigid expanse, wispy patches of polar fog snaked across the ice. The only signs of life were occasional seals, polar bear tracks and a few birds. After nearly a day of travel the fog cleared to reveal, once again, a featureless, wind-blown plain of white nothingness. It was empty, eerie and haunting in its desolation, particularly for anyone not used to the polar environment. On the other hand, it was a routine flight in terms of the activity required of the crew, distinguished chiefly for its cold temperatures and the men's trepidation at entering the unknown.

All the crew had small tasks to do as they operated various propulsion or steering machines. Piloting an airship was certainly not a one-person job. There were ten men in the cabin, and six others out in the rigging checking the gas cells and valves, while others checked on and maintained the engines at the rear of the enormous airship. Men from the cabin crew continuously rounded the vessel on its catwalks, their eyes always scanning for possible problems, spelling each other off when they could no longer endure the bitter cold. Nobile's dog stayed close to her master, though her presence was technically a breach of the rules. (Amundsen overlooked this, perhaps in a spirit of generosity.) Cooking on board ship was prohibited, to avoid the risk of an explosion resulting from escaping gas. It can hardly have been a relaxing flight for the crew, clothed in fur garments in the unheated cabin, comforted with thermoses of coffee and tea and cold sandwiches, hardboiled eggs frozen as solid as rocks, all the while wondering about gas leaks.

Most of the actual piloting was done by Oscar Wisting, as Lieutenant Emil Horgen controlled the lift and horizontal rudder wheels. Riiser-Larsen was the principle navigator, doing the calculations by hand and relaying the information to Nobile, who then made judgments and told the pilots what to do. The radio operator kept busy relaying messages of the airship's progress across the top of the world to eager newspapers. Although there was a perpetual drone from the engines and occasional engine trouble caused by frozen water vapour, the only real danger came from ice forming on the dirigible as it entered fog, which made it heavier and harder to control when its valves and flaps jammed. Whereas it needed to be low to the ground for better visibility in the fog, it risked a deadly ice build-up at lower altitudes as well.

Other navigators, including Ellsworth, were busy with sextant observations, sun readings and magnetic compass bearings, in an effort to determine position. The *Norge* neared the North Pole at around 1:30 a.m. on May 12. As Riiser-Larsen squinted into his sextant, he announced: "Ready the flags. Now we are there." Nobile called for the engines to be cut, and all went quiet as the giant dirigible slowly drifted over an unremarkable icy spot. It then began to slowly circle the lifeless location at about 100 metres elevation. In the great cabin, Amundsen stared over at his old companion Wisting, who had been at the South Pole with him. Now they were together at the opposite end of the earth, the first people in history to obtain this distinction. They did not say anything, merely exchanging a quiet handshake. No doubt it was an emotional if undemonstrative moment. Amundsen, then Ellsworth, and then Nobile, brought out their national flags, attached to sharp metal poles, and dropped them to the ice below, where they stuck upright, fluttering slightly in the wind.

Nobile had firmly told Amundsen and Ellsworth to bring only small flags, about the size of handkerchiefs, to keep the weight down on the airship, so they stared in astonishment when he brought forth an enormous Italian flag, carried reverently in a special casket under Mussolini's orders. Nobile also brought forth several other pennants and flags representing various cities and associations, which he dumped out the window of the cabin making the airship look, in Amundsen's words, "like a circus wagon in the skies." One of Nobile's fluttering flags was so large that it drifted toward one of the engines and was caught in the slowly spinning propellers, nearly damaging the rotor. Amundsen laughed at Nobile, annoyed both at the duplicity and the Italian's conceit. It was reminiscent of the time when Nobile told all the men on the voyage to reduce their clothing allowance and then provided all of his own men with ceremonial uniforms. Nobile ignored the derision and wrote in his log book: "Planted the Italian Flag at the Pole." From here all directions led south.

How many men could claim to have been at the North Pole by 1926? Frederick Cook's claim to have been the first arrival had never really been accepted, and he was widely believed to have provided fraudulent evidence. Peary was widely believed at the time to have been there on foot, but that claim has been challenged and is no longer universally accepted. He may not have been deceitful, but he failed to account for the drifting of pack ice in his calculations and was overly generous in his estimations of the distance he travelled over the ice. He probably never came within a reasonable distance of the North Pole, certainly not enough to be credited with attaining it. As for Byrd, the controversy over his flight was to come in the following years, when the true distance he claimed to have flown was calculated to have been unrealistically far for that type of airplane and that duration of flight. The crew of the *Norge*, on the other hand, were the first to indisputably reach the North Pole. All of Amundsen's records have stood the test of time. This is something uncommon for that era, when assessing an explorer's claims was difficult and yet the fame, prestige and money awarded for claiming an exotic geographical conquest were great enough to propel men into fraudulent claims for their achievements.

After an hour of circling the North Pole, the *Norge*'s engines roared and the airship turned to cross the unknown expanse toward Alaska. For Amundsen and Ellsworth, the exciting part of the journey was just beginning—the search for new land. Every hour brought never-before-seen terrain and the possibility of bumping into the mountain range Peary claimed to have sighted years earlier. The two explorers hovered near the airship's windows, their eyes scanning the horizon for any variation in the ice plain. Meanwhile, exhaustion was beginning to take its toll on the crew. They had already had a night of interrupted sleep before they left, and then another aboard the airship, where the incessant noise of the engines and the howling of the wind, freezing temperatures and cramped conditions were not conducive to relaxation or sleep. Discarded thermoses and food littered the cramped cabin floor. Although excitement had accompanied them to the North Pole, weariness now set in. Nobile got some sleep—a lot, according to Amundsen; barely a few hours, Nobile claimed afterward.

A couple of hours after they left the pole, mysterious pools of fog began to appear. They grew larger, until finally the *Norge* was enveloped in fog. Not only did this hamper visibility, frustrating Amundsen and Ellsworth, but it began to slowly condense into ice on the exterior of the airship. Eventually the ice formed an enormous crust and made the airship much heavier, ruining Nobile's carefully arrived-at weight-to-gas-and-ballast calculations.

Occasionally chunks of ice would break off and slide down the canvas coat of the airship, falling into its engines. When a chunk hit the whirling propeller blades it was shot into the outer shell, rending it in several places. The real worry was that the shards of ice would puncture a gas chamber or damage a propeller blade, either stalling or deflating the airship, and causing it to crash on the ice. So Nobile reduced the rotational speed of the outer engines, slowing the airship down and prolonging their journey. The irregular positioning of the remaining and accumulating ice continued to create a great danger, however: it was forming more heavily on the bow of the ship, pulling the nose down until the crew's frenzied shifting of ballast compensated for it. Soon ice coated the aerial wire that dangled behind the airship, too, cutting off all contact with the outside world; a situation only Amundsen regarded as normal. Not only could the *Norge* not report its position and observations, it no longer had access to updated weather reports in Alaska. Rescue ships were put on alert because no one knew why radio contact with the airship had ended. But no rescue ship could reach the crew where they were now. Nobile later accused Amundsen of deliberately cutting radio contact, for which there is no evidence; but the dire situation no doubt heightened the tension and excitement of the expedition in a way that regular check-ins could never do.

After a few hours, the fog dissipated and the airship droned onward, looking for land. The crew saw no land, only ice covering a vast sea. Then, as chunks of ice continued to slide off the exterior of the airship, causing more tears in the outer coating, Riiser-Larsen called out "Land ahead to starboard!" And when the crew took their measurements, they determined that the *Norge* was drifting along the north coast of Alaska. The last great unknown region of the earth had been crossed, and there was no new land to be found. Later that morning the airship cruised slowly over a frozen beach. Amundsen thought the land looked like Point Barrow, but with visibility poor he couldn't be certain. Pushed by an increasing tailwind and turbulent conditions, the ship headed along the coast until the crew saw some Inuit below, looking up at them and waving. Then they saw the red roofs of a caribou farm that Amundsen and Omdal knew to be near Wainwright; in fact, they could see Amundsen's cabin, where people stood on the roof cheering and waving. Among the crowds were George Wilkins and his co-pilot, the Norwegian Ben Eilson, the other competitors in that summer's race to the North Pole, who had been unable to fly after their earlier crash due to fog.

But the voyage wasn't over. The final day of the four-day flight was the most dangerous and most difficult. The men were exhausted. Riiser-Larsen reported having hallucinations, and others fell into stunned slumber where they stood, having slept little since leaving Kings Bay. Amundsen and Nobile were faced with yet another decision: take the long route, following around the coast to Nome, or turn inland and over the mountains to reach Nome directly. These mountains had never been crossed by a flying machine and their elevation was unknown, making the trip particularly dangerous.

Soon the decision was made for them. Erratic winds began to buffet the *Norge* and more ice began to form as the airship drifted uncontrollably out over the Bering Strait. The crew scrambled out along the rigging to knock off the ice, its weight threatening to drag the craft into the frigid waters. The men were poorly equipped to respond to this emergency. Many had received only basic training, and they were still unable to converse in a common language. The airship was alternately driven low over the water and tossed into the air. "I cannot attempt to give any details of this breathless race under the implacable fog, among the hills, over the ice of Kotzbue Bay, over frozen lagoons," Nobile wrote afterward. "Who can tell what route we followed, or how we wound in and out of the fog? Even today I can still live through the emotions of this wild flight under the fog, without knowing where we were or where we were going; but the recollection is confused, as in a nightmare."

The temperature fluctuated with the *Norge*'s altitude changes, making it nearly impossible for Nobile to accurately estimate how much hydrogen to valve off in order to keep the airship as high as possible. There was no more ballast to drop to make the craft lighter, but if Nobile released too much gas it would be too heavy when the storm cleared. Should they fly under or over the fog? What was the weight of the ice on the outside of the ship? When the airship finally made its way back toward the coast, Nobile feared that a rogue gust of wind would knock the airship into the mountainous terrain. If it did hit, there might only be seconds to jump from the damaged airship before it exploded—the vast volume of hydrogen would go up in flames instantly with a spark of electricity or an open flame. So the airship continued south along the coast, weaving between hills, trying to keep below the fog. Villages appeared and disappeared, people waved. There was little the crew could do to change their predicament.

Riiser-Larsen decided to check their position by using his sextant to take a reading on the sun. He climbed along the ladders to the bow to get out from underneath the shadow of the airship, as Nobile was steering it higher to get above the fog. As soon as the airship cleared the fog, the sun heated up its surface and the hydrogen gas expanded, swelling the chambers to bursting. The automatic valves started releasing gas, but not fast enough to solve the immediate crisis of the chambers nearly bursting. The airship was still pointed up for the ascent. Nobile desperately spun the elevator wheel, but it didn't respond. In desperation he began yelling in Italian and gesticulating wildly in the direction of the front of the airship, while the Norwegians looked on in bewilderment.

Only after a few agonizing moments did they realize what he was saying. They rushed to the nose of the airship, clambering along the gangplank and shifting their weight until the airship slowly tilted downward before its gas chambers exploded. But now the airship was plunging precipitously through the fog toward the ground. The men dashed back to the cabin. During a period of only a couple of minutes, the *Norge* had soared to 1,650 metres before plummeting to little over 180 metres while being blown inland with the wind.

On another occasion Nobile forgot to respond to Riiser-Larsen's shout to fly up—he stood at the elevator wheel stunned and unresponsive, probably literally asleep at the wheel, while the airship roared toward a hilltop, until Riiser-Larsen pushed him aside and cranked on the wheel. The ship reversed direction again, barely avoiding the ground. And once, they came so close to a hilltop in the fog that the dangling antenna hooked on some rocks and snapped off. Although Amundsen saw these incidents as yet further evidence of Nobile's poor flying ability, they more likely pointed to the unsuitability of using hydrogen-filled dirigibles to fly in regions where temperatures and winds fluctuate wildly.

More storms followed along the coastline while the *Norge* bucked in the headwinds, at one point making no progress at all. Nobile, totally exhausted, fell asleep in Amundsen's chair. Nevertheless they continued, and a few hours later spied the roofs of houses below. They agreed to land the airship, even though Amundsen knew the community wasn't Nome. The *Norge* cruised over a three-masted ship in the frozen bay and readied an enormous anchor and the landing ropes. But it was still not over. Before anyone had climbed down, a sudden gust pushed the airship toward the shore, pulling loose the anchor. Nobile cranked the valves to release hydrogen. The great machine began to sag and shrink, accompanied by the sounds of a tonne of ice cracking and falling from the outer shell. Its terrified crew slid down the ropes while the great beast collapsed around its skeletal framework, limp and unresponsive, in a field not far from the cottages. A group of onlookers gathered round, quietly staring at the deflated behemoth. Where were they? "Teller" came the reply—still about 160 kilometres north of Nome, but safe enough. The *New York Times* promptly ran a curious story, "Amundsen Visited Teller Back in 1922," detailing his previous visit to the community in the *Maud* to purchase reindeer meat.

The world's final patch of undiscovered geography was discovered not from the deck of a heaving ship or from behind a pack of panting dogs, but from inside the technological wonder of a flying ship, where the explorers were curiously removed from the event. Outside the window of the droning machine the surface of the earth had passed unremarkably beneath them, as if in a dream. It was a strangely modern end to the age of exploration, ushering in an age of passive observation, in which the machine was as much the hero as the people who operated it.

Amundsen and Ellsworth didn't fully appreciate the technical challenges of flying an airship under any conditions, let alone in the Arctic. They just wanted someone to pilot the craft according to their instructions, much as they hired men for many other jobs requiring technical proficiency. Nobile was the wrong person for this arrangement—picky, proud, an academic and a high-ranking military officer—he was a man of distinction in Italy who felt he should have been given greater respect in the Arctic. When this was not forthcoming from Amundsen and Ellsworth, Nobile felt no compulsion to honour his agreements with them. He was also the wrong man by profession. He wasn't a pilot for hire, a private individual looking for employment; he was a high-ranking officer in a foreign armed force, and as such was not entirely at liberty to make his own personal decisions. Clearly, Amundsen and Nobile were incompatible personalities grappling for respect and leadership; but it was the fallout from publicity that turned irritation to hatred.

After a few days in Teller, Amundsen, Ellsworth, Wisting and Omdal boarded a launch for Nome. The wireless in Teller wasn't working, and Amundsen wanted to get his story out. Nobile and Riiser-Larsen stayed behind to supervise the packing of the airship for its trip back to the southern United States, though it was severely damaged and might never fly again. The Teller wireless transmitter was soon repaired, and Nobile sent off his own press report to the world detailing the adventures of the *Norge*, highlighting his own and the Italian role. This news was received with great fanfare in Italy, where 100,000 fans cheered a speech marking the event given by Mussolini, who was flanked by a large Italian flag alongside smaller Norwegian and American flags. According to his contract, Nobile had no legal right to do this. The contract stated that "Nobile shall be under obligation not to publish any papers, articles, photographs or designs relating to this expedition without the authorization of the Norwegian Aero Club. . . . [This] includes radio or other telegraphic communications sent from the airship or from land stations during stops." He was entitled to send a communication to the Italian government "on the condition that these communications shall in no case be published before the press-telegrams"— which, of course, they were.

Amundsen and Ellsworth finalized their version of the story later in May and sent it to the American newspapers that had paid a great deal of money for the story (first to the *New York Times*, which had paid $55,000 for exclusive first rights). But Nobile's attempt to scoop them damaged their newsworthiness: parts of the story had already been poached and had made the rounds as general news. This threat to their exclusive contract must have reminded Amundsen of the Northwest Passage scenario all over again.

He and his comrades were not received as enthusiastically in Nome as they had hoped. Amundsen had promised that the airship would land in Nome, and according to a newspaper account "the Chamber of Commerce had gone to considerable expense placing a cable and four anchors on the Nome landing field. A triumphal arch had been erected on the main street and streamers and banners lined the street, while all the buildings and homes were decorated." Over one hundred men had been readied to haul the landing ropes of the airship. Not surprisingly, they didn't understand the difficulties of airship landings, and "a feeling of resentment against Amundsen was expressed by many over the failure of the explorer to bring the *Norge* to Nome." Then Nobile made a separate and ostentatious display of his arrival a few days later and kept his Italian crew separate from the Norwegians, even organizing a celebration ceremony in honour of the flight to which neither Amundsen nor Ellsworth was invited. The three explorers and their crew departed together on a steamship bound for Seattle, frequently posing for photographs but with the two sides never actually speaking to each other during the twelve-day voyage.

Whether Amundsen had a premonition of the public relations disaster that was brewing or whether he was pondering more personal matters, Ellsworth noted a certain melancholy in his partner as the steamship pressed south. "I saw Amundsen standing at the rail, his chin on his hand, looking at the receding coast of the land of his choice. I stepped beside him and observed that his eyes were moist."

"I suppose I will never see it again," Amundsen said.

PART FIVE
LOST

✦ NORTH POLE

17

No More Poles to Conquer

My work is fulfilled. All the big problems are solved.
The work that remains in Polar exploration is a mat-
ter of detail. Let others handle it.

LARGE CROWDS WERE awaiting the famous-again explorers in Seattle. But Amundsen noted with dismay that many in the crowd were either waving Italian flags or flying Italian flags on their boats. The Italian community in Seattle was better at organizing a public turnout than the Norwegian community, and it had spread the word that the expedition had been an Italian one. At the gangplank of the ship Nobile, resplendent in his glittering military uniform, stepped forward to give the Fascist salute to the cheers of the Italian American congregation. When a little girl approached the explorers to present them with a bouquet of flowers, she handed it to the stylish and impressive-looking man in a shining uniform who had the small dog at his feet rather than to Amundsen or Ellsworth, who seemed like weary prospectors. Newspaper reporters noted that Amundsen "looked tired and worn," sporting a bushy grey moustache and garbed in a prospector's outfit he had purchased in Nome, instead of the stylish suits he usually wore when meeting reporters.

After a short stay in Seattle, Amundsen, Riiser-Larsen, the other Norwegian crew and Ellsworth boarded an eastbound train in two reserved cars. When they pulled into New York's Grand Central Station several days later, "the party was cheered" and Amundsen was "smothered under armfuls of roses until he looked like a moving flower bed." Once again there were speeches and the singing of the American and Norwegian anthems. A police-escorted cavalcade led them through streets teeming with enthusiastic crowds. Amundsen was now described as looking "ten years younger"—clearly the adulation was counteracting the trials of the expedition. "He was clean-shaven. . . . He wore a smartly tailored double-breasted suit and looked very rosy and plump. He expressed some horror when he was told that he was putting on flesh."

Amundsen announced that "I never felt better in my life. I'm a free man now. I'll never explore again." He had accomplished all the goals he had set out for himself as a youth, he said, and "felt the relief and happiness of an emancipated slave." He also proclaimed, "I'll never lecture again. Riiser-Larsen can do that—I've lectured for twenty years. I don't know what I'll do with the rest of my life, but it will be what I feel like doing." In a speech at a public luncheon, he claimed that Ellsworth would also have to keep exploring: "He's a fine young man of courage and spirit. There may still be work worth while for him to do." Part of Amundsen's sudden feeling of freedom no doubt had to do with the accomplishment of a goal he had contemplated since adolescence, but it also stemmed from the finalization of his bankruptcy proceedings; his brother Leon had not publicly revealed that Amundsen had at one time signed over his properties to Kristine Bennett in his will—the secret of their affair was safe. Uranienborg, which was included in his estate, was sold to Herman Gade and Peter Christophersen with the provision that Amundsen could live there for the duration of his life. The proceeds went to pay off some of the debts.

Among the crowd at the culminating luncheon, Amundsen noticed Richard E. Byrd, who had made the trip from Washington,

D.C., to greet him. Amundsen heartily called out "Byrd!" and pushed through the crowd to shake his hand before introducing him to the throng, "his face all smiles." He dragged Byrd onto the stage, happily sharing the spotlight with the other man who had purportedly flown over the North Pole. Then the nine Norwegians and Ellsworth boarded a steamer for Bergen, where they were received as heroes on July 12, pushed into gilded chairs and lofted off the gangplank and on to the celebrants' shoulders. A few days later, in Oslo, they were escorted into the city by a flotilla of small boats and military airplanes flying in formation. The streets were crowded with thousands of well-wishers. A red-carpet reception awaited them, and the quiet and unassuming Ellsworth was proclaimed "a modern Viking."

Umberto Nobile was supposed to travel on to Japan to help with an airship installation there, but he had received new orders from Mussolini: he was remain in the United States to undertake a tour of the "Italian colonies." He would promote his own and Italy's role—and, naturally, Mussolini's role—in the successful and famous polar endeavour. Mussolini also promoted him to the rank of general. Nobile and his men toured thirteen major cities in the United States. This was a breach of the spirit of the contract Amundsen and Ellsworth had drawn up with Nobile, whom they viewed as their employee. But Nobile was engaged in state propaganda and was impervious to any attempts by Amundsen or Ellsworth to control him. Although Amundsen had always promoted his country of origin, he remained a private individual in all his expeditions, making his living by selling the spectacle of his thrilling accomplishments to the public. Nobile and his five Italian crew were agents of their government, and as such may not even have had the right to enter into civil contracts that might obligate them to act against the will of their commanding officers.

In November 1926, after some months in Norway spent working on the draft of *First Flight Across the Polar Sea*, Amundsen sailed

back to New York to begin his lecture tour of the United States—
only to find that Nobile was doing his own tour, presenting the
whole affair in a light most favourable to Mussolini and Fascist Italy.
During the next several months, the quarrel between the Norwegian and the Italian contingents intensified. Nobile made a series of
outrageous claims: that he had conceived of using a dirigible to cross
the Polar Sea himself in 1925, before being approached by Amundsen: "While this Italian project was ripening, Amundsen asked to
meet me. . . . In fact, to Italy full credit must be given for the technical organization of the entire flight from Rome to Alaska. It was
made entirely through our own initiative and under our responsibility." Nobile graciously thanked Ellsworth for contributing financing to "his" expedition. In an interview with the *New York Times* on
December 6, he declared that "I was the commander of the *Norge*
and everybody on it, including Amundsen, was under my orders."

Nobile also claimed that the Norwegian crew did little besides
sleep, while the Italians did all the work. All of these statements
were of course blatant falsehoods. How could Amundsen and
Ellsworth not be infuriated by them? These nasty personal attacks
were clearly inspired by far more than the explorers' brief time together on the airship; they were in a competition for public attention
and the storyline of the adventure. Amundsen and Ellsworth wanted
this for themselves, both to recoup their costs and for personal reasons. Nobile wanted it to assuage his wounded pride and for the
greater glory of the Fascist state; now that the expedition was a success, Mussolini promoted it as an example of Italy's new and powerful position as a world leader in technical and scientific matters. If
Nobile had been instructed by Mussolini to make his outrageous
pronouncements, he certainly could not have refused. Eventually,
the publicity-shy Ellsworth joined the public quarrel, pointing out
that Riiser-Larsen did more flying than Nobile and that Nobile
hadn't done *any* of the navigation—so vital on a featureless expanse
of frozen water. Nobile immediately attacked Ellsworth, claiming

in the *New York Times* that the American, who had performed a fair amount of the navigation as well as the general conceptualization of the entire enterprise, "was merely a passenger whom I took on board at Spitsbergen and left at Teller."

In Italy, the voyage of the *Norge* was elevated into a propagandistic story of two great peoples and their national temperaments—Norwegian discipline and willpower melded with Italian creativity and inventiveness—united in the conquest of the last geographical prize on the planet, a symbol of Norwegian co-operation with the "New Italy." Yet neither Amundsen nor Ellsworth wanted the Italian state as their partner. Amundsen himself became increasingly nationalistic in the wake of his public fight with Nobile, wrapping himself in his nationality as never before, dedicating *First Crossing of the Polar Sea* to "The Norwegian Flag." Resisting Mussolini, who would later reveal the vicious and aggressive nature of Italian nationalism, brought out Amundsen's own tribalism. This intense nationalism was increasingly becoming the spirit of the age.

The quarrel with Nobile was in part related to Amundsen's and Ellsworth's quarrel with the Norwegian Aero Club, whom they charged with mismanagement, including failing to sell film rights to an American company and giving additional rights to Nobile. Amundsen's quarrel with the club had begun the year before, when it had turned down a significant offer from First National Pictures for the film rights to his and Ellsworth's polar flight. He later remarked that "anybody with the slightest knowledge of the motion picture business realizes that the great market is the United States, and that the value of news pictures diminishes in geometrical ratio with the passage of time between the events portrayed and the day they are exhibited in theatres." This "stupid error" cost the expedition, by Amundsen's estimate, about $42,000—a huge sum in those days.

Amundsen and Ellsworth publicly resigned their memberships when they discovered that the club was sponsoring and endorsing

Nobile's lecture tour of the United States. Rolf Thommessen, the Aero Club's president, claimed he had to endorse Nobile's lecture tour because Ellsworth and Amundsen refused to give the Italian equal credit for the expedition and would not allow Nobile to contribute to the official book of the expedition. Thommessen was in fact an admirer of Mussolini, which may explain his willingness to alter the terms of the contract between the Aero Club and Nobile. He ran sympathetic portraits of the Italian dictator in his newspapers, and contrasted positive portraits of Nobile's competence with denigrating comments about Amundsen's leadership. The fact remains that there is no way that Nobile or the *Norge* could have flown anywhere near the North Pole or Alaska, or even have left Italy, if not for the lofty dreams of Amundsen and Ellsworth.

The Aero Club held the world copyright to the newspaper and magazine articles produced by Ellsworth and Amundsen except in the United States, where these rights were held by the *New York Times* and the *St. Louis Globe-Democrat*. The Aero Club's actions were obviously contrary to what Amundsen and Ellsworth had intended—why would they invest time and money in a venture to which a paid employee would then be given the rights to the fame and financial rewards? Amundsen vented his frustration with the club's senior members when he wrote that they "caused us troubles so numerous as to outweigh any services they rendered us. Indeed, most of the misunderstandings that have arisen in the public mind about the facts of the flight of 1926 are traceable directly to the mismanagement and weakness and vacillation of the Aero Club of Norway." Because the club was endorsing Nobile's right to tour, Amundsen refused to turn over to it the proceeds either from book sales or from his and Ellsworth's American lectures from the fall of 1926 and the spring of 1927, according to the financial arrangements of the enterprise. Eventually the matter went to court.

Amundsen considered Nobile's lecture tour to be not only the theft of money that belonged to the expedition but also the grossest of betrayals. Amundsen had had plenty of personal and professional disagreements and quarrels over the years, but he had kept silent so long as others did the same. It was his conviction that personal acrimony was tolerated so long as the rules were obeyed—all expedition members, including Amundsen as the leader, had an obligation to the expedition first; dirty laundry was to be kept private. But when this rule was broken by Nobile, Amundsen responded in kind. This did not have the intended effect. One American reporter wrote in the *New York Times*: "When the polar explorers landed in Teller there was honour and glory enough to go around, but if this quarrel continues there will be neither honour nor glory for anyone."

Amundsen was now fifty-four years old and tiring of the strenuous life he had chosen for himself many decades earlier. "My work is fulfilled," he claimed in one interview. "All the big problems are solved. The work that remains in Polar exploration is a matter of detail. Let others handle it." He pointed out that Riiser-Larsen and Ellsworth might lead their own expedition the following year. At a private dinner in Washington, D.C., he, Ellsworth and Byrd decided to form the Polar Legion, a club with a very select membership: it would be open only to leaders of expeditions that had reached either of the two poles. Because these requirements included only three living people—the three explorers sitting at the dinner table—they voted to posthumously induct Peary and Scott into the august ranks, and sent off the notification to their respective widows. "The Club is not likely ever to be crowded," Amundsen wrote, "though possibly Magellan may have thought the same thing about the Circumnavigators' Club, which now has a numerous membership."

Despite the acrimony of his public dispute with Nobile and the bitterness they felt over lost revenue and time, Ellsworth wrote fondly of the time he spent with Amundsen on their lecture tour of the United States. He noted that on one occasion Amundsen had turned to him and proclaimed: "Do you know I have adopted many of your ways. I have learned to smoke my pipe in bed of evenings and have written Montreal for fifty pounds of that French-Canadian tobacco you smoke and I only eat two meals a day now. I never have the tight feeling around the belt any more." Amundsen was still having fun in America, where, ensconced in his room at the Waldorf-Astoria, he felt he could relax and mingle socially, with periodic forays to deliver lectures and attend ceremonies. He again joked with a reporter that he might now be ready to contemplate marriage, although to whom he did not say, and he offered no further details.

In June 1927, he sailed across the Pacific for a tour of Japan, departing from Vancouver, British Columbia, on the steamship *Empress of Asia*. He was treated grandly during his ten well-attended lectures there over the course of three weeks. Then he moved on to a tour of Russia that eventually brought him back to Norway by September 6, "a very tired man," just a month before the publication of his incendiary memoir, *My Life as an Explorer*. With the publication of this book, his façade was cracked. In place of a near-invincible risk-taker who seemingly could compel himself to victory through sheer force of will, was a vulnerable man who complained and pointed fingers. Here was a seeming joker who wrote in a tone that was alternately superficial, mocking and tediously earnest. He referred to himself as a pirate who deliberately fled his creditors. Here was a man whose dash to the South Pole was mere sport, accomplished by deceiving his investors, without any legitimate scientific motive, a man who publicly quarrelled with one of his partners, rehashing all their dirty laundry for the world to see. This was not The Last of the Vikings, the Norwegian national hero and famous polar pioneer who had pushed away the mists of obscurity from the map's remaining major geographical mysteries for the good of humankind, but a weary, aging adventurer making light of his own accomplishments and motives. Was the public now to believe that it had been taken in by this charlatan, a character who was merely fabricating stories for his own amusement and to make a quick buck?

The book seemed to have been slapped together in a hurry; indeed, it was hastily scrawled out by Amundsen in the final months of 1926, in his room at the Waldorf-Astoria, without the benefit of a coauthor, ghostwriter or editor to fill in the technical details, an arrangement that had enhanced his previous books and articles. He wrote *My Life as an Explorer* from memory rather than making any effort to provide useful documentation of his life's adventures. He omits all details of a personal nature, and the details of some of his earlier adventures are vague and imprecise. When detailing his Antarctic expedition in the *Belgica*, Amundsen does not even bother to mention his commander's name, either because he forgot how to spell it and couldn't be bothered to look it up after thirty years, or because he considered Adrien de Gerlache to be inconsequential in this brief overview of his life. The chronology is sparse and inaccurate, and the names of people not of personal interest to him are missing—but not necessarily deliberately so.

Amundsen's motive in writing the memoir was to defend himself against the bad press and charges stemming from his expedition with Nobile, and to counter those charges with his own presentation of events. The usually indulgent *New York Times* commented in its review of the book that "the reader's sympathy cannot fail to go out to Roald Amundsen in this controversy, but it may still be said that the space given to the feud, about a third of the book, is disproportionate." Another large portion of the memoir defends his actions in racing Scott to the South Pole, and yet another significant portion is devoted to an attack on his brother's handling of his financial affairs, blaming his bankruptcy on Leon. The fact that the book was published in this state, with so much vitriol, reveals little about Amundsen's character in a general sense (at the time he did feel and believe all the things he wrote about his ill-treatment in Britain and the betrayal by Nobile and the Norwegian Aero Club), but it does reveal something about the extent to which he was let down by his publisher, who should have waited for the author's temper to cool and offered him the chance to rewrite it the following year.

But the memoir isn't entirely without merit. The part of his autobiography that isn't concerned with his recent quarrels definitely falls into the category of the unvarnished. Amundsen was old enough to have the confidence to speak his mind, and free enough that he no longer needed to bow to tradition. In many ways, he was just saying "to hell with it," this is how things were: Everyone wanted to bask in the glory of his success after the fact, but no one wanted to support him at first. His early expeditions would never have been possible if he hadn't taken drastic, quasi-illegal, measures. Why should he go on pretending it was otherwise, decades after the fact? The memoir is that of an older man reflecting, a brooding rumination on all the injustices of his life, his chance to set the record straight before it was too late. Amundsen was magnanimous in victory, but at this time in his life he was not celebrating a victory; rather, he was struggling with a sense of defeat and an awareness of the diminishing possibility of his rising again. An American reporter who visited him at Uranienborg in September 1927 noted that Amundsen "said wistfully, as if regretting that he could not begin his career over again . . . 'There is nothing left for me to do.'" There were no more poles to conquer. What was he to do with the years that lay ahead?

After only a month in Norway, in the early fall of 1927, Amundsen unexpectedly packed again and set off on a steamship across the Atlantic for another extensive trip to the United States, and perhaps other countries as well. He was as restless as ever, and may have been uncomfortable with the contents of his memoir, which if he had ever glanced over the published version must surely have struck him as amateurish compared with his other works. Having spent so much of his life on the road, he could never just settle down to quiet obscurity and a peaceful life of contemplation in Uranienborg. It would require too much thinking—thinking about his past and, perhaps more importantly, about his future. Besides, he had spent far more time living in the Waldorf-Astoria than he had in his house in Norway. In a sense, he was returning home when he crossed the Atlantic to New York.

After spending a month in New York, Amundsen again abruptly packed up from the hotel, cancelled his speaking engagements and boarded a steamship for Norway. Near the end of his memoir he had written, "My explorations have brought me welcome formal honours, but, better than these, they have brought me the joys of enduring friendships. Many of my best friends are Americans. Their homes are open to me and their hearts as well." This time, however, one particular friend wasn't in New York. Amundsen's relationship with Bess Magids was becoming more serious, and the rumours were that she was the reason for his abrupt departure from New York. But as with all of Amundsen's previous romantic relationships, he was thoroughly discreet, particularly since Magids was still married.

She arrived in Norway on December 22, 1927, in secret. The Magids Brothers trading company was involved in business around the world, and Bess easily could have been in Europe on business. In any event she stayed at Uranienborg for several months, returning to the United States at the end of February to finalize her divorce. She may have returned to Norway in March, but by May and June she was in Seattle, packing up her life for a permanent move to Norway. She was 30, Amundsen 55. Her unusual level of comfort with the Arctic frontier and also with large urban centres was surely one of the foundations of their relationship. But their story was to be altered by the inexorable unfolding events of the next few months.

The public quarrel with Nobile was stressful for Amundsen, and the public reaction to his memoir was less than enthusiastic, in some cases hostile. The book was routinely dismissed as petty and peculiar, a drastic departure from his usual subtle and self-deprecating style. One of Scott's South Pole expedition members, Herbert Ponting, wrote a letter to the *London Times* deriding Amundsen's claims of the British being "bad losers" and claiming that the Norwegian explorer's entire South Pole expedition was nothing more than "a desire to deprive the British of the glory of crowning their long and valuable work in the South." The claims were reprinted in the *New York Times* and other papers, reviving the now fifteen-year-old controversy to no one's benefit, least of all Amundsen's.

He had also burned many professional bridges—with the Royal Geographical Society in London and the National Geographic Society in Washington—by including undiplomatic accounts of events that placed those institutions in an unflattering light. *My Life as an Explorer* raised the spectres of these past quarrels, which would otherwise have remained dormant. Time has shown that Amundsen was right to question Robert Peary's claim to have reached the North Pole, and he was right that Frederick Cook's and Peary's evidence was equally compelling—that is, equally fabricated. Amundsen's quarrel with the National Geographic Society stemmed from its cancellation of one of his lectures; the society had endorsed and supported Peary, and didn't want anyone challenging its version of the truth. But Amundsen had refused to be muzzled.

The publication of his memoir also led directly to "the Amundsen Affair," a diplomatic issue between Britain and Norway that Amundsen probably had no idea could result from revealing the thoughts and ideas that he harboured deep within himself—resentments, bitter reminiscences and memories of perceived slights that were decades old and deeply personal to the aging explorer. Many of his friends and colleagues believed that he had not been in his right mind when he allowed his memoir to be published in its current state. Fridtjof Nansen wrote letters to the Royal Geographic Society informing it that he believed Amundsen was not of sound mind and that whatever Amundsen might say should not be trusted.

Whether Nansen believed Amundsen to be deranged or not, his comments were intended to stem the disintegration of co-operation and goodwill between prominent individuals in Norway and Britain; it was a political, rather than medical, claim. Such was Amundsen's international stature that international relations could easily be damaged by nationalistic feelings. For many, Amundsen was a stand-in for Norway, and attitudes toward him transferred to the nation. If it was believed that Amundsen had lost his mind and was no longer to be trusted, the potential diplomatic damage resulting from his statements could be minimized.

Amundsen certainly harboured some bitterness over his current state of affairs. He had reached the age when intrepid adventuring in the remote wilds of the polar regions was beyond him, and yet he was barely financially solvent after a lifetime of dangerous work. He had never married and had no children. He felt that he deserved more, after all he had risked; that it was unjust that he should end up with so little. And he would have been correct in his assessment, but as Amundsen himself was aware, seldom does the world mete out justice and success based upon merit alone. Many people live and die in poverty and obscurity only to be revered later, and many have seen their tide rise through no great effort of their own.

It is also possible that Amundsen's health was not good after his many years of hard living in frozen lands, compounded by years of cocktail parties, endless travel and public engagements, and his long-time smoking habit. On several occasions he had visited physicians concerning the heart troubles that resulted from the poisoning on the *Maud* expedition, including consulting a doctor in Los Angeles for an unspecified treatment involving radium. He had instructed his lawyer, "Make me a free man. See to it that my debts are paid." But the stress of paying off his creditors, which was nearly complete after several years of applying all his surplus income to the task, as well as selling off many of his medals and decorations (which were purchased by a benefactor and donated to the Norwegian state), could easily have exacerbated any lingering or underlying health problems. Fortunately he still had his monthly stipend from the Norwegian government. Any discussion of Amundsen's health is speculation, however, in the absence of any direct evidence. His older brother Jens had recently died, and that event was sure to provoke ruminations on his own mortality.

It was during this time that Amundsen was also intensifying his relationship with Bess Magids, whom he had visited in New York for several years. He hosted her at Uranienborg for several months, and she had plans to return to Norway to marry him in June 1928. It has often been claimed that at this time in his life Amundsen was a bitter, lonely and resentful man, but he couldn't have been too lonely—Magids was visiting him during much of this period, and he was excited enough about her visit to cut short his American lecture tour. Furthermore, she was returning to the United States to organize her affairs before coming back to Norway to share her life with Amundsen—an act that involved getting divorced (her husband was probably ill at the time; he died the following year) and likely sacrificing a substantial amount of money. So, at the very least, Amundsen was able to muster enough energy and charm to move forward with this aspect of his life. It couldn't have been all bad, despite the unresolved issues that preyed on his mind.

Many people who retire experience problems in adjusting to a quieter life, a life without responsibility. Could Amundsen be a romantic and charming gallant for an extended period? He had never been in a committed public relationship, had always followed his own schedule. Perhaps, like many an older bachelor, and particularly for one who spent far more time in hotels than he ever did at home, he feared that he was permanently unmoored from the rhythms of regular life, that he was incapable of a committed relationship or of settling down. Perhaps Magids herself operated under a set of false expectations, such as about the state of Amundsen's finances?* Perhaps Amundsen feared he wouldn't be able to succeed at commitment. It couldn't be planned like an expedition, and at the age of fifty-five he had no precedent.

On May 26, 1928, while Magids was in Seattle settling her affairs, Amundsen was attending a public luncheon celebrating the successful airplane flight of Hubert Wilkins and Carl Eielson from Alaska to Spitsbergen. The host of the lunch, the editor of the newspaper *Aftenposten*, was called to take a phone call: Nobile's new airship *Italia* had been lost near Spitsbergen. There was no radio communication with Nobile. His highly publicized second airship expedition to the North Pole had been undertaken chiefly to prove that he didn't need Amundsen to lead an expedition in the Arctic. Questioned by a reporter, Amundsen made a public statement of support and offered his assistance. And so followed the series of events that led to Amundsen setting off in his French Latham biplane.

Having publicly announced his intention to help with the search and rescue, and having such a storied relationship with Nobile, Amundsen felt compelled to push for a role in the rescue operation.

---

*Bess Magids returned to Alaska and eventually took over Magids Brothers Trading Co., becoming a noted figure in early-twentieth-century Alaskan history. In 1931, she married a younger man, Arthur Chamberlain, with whom she had a daughter, and in 1937 she married John Milton Cross. In 1945, she was elected to the Alaska Territorial Legislature, where she voted for Alaska statehood. She died in 1971.

An emotional and temperamental man, he probably regretted his feud with Nobile. Their quarrel likely would have petered out much sooner if not for the constant reporting of each other's statements in the press. By the spring of 1928, after four months in Norway, Amundsen had spent a greater block of time at Uranienborg than he had in years, and if his past behaviour is any indication he may have been anxious to leave and do something. Contributing to Nobile's rescue would be a chance to gain some final fame, to feel he was doing something useful, to show that he still had something to contribute.

But he was no longer the leading man. He was a bit player dutifully performing his role—workmanlike, predictable and competent—but not in control. He was annoyed when the Norwegian government, at Mussolini's request, denied him an official role in the rescue and selected Hjalmar Riiser-Larsen to lead the Norwegian rescue operation. Mussolini was trying to salvage Italian pride by downplaying the international rescue operation. (He had warned Nobile about tempting fate with a second expedition and had advised against it.) Amundsen quickly sought other means of joining the operation, to counter the taint of being overlooked by his own country. If he at least made the appropriate gestures, none could claim that he had been cowardly or had accepted the official slight without a fight. At the same time, he was a reluctant rescuer—his participation was all to save face and honour. Many countries were participating in the extravaganza for a similar reason—not in a genuine attempt to rescue a handful of injured and stranded men, but to bolster their national prestige. Twenty-one airplanes and numerous ships from the international community were involved in the search, so it was only a matter of time before Nobile was found.

Amundsen may have been surprised and perhaps annoyed when the French government, which certainly didn't mind upstaging or humiliating Mussolini, had a plane and crew ready for him. Many possibilities can be advanced as sources of the guilt and misguided sense of duty that drove Amundsen at this time: he knew that Nobile had ventured to the Arctic again merely to prove that it could be done without Amundsen's leadership; he didn't want another life on his conscience, in addition to Wiik's, Scott's and Johanssen's. Perhaps he lacked the courage to say no, he wasn't going, it wasn't his job. We will never know.

Amundsen's life seemed to be narrowing. His old companion Sverre Hassel, one of the four men with whom he had reached the South Pole, came to visit him in Uranienborg and died suddenly of a heart attack while they were talking. In a telephone interview with a *New York Times* correspondent, Amundsen specifically asked the man to "give my greetings to my numerous friends in America and thank them for me for all the cables of encouragement they have sent to me." With his companions Leif Dietrichson and Oscar Wisting, Amundsen boarded the train for Bergen with a certain reluctance, lingering on the walkway even after the train began to move, with a tear in his eye, staring at the ground while the crowd cheered.

After a lingering meeting in Tromsø, his friend Fritz Zapffe, who had known him for nearly two decades and had been part of the support crew for several expeditions, wrote "I even felt slightly embarrassed—as I would in the company of someone ill, to whom one does not quite know what to say." When Zapffe saw Amundsen crawl into the fuselage of the biplane, he saw a man already defeated. "I shall not forget the expression on his face, sitting astern, something extraordinary and resigned was over him. It appeared that nothing concerned him and yet it was maybe all about him. He sat quietly just looking at me." Amundsen had played the showman for so long now that he could not back down; he had to keep acting for the crowd as if he still needed their goodwill to finance his next expedition. Rueful and sheepish, propelled toward his fate, Amundsen was caught up in a media frenzy of his own making and was unable to stop himself.

The French Latham biplane, with its crew of young Norwegian and French men headed by Amundsen, set off into a bright sun on

June 18. Underpowered and overloaded, the Latham also had the disadvantage of being unsuited to landing safely on either choppy water or ice. A fisherman reported the airplane flying into "a bank of fog that rose up over the horizon and then the machine began to climb presumably to fly over it but then it seemed to me she began to move unevenly but then . . . she ran into the fog and disappeared before our eyes." It was the last anyone ever saw of the biplane, and soon radio contact was lost.

Amundsen had often telegrammed Bess in Seattle in June before she rode the train to New York. He sent her a final telegram from Bergen on his way north, just before she boarded the steamship *Hellig Olav*. When she arrived in Oslo on July 2, he was missing and presumed dead.

The End of the Heroic Age

Amundsen! The very name carries the song of the Arctic winds; the mystery of the white places on the earth. Of all men, he alone had stood at both frozen tips of our spinning world. From boyhood, his life was dedicated to the lonely polar trails, and when, a weathered old man, he roared away into the white silence, on a winged quest of rescue, it was his beloved land of snow that claimed him at last. Even today, as Byrd and Wilkins plow southward toward the Antarctic, it is the spirit of Amundsen that leads on.

—Boyden Sparkes, "The Last of the Vikings,"
Popular Science Monthly, December 1928

IN THE MONTHS after his disappearance, Roald Amundsen was eulogized as a hero in both Norway and the United States in countless speeches, articles and radio broadcasts. This was particularly the case on December 14, 1928, when South Pole Day, the seventeenth anniversary of Amundsen and his party's reaching the South Pole, was proclaimed a national holiday in Norway. The entire country observed two minutes' silence in Amundsen's honour; thousands crowded the streets of Oslo, and Norway's schools devoted lessons that day to the man and his explorations. Lincoln Ellsworth delivered a heartfelt speech that was broadcast in New York and, in translation, in Oslo: "The end, no doubt, was as he himself would have wished it," he said. "For Amundsen often told me that he wanted to die in action. . . . I cannot see him other than as the great leader he was."

Even Umberto Nobile, rescued from the ice five days after Amundsen went missing and now disgraced in Italy for his role in the *Italia*'s failure, paid tribute to the Norwegian hero: "On the day that Norway commemorates Roald Amundsen my thoughts are turned with deep respect to the memory of that great explorer. I ask you to consider me present in spirit at your memorial festival." In the United States, the *New York Times* boldly proclaimed that the "Whole World Honors Amundsen's Memory."

Nevertheless, Amundsen soon faded from public memory. The technology of exploration changed, new records were set and then broken, and other world-shaking events came to dominate the news: stock markets crashed, the Great Depression set in, Fascism gained strength and the world moved toward another war. In Britain, Robert Falcon Scott was transformed into a national hero, a martyr who had died in a gallant struggle, while Amundsen was denigrated as the dastardly foil to Scott—Scott was good, therefore Amundsen was bad. It was a task made much easier by Amundsen's ill-considered claim, fifteen years after the fact, that the British were "bad losers" for not celebrating his achievement with the same vigour with which they celebrated Scott's tragedy. For decades in Britain, Amundsen was considered only in reference to Scott and their so-called race to the South Pole, at the same time receiving only occasional mention in books about the exploration of the Arctic and aviation history.

The tenor of the debate changed after the publication in 1979 of Roland Huntford's epic and revisionist *Scott and Amundsen*, a ground-breaking work that was republished in 1999 as *The Last Place on Earth*. Huntford's book, which focused on contrasting

Amundsen's and Scott's journeys to the South Pole, shattered many of the myths fuelling the disparaging British view of Amundsen. Yet the debate concerning the relative virtues of Amundsen and Scott has continued, unfortunately without much subsequent discussion of Amundsen's substantial accomplishments following his exploits in Antarctica. This book is intended to address the dearth.

With the exception of Huntford, many who have written about the conquest of the South Pole have seemed to believe that Amundsen could do no good. Instead of portraying a firm and visionary leader, they present Amundsen as an autocrat. Rather than recognizing him as a curious explorer, they see him as single-mindedly in pursuit of glory. Rather than acknowledging his talent for self-deprecating storytelling, they describe him as a shallow and narcissistic manipulator. And rather than praising him for making skilful use of indigenous polar traditions and technology, they disdain him for being heartless in the treatment of his dogs. To diminish his achievements, his critics claim that Amundsen was merely lucky.

There was actually a time when British schoolchildren were taught that Scott the Briton was the first person to reach the South Pole, and that Amundsen had cheated in "the great race." Amundsen's legacy certainly raises questions about our knowledge of the past: What do we really know about past events—and hence the present—when our understanding of those events (and the people involved in them) has been shaped, perhaps manipulated, by the political and social agendas of vested interests and longstanding prejudices?

Some portrayals of Amundsen are bizarre. There are claims that his entire life's goal was to reach the North Pole, and that everything he did was for his own aggrandizement. Also, that contemporaries who thought well of him were "bootlickers." In this view there is only one actor, Amundsen; all the other members of his expeditions were apparently bit players in the drama of the Norwegian explorer's life. The truth is that all the members of his expeditions were keen participants in those death-defying adventures over the years.

Some writers muster up shock that Amundsen had affairs with three married women, regarding it as evidence of his pathological desire to defeat others—in this case, their husbands—just as he would stop at nothing to conquer Scott and the South Pole. But what other women was Amundsen likely to meet, given the circumstances of his life? In the early twentieth century, women married early and usually had children. Amundsen had little time to socialize in the periods between his multi-year expeditions to the wilds. The first opportunity he had to consider settling down was upon his return from the South Pole, when he was already forty years old. Most women within a decade of his age were in all probability already married. And what of the possibility that Amundsen was the object of pursuit for mature women seeking an escape from their dull or otherwise unfulfilling marriages? He was famous, a man of mystery, and undoubtedly carried about him a hint of danger and a whiff of scandal—worthy of a fling or a brief engagement, perhaps, but not of a lifelong commitment.

Ultimately, however, we know little about Amundsen's relationships because he was not one to kiss and tell. He knew that anything he said might irreparably damage the reputations of the women with whom he was involved, and remained silent even when things did not work out as he had hoped. In those conservative days, this was an honourable trait. His endless travels and occasional affairs didn't lead to happiness or contentment; discontent was the price the voyager paid for fame and adventure.

Amundsen has remained an enigmatic figure in the literature devoted to him, his reputation depending upon the time and source. High achievers tend to be much more complicated than the stereotypes employed to portray them, which in Amundsen's case appear to have been repeated from book to book over the years. Amundsen was multi-faceted, and he could be taciturn, rude and brusque. Many accounts attest to this. In his final years, following his quarrel with Umberto Nobile, he appeared to be erratic and, some feared, unmoored. But even more numerous than these accounts are those from comrades who praised his leadership qualities, his warmth, his sense of humour and generosity.

Amundsen could be a hard taskmaster. He was temperamental, unstinting in his attention to detail and occasionally rough with his words. Many of his men complained in their private journals of his abrasiveness and brusqueness while under stress, yet they willingly signed on for more adventures with Amundsen when the time came. Some of their comments are reminiscent of those in which soldiers might gripe about their famous general between battles but rally passionately to him once the fighting starts. Amundsen's men recalled their journeys fondly in hindsight, even while the day-to-day record in their diaries suggests that these journeys were mostly unpleasant and frustrating, filled with hardships and tedious delays. Clearly, their feeling of accomplishment and camaraderie prevailed long after the expedition was over.

Although it could be infuriating to heed the seemingly endless details of Amundsen's instructions, most of his men knew that it was this apparent fussiness that brought them back alive and victorious rather than in a body bag or with their heads hung in failure. Amundsen's attention to detail made his expeditions successful, and as the expedition leader he was merely the enforcer of what all knew were the necessary logistics of his operations if they wanted to succeed. They knew what was expected of them before they signed on. On a day-to-day basis the personal dynamics of any small, endangered group could be trying. Living together for months, or even years, hearing the same old jokes and stories, dealing with the same irritating aspects of other personalities, is bound to drive anyone a little mad. It wasn't Amundsen's job to make his men happy, but to lead them to victory, alive.

It's hard to know whether members of Amundsen's crews knew that it was equally frustrating for their leader to be preoccupied with these annoying interpersonal details. He was forced to make hard choices, sometimes life-and-death decisions, quickly and frequently. Rarely was there time for reflection as events unfolded, and in hindsight some of his decisions proved unnecessary or wrong. The stress must have been great—the second-guessing, planning and rethinking of various scenarios over and over again, anxiety-inducing as the possibilities of defeat or victory alternately preyed on Amundsen's imagination. At the same time, Amundsen was perceptive enough to know what others were experiencing or feeling, and he was generous with his praise of others' abilities and contributions. He shared credit willingly and the public acclaim widely.

Sverre Hassel, Amundsen's expert dog-driver and an experienced polar sailor, seems to have been the one who was most irritated by Amundsen during their South Pole expedition. Nevertheless he kept his work in perfect form and never quarrelled much with either his leader or other crew members. He vented his frustrations in a private notebook but did not engage in quarrels or make them public. After a "victory banquet" in Buenos Aires, Hassel wrote that Amundsen "said he knew he was an unpleasant man to work with. And he is right. However, it is extraordinary how an honest admission of one's faults can help alleviate the dislike they create." Like the other members of Amundsen's party, Hassel forgave his old boss his cantankerous moments. He remained in touch with Amundsen throughout his life and died while visiting him at Uranienborg many years later in 1928.

In later years Amundsen arranged work for the men who had remained loyal to him, pushing for their promotion and fighting for government recognition and pensions for them, even lending them money. Although expedition member Olav Bjaaland chose to remain in Norway for the rest of his life after returning from the South Pole and did not join in any further expeditions, Amundsen lent him money to start a ski manufacturing business. On another occasion, Amundsen threatened to cancel one of his expeditions when the Norwegian government appeared to be reneging on promises made to his crew about their positions and decorations. He was loyal to a fault, using his fame and influence as well as his own money, or the expeditions' money, to work for the interests of his former comrades. In Britain, Ernest Shackleton, responding to Amundsen's self-effacement in a speech to the Royal Geographical Society, noted that "throughout the lecture tonight I never heard the word 'I' mentioned; it was always 'we'. I think that is the way in which Amundsen got his men to work along with him, and it brought the successful conclusion."

Amundsen's most fascinating trait was his ability to constantly reinvent himself as an explorer, devising new techniques for new goals. He dreamed up new ventures that combined geographical exploration and public spectacle. With an almost unparalleled ability to conceive, plan and execute seemingly crazy schemes, he also had a good grasp of how to publicize his adventures. Like an artist constantly changing mediums, Amundsen made transitions from sailing ships to skis and dogsleds, to open-cockpit airplanes, to a prototype airship. An uncompromising individualist, he refused to be discouraged by the changing times or his aging body, was never content to return again and again to the same place or the same methods, or to settle into comfortable respectability. Not for him the dwelling on past glories as the world passed him by.

Amundsen pursued travel to feed an insatiable hunger for the excitement he felt in anticipating his next destination; he was never more alive than when he was dreaming of and planning a new adventure. He devoted all his personal resources to his expeditions, sums of money that on several occasions would have allowed him to retire comfortably. Money meant nothing to him, except as a means of making possible his latest plan. Yet regaining this feeling of exuberance and vitality became more difficult as he got older and as the number of things that were new to him diminished. Amundsen wanted the excitement never to end; nor, perhaps, did he want the public adulation and respect that came in its wake to subside. He had no career other than exploration; telling the tales of his adventures was his source of income, even when he was bored with the lecture circuit. Yet he shunned institutions and respectability, even refusing the prestige offered by a Norwegian university appointment and the security of a regular salary.

There is an integrity and consistency in Amundsen's life. He was a man of action rather than a philosopher; angst-ridden questioning and self-doubt, circular musings on the meaning of life and the nature of God, or fretting about either the immediate future or eternity were not for him. He knew what goals he wanted to achieve in his life and he set out after them, again and again, in a intriguing cycle of reinvention and novelty. This approach to life may have contributed to his loneliness and a certain detachment from the rhythms of others' lives, but for Amundsen it also prevented stagnation, regret and boredom. Perhaps he would indeed have been more conflicted and meditative if he had been thwarted in his quest for heroic adventure, but thankfully that was not the case—he created an unparalleled legacy of real-life adventure, of daunting physical and mental challenge, while engaged in an uncompromising pursuit of the chimera of acclaim. What makes him such an intriguing character is that he chose his life, rather than having it thrust upon him.

Amundsen towers in the pantheon of great explorers, and his death marked the end of an era. It is now impossible to do what Amundsen did, just as it is not possible to accomplish what Magellan did. The corporate-funded, technology-dependent, risk-averse expeditions of today seem sterile compared with the gambles of the heroic age in which pioneers such as Amundsen were exploring unknown geography with untested technology. Amundsen ushered in the end of grand-scale terrestrial exploration by claiming the most desired geographical prizes, at the polar extremes of the earth. At the same time he developed a business model that would be used by future explorers to finance their expeditions.

Amundsen's conquests gave rise to the phenomenon of the explorer as entertainer, one who is unfettered by the constraints of past generations that travelled under the orders of a government or a commercial patron with geopolitical objectives. His accomplishments are all the more noteworthy because he achieved them as a private citizen, with mostly private financing, but did so in an era when geographical conquest was a proxy battle between nations, fought in a highly publicized manner for political prestige and national honour. In some ways he was like a private, self-funded athlete competing in the modern Olympic Games.

Amundsen packed more travel, excitement, danger, tragedy, pathos and triumph into his fifty-six years than seems possible, even now. He led as successful a life as can be imagined, creating a record of sensational geographical feats that were front-page news in their day and that will never be forgotten. He fulfilled all his youthful dreams and then, as far as we know, died according to his professed desire, in a dramatic burst of publicity and mystery. He had earned the title bestowed on him by the popular press—"the last of the Vikings."

A Note on Sources

There are many ways to interpret a life. I have approached Roald Amundsen's life in such a way as to not only reveal the astounding adventures of a unique and compelling personality, but to place these exploits in their historical context: Why was Amundsen so important, and why did anyone care about what he was doing? I am not a polar expert; I have never been to either of the poles and I have no plans to travel there, but in the early twentieth century the quest to explore these last remaining uncharted places was an obsessive goal for some nations, and they fought to be the first to dispel the few geographical mists that still shrouded the planet. My interest is in Amundsen as an individual working within the technological and psychological limitations of his day—a person who struggled to accomplish what was important in his era, not what was or is universally important, if indeed there is any such thing.

In viewing Amundsen as a historical character, I am interested in how the world viewed him, as much as I am interested in how he viewed the world—in how he changed the world, as much as how the world changed him. This broad view of his actions speaks to his character: he spent nearly his entire adult life engaged in publicity-financed exploration, recording the details both to earn his living and for posterity. Amundsen viewed himself as a public figure, and it is this public persona that has been my chief interest, rather than the minutiae of his private life. His public life is very well documented, both by Amundsen himself in his prolific articles, lectures and books, and by others in articles, interviews, photographs and motion pictures. His private life, however, is more obscure. He purposely hid it behind a daunting façade of grim, heroic determination. The concealment itself was part of his character. *The Last Viking* is intended as a large-canvas story of Amundsen's life and times rather than as a meditation on his character.

As a Canadian historian and biographer, my interest in Amundsen stemmed from his activities in the Northwest Passage rather than at the South Pole, and as a result I had no preconceived notions of Amundsen in relation to Robert F. Scott. I didn't begin with the thesis that Amundsen was either superior or inferior to Scott and then set out to prove my case. I was just curious—and then stunned to realize that Amundsen was usually discussed only in relation to Scott and Antarctica. Almost everything written about Amundsen is in the context of "the race to the South Pole," and the sixteen years following his return from Antarctica are often summed up in a paragraph or two. The post–South Pole years of his life, however, take up nearly half of *The Last Viking* and include the years when he was an American celebrity, as well as his experimentation with pioneer airplanes, his five years of sailing the Northeast Passage, his failure and then success in flying open-cockpit airplanes toward the North Pole and his pioneering use of an airship to fly over the North Pole and Polar Basin. Amundsen achieved his greatest popularity during these years, particularly in the United States.

Amundsen and many of his friends wrote primarily in Norwegian. Until recently much of this material was unavailable in English, contributing to the relative lack of information about him in the English-speaking world. More than any other factor, the language barrier to accessing some of Amundsen's correspondence is probably the reason for his waning popularity in the English-speaking world. This raises questions concerning what we know about important individuals, their ideas and actions: if they left a great deal of source material in a widely spoken language, then we learn about them and they are considered important; if their surviving correspondence was minimal or lost or in a language spoken by fewer people, or they were not from a dominant culture, then our portrait of the past does not include them.

I was aided greatly in my research by the recent translation—made in preparation for the 2011 celebrations in Norway commemorating the centenary of Amundsen's reaching the South Pole—of diaries and letters and other documents, including copies of Amundsen's lectures, letters from his agents, promotional brochures and so on. The Fram Museum in Oslo, Norway, is the source of much of this information. The museum's publication *Cold Recall: Reflections of a Polar Explorer*, edited by Geir O. Klover, provides the original text of Amundsen's Northwest Passage and South Pole lectures, his correspondence with his lecture agents in the United Kingdom and the United States, and examples of advertisements for Amundsen's lectures and product endorsements. There has been a fair amount of other new material about Amundsen made available in recent years as well, particularly information about his possible Inuit descendants in northern Canada and the fate of his adopted daughter Kakonita, who settled near Vancouver, B.C. This has been written about only in a few recent magazine articles; see particularly George Tombs's "Amundsen's Family Secrets: Another Side of the Polar Explorer Emerges as an Inuit Family Connection Comes to Light" in the October/November 2011 issue of *Canada's History.*

The heart and soul of *The Last Viking*, however, is a collection of more than four hundred newspaper articles about Amundsen, primarily from the *New York Times* (which published articles that also appeared in other newspapers), which I relied upon extensively to enliven his story and to enrich the understanding of his personality. There are literally thousands of extant newspaper articles about Roald Amundsen, if one chose to search for them. Every city he visited produced a story about his latest exploits. In general, however, little of unique interest is contained in these reports that differentiates them from the reportage in the *New York Times*, which frequently ran a similar version of a local story submitted by correspondents. Many of these stories can be searched and read online at little cost, or for no cost at a university microfilm station.

I have elected to quote mainly from the *New York Times* for several reasons: because it was the newspaper of record at the time and had a large national and international audience, and because it reproduced variations on almost everything written about Amundsen from other sources, including articles from European correspondents and reprints from smaller local newspapers. Amundsen also had a special relationship with the *New York Times*: he sold the newspaper exclusive rights to the stories of his adventures, ensuring that he received a great deal of publicity even when he wasn't returning from an expedition. If a story made the *New York Times*, it must have been important enough to be of more than purely local interest and therefore is a good reflection of American sentiment about and interest in Amundsen and his exploits.

Amundsen spent most of his adult life either on his expeditions or in the United States (where he was particularly fond of the Waldorf Astoria in New York), rather than in Norway, as is commonly assumed. In fact, he was hardly ever in Norway; nevertheless he was a national hero there. But he was equally famous in the United States. In the 1920s the American coverage of Amundsen picked up dramatically, even though many of his exploits then lacked the unique flare of capturing the South Pole; it was during this period that he became a celebrity and every detail of his public life was reported.

These articles have never been brought to light in a book, apart from the obvious headlines concerning the Northwest Passage and the South Pole. I was able to discover and access this extensive source of new information because of the digital searching capabilities of the *New York Times* Article Archive. These articles were probably never previously used because of the Herculean task of searching for them. Yet they reveal a whole new perspective on Amundsen. Who knew that in early-twentieth-century America Amundsen was constantly in the news, like a modern rock star?

The articles provide wonderful insight into Amundsen's activities and character. In an era before television, radio and the Internet, newspaper and magazine articles were the main source of public news and entertainment. The articles on Amundsen are not primarily what we would consider news. They are lingering biographical treatments, full of quotes, descriptions of his unusual life and his opinions on all matters, including polar exploration. A different portrait of Amundsen emerges from these articles—not the typical one of Amundsen as the stern and ruthless foil to Scott, but that of a droll, self-deprecating storyteller who had unusual opinions and strange dreams.

I could not have written this book without the prior work of Roland Huntford, especially his book on Scott and Amundsen, *The Last Place on Earth*. Huntford focused on Antarctica and on how Amundsen's career and life were melded with Scott's. *The Last Viking* seeks to extend and expand on Huntford's work to include all of Amundsen's adventures, including his numerous publicity tours of the United States.

Also valuable was the work of the Norwegian biographer Tor Bomann-Larsen, who has gone through a collection of Amundsen's voluminous correspondence in Norwegian that provides details about Amundsen's relations with his family and about his financial records, which are helpful in creating a full chronology of the less-public periods of his life, particularly in Europe. Bomann-Larsen focuses more on what the world (especially Norway) was to Amundsen and on the details of the people, primarily the Norwegians, who shared his life. As a reassessment of a national hero, his book *Roald Amundsen* is perhaps unjustifiably critical of Amundsen's personal attributes. While I appreciate the great work Bomann-Larsen has done in bringing to light new documents concerning Amundsen, I have come to very different conclusions regarding Amundsen's character and historical significance. But that is to be expected from two authors from different backgrounds; Bomann-Larsen is looking at his famous countryman and challenging some of the myths surrounding him in his native land, whereas for me Amundsen has always been an international figure. His accomplishments are of global significance, and his greatest fame was in the United States.

I sincerely hope that the public interest in Amundsen stemming from the centenary of his and Scott's conquest of the South Pole will inspire further interest in this most fascinating and enigmatic of polar explorers and will result in greater access to the documents that provide information about his life.

Further Information on the Web

Motion pictures, black-and-white and silent, were in their infancy when Amundsen was engaged in his later expeditions. One fascinating film includes footage of Amundsen's flight to the North Pole with Lincoln Ellsworth in 1925. Amundsen's brief appearance on camera is intriguing; it starts with the familiar stern face common in his still photographs, and then, after a moment, he transforms into the smiling, somewhat shy and self-effacing character described by his friends. View the footage online at www.youtube.com/watch?v=xEHmD-FDUEU. The close-up of Amundsen begins at 2:11.

The Fram Museum in Oslo is a fantastic source of information about Amundsen, including a photo gallery, short biographies of Amundsen's men and excerpts from their expedition journals, and information about all of Amundsen's expeditions as well as those of other Norwegian explorers. Visit the museum online at www.frammuseum.no.

The *New York Times* Article Archive is a great place for those interested in reading Amundsen-related articles in full or in researching a specific aspect of Amundsen's storied life in the United States. They are organized by date, and many of the early articles are free. Visit the archive online at www.nytimes.com/ref/membercenter/nytarchive.html.

Selected Bibliography

Amundsen, Roald. *Roald Amundsen's Belgica Diary: The First Scientific Expedition to the Antarctic.* Bluntisham, UK: Erskine, 1999.

————. *The North-West Passage: Being a Record of a Voyage of Exploration of the Ship Gjøa, 1903–1907.* New York: Dutton, 1908.

————. *The South Pole: An Account of the Norwegian Antarctic Expedition in the Fram, 1910–1912.* New York: Keedick, 1913.

————. *Nordostpassagen.* Kristiania: Gyldendalske Boghandel, 1921. There is no English translation.

————. *My Life as an Explorer.* Garden City, NY: Doubleday, Page, 1927.

Amundsen, Roald, and Lincoln Ellsworth. *Our Polar Flight: The Amundsen-Ellsworth Polar Flight.* New York: Dodd, Mead, 1925.

————. *First Crossing of the Polar Sea.* New York: Doran, 1927.

Arnesaon, Odd. *The Polar Adventure: The Italia Tragedy Seen at Close Quarters.* London: Gollancz, 1929.

Atwood, Evangeline. *Who's Who in Alaskan Politics: A Biographical Dictionary of Alaskan Political Personalities, 1884–1974.* Portland, OR: Binfords & Mort (for the Alaska Historical Commission), 1977.

Balchen, Bernt. *Come North with Me.* New York: Dutton, 1958.

Bomann-Larsen, Tor. *Roald Amundsen.* Translated by Ingrid Christophersen. Stroud, Gloucestershire, UK: History Press, 2006. Originally published in Norway in 1995.

Bryce, Robert M. *Cook and Peary: The Polar Controversy Resolved.* Mechanicsburg, PA: Stackpole Books, 1997.

Byrd, Richard. *Skyward.* New York: Putnam, 1928.

Eber, Dorothy Harley. *Encounters on the Passage: Inuit Meet the Explorers.* Toronto: University of Toronto Press, 2008.

Ellsworth, Lincoln. *Beyond Horizons.* New York: Doubleday, 1938.

Gade, John G. *All My Born Days.* New York: Scribner, 1942.

Goldberg, Fred. *Roald Amundsen: Expedition Mail, Letters, Postcards and Stamps.* Oslo: Fram Museum, 2000.

Hanssen, Helmer. *Voyages of a Modern Viking.* London: Routledge, 1936.

Hayes, Derek. *Historical Atlas of the Arctic.* Vancouver, B.C.: Douglas & McIntyre, 2003.

Hensley, William Iggiagruk. *Fifty Miles from Tomorrow: A Memoir of Alaska and the Real People.* New York: Farrar, Straus & Giroux, 2009.

Holland, Clive, ed. *Farthest North: A History of North Polar Exploration in Eyewitness Accounts.* London: Robinson, 1994.

Huntford, Roland. *Race for the South Pole: The Expedition Diaries of Scott and Amundsen.* London: Continuum, 2010.

Huntford, Roland. *The Last Place on Earth: Scott and Amundsen's Race to the South Pole.* New York: Modern Library, 1999. Originally published as *Scott and Amundsen* in 1985.

Huntford, Roland. *The Amundsen Photographs.* New York: Atlantic Monthly Press, 1987.

Kenney, Gerard. *Dangerous Passage: Issues in the Arctic.* Toronto: Natural Heritage Books, 2006.

Kershner, Howard Eldred, ed. *Air Pioneering in the Arctic: The Two Polar Flights of Roald Amundsen and Lincoln Ellsworth.* New York: National America Society, 1929.

Klover, Geir O., ed. *Cold Recall: Reflections of a Polar Explorer.* Oslo: Fram Museum, 2009.

Langner, Rainer K. *Scott and Amundsen: Duel in the Ice.* London: Haus, 2007.

MacPhee, R.D.E. *Race to the End: Amundsen, Scott, and the Attainment of the South Pole.* New York: Sterling Innovation, 2010.

Mason, Theodore K. *Two Against the Ice: Amundsen and Ellsworth.* New York: Dodd, Mead, 1982.

Maynard, Jeff. *Wings of Ice: The Mystery of the Polar Air Race.* North Sydney: Random House Australia, 2010.

McCutcheon, Campbell. Introduction to Roald Amundsen, *My Life as an Explorer.* Stroud, UK: Amberley, 2008. Reprint of a 1927 original.

McKee, Alexander. *Ice Crash: Disaster in the Arctic, 1928.* New York: St. Martin's, 1979.

Montague, Richard. *Oceans, Poles, and Airmen.* New York: Random House, 1971.

Neider, Charles. *Antarctica: Authentic Accounts of Life and Exploration in the World's Highest, Driest, Windiest, Coldest and Most Remote Continent.* New York: Random House, 1972.

Nobile, Umberto. *My Polar Flights.* New York: Putnam, 1961.

Pinson, Elizabeth Bernhardt. *Alaska's Daughter: An Eskimo Memoir of the Early Twentieth Century.* Logan: Utah State University Press, 2004.

Roberts, David. *Great Exploration Hoaxes.* San Francisco: Sierra Club Books, 1982.

Stevens, Robert W. *Alaskan Aviation History.* Des Moines, WA: Polynyas, 1990.

Sverdrup, Harald. "Roald Amundsen, Biographical Sketch." *Journal of the Arctic Institute of North America* 12, no. 4 (1959).

Thomson, David. *Scott, Shackleton and Amundsen: Ambition and Tragedy in the Antarctic.* New York: Thunder's Mouth, 2002. Originally published as *Scott's Men* in 1977.

Tombs, George. "Amundsen's Family Secrets: Another Side of the Polar Explorer Emerges as an Inuit Family Connection Comes to Light." *Canada's History* 91, no. 5 (October/November 2011).

Acknowledgments

I wish to thank a number of people for their contributions to this book. First, my wife, Nicky Brink, for encouragement, numerous discussions, and for reading the first draft. My editor John Eerkes-Medrano once again provided his insightful comments, suggestions and opinions, strengthening the book and leading me to some new ideas; also to copyeditors Ann Delgehausen and Ruth Wilson. Merloyd Lawrence offered valuable and enthusiastic suggestions and an exciting vision of the book's potential. Scott Manktelow created the stylish maps (www.scottmanktelow.com). A big shout out goes to the Canmore Public Library for bringing in numerous old and obscure books for me, the Arctic Institute of North America for maintaining such a good selection of Amundsen's books, and to Café Books for its support and for at one time devoting an entire table to my books. Thanks to the Alberta Foundation for the Arts. Last but not least, thanks to Roald Amundsen for living such an unusual and adventurous life.

Photo Credits

The photographs in this book's inserts originally appeared in the following books by Roald Amundsen:

Opdagelseseiser: images 1, 2, 12, 13, 14, 16, 17, 19, and 20
The North-West Passage: The Gjoa Expedition, 1903–1907: images 3, 4, 5, 6, 7, and 8
The South Pole: An Account of the Norwegian Antarctic Expedition in the Fram, 1910–1912: images 9, 10, 11, and 12
Voyages of a Modern Viking: image 15
Nordostpassagen: images 18 and 21
My Polar Flight: images 23, 24, 25 and 31
The First Flight Across the Polar Sea: images 29 and 30
Image 22 appears courtesy of the Museum of History and Industry, Seattle.

Index

Stephen R. Bown is the author of several critically acclaimed, award-winning books on the history of exploration, science, and ideas. These include *1494: How a Family Feud in Medieval Spain Divided the World in Half*, *Merchant Kings: When Companies Ruled the World, 1600–1900*, *Madness, Betrayal and the Lash: The Epic Voyage of Captain George Vancouver*, and *Scurvy: How a Surgeon, a Mariner, and a Gentleman Solved the Greatest Medical Mystery of the Age of Sail.* The *Globe and Mail* has called him "Canada's Simon Winchester." Bown lives with his wife and two children in Canmore, Alberta.

Author website: www.stephenrbown.net

Author Facebook page: www.facebook.com/srbown